AGRARIAN REFORM AND CLASS CONSCIOUSNESS
IN NICARAGUA

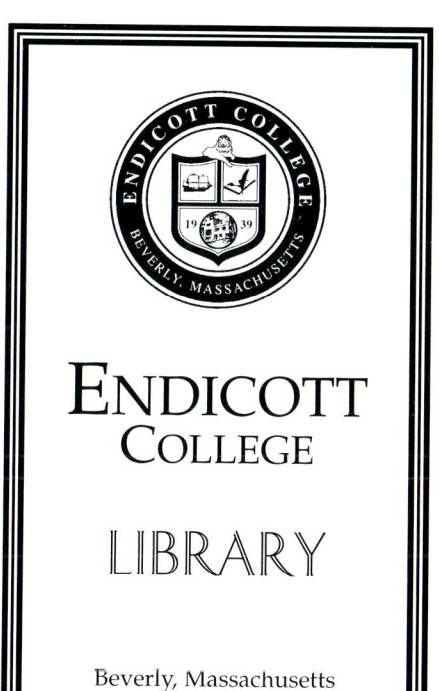

Endicott
College

Library

Beverly, Massachusetts

Agrarian Reform and Class Consciousness in Nicaragua

Laura J. Enríquez

University Press of Florida
Gainesville/Tallahassee/Tampa/Boca Raton
Pensacola/Orlando/Miami/Jacksonville

Copyright 1997 by the Board of Regents of the State of Florida
Printed in the United States of America on acid-free paper
All rights reserved

02 01 00 99 98 97   6 5 4 3 2 1

Library of Congress Cataloging-in-Publication Data

Enríquez, Laura J.
Agrarian reform and class consciousness in Nicaragua / Laura J. Enríquez.
    p.   cm.
Includes bibliographical references and index.
ISBN 0-8130-1489-1 (alk. paper)
1. Land reform—Political aspects—Nicaragua. 2. Peasantry—Nicaragua—Political activity. 3. Frente Sandinista de Liberación Nacional. 4. Nicaragua—Politics and government—1979-1990. 5. Nicaragua—Politics and government—1990- . I. Title.
HD1333.N5E569   1997
322.4′4′097285—dc21   96-39604

The University Press of Florida is the scholarly publishing agency for the State University System of Florida, comprised of Florida A & M University, Florida Atlantic University, Florida International University, Florida State University, University of Central Florida, University of Florida, University of North Florida, University of South Florida, and University of West Florida.

University Press of Florida
15 Northwest 15th Street
Gainesville, FL 32611

Contents

List of Maps and Tables   vi

Acknowledgments   viii

Abbreviations   ix

Introduction   1

1. The Theoretical Debates Concerning the Impact of Development on Politics   7

2. How the FSLN Lost the Hearts and Minds of the Peasantry   31

3. Los Patios: Its Roots   58

4. Los Patios: Its Social and Political Impact   73

5. Plan Masaya: Its Roots   95

6. Plan Masaya: The Social and Political Impact of the Project   110

7. The Lessons to be Drawn from Los Patios and Plan Masaya   137

A Brief Discussion of Methodology   163

Notes   171

Bibliography   189

Index   201

Maps and Tables

Maps

1. Region IV within Nicaragua   2
2. Los Patios areas of influence   18
3. Plan Masaya areas of influence   19
4. Municipalities in Granada, Masaya, and Carazo   82

Tables

2.1 Electoral support for the FSLN, 1984 and 1990   35
3.1 Land concentration in agroexport production, Region IV   62
3.2 Changes in Region IV land tenancy following the agroexport boom   63
3.3 Economic activity of two generations of Los Patios campesinos   68
4.1 Agricultural production of two generations of Los Patios campesinos   76
4.2 Reliance of Los Patios beneficiaries on agricultural credit   78
4.3 Voting pattern of Los Patios beneficiaries   83
5.1 Economic activity of two generations of Plan Masaya campesinos   106
6.1 Land redistributed and families benefited, nationwide and Region IV, Oct. 1981–Dec. 1988   111
6.2 Access of Plan Masaya beneficiaries to productive resources   114
6.3 Access to technical assistance among Plan Masaya beneficiaries versus non nonbeneficiaries   115
6.4 Evolution of cotton, corn, and bean production, nationwide and Region IV   118
6.5 Voting pattern of Plan Masaya beneficiaries   130
7.1 Profiles of project participants   139

Acknowledgments

The list of people who assisted me in completing this study is longer than I could fit in this space. What follows is an attempt to express my gratitude to those who stand out most in this sense, while not burdening them with any responsibility for the final product.

Above all, the peasants who spent hours conversing with me—on repeated occasions—and who form the subject of this book deserve my special thanks. Despite the fact that farming is an all-consuming occupation, which was only made more so by the hard times that coincided with this study, they were willing to share their experiences, trials, and tribulations with a neophyte in the field of peasant life.

Another key ingredient was the participation of a group of faculty and students from the Central American University. Marlen Llanes, Nahela Becerrill, Pio Martínez, Guillermo Mesa, Ileana Muñoz, Rafael Ramagoza, and Guido Eguigure not only made certain aspects of the study feasible but helped to fill our many days of fieldwork with laughter and stories and lightened the load when we occasionally found ourselves in distressing circumstances.

Among these assistants, Marlen Llanes merits particular mention. Marlen worked with me from the day the project started, and has continued to throw in a helping hand even as it was in its final stages of completion. Her seriousness, insights, and commitment made a major difference in the quality of this study.

As we began the fieldwork for this study, and throughout its duration, many individuals whose work was related to agricultural production and agrarian reform opened the way, giving us ideas, information, and other essential assistance. Thus, officials from the local, regional, and national offices of MIDINRA (especially Carlos Collado, Martín Medina, Mariano Vásquez, Marvin Ortega, Bismarck Hueck, Carlos Lorente, and Jorge Zuniga), UNAG (particularly Bernardo Cardenal and Ignacio Valladares), the BND (especially Denis López and Wilfredo Aguilar), and the FSLN (particularly Carlos Barrios) played a crucial role in facilitating the completion of our work. And Noel León, from the CSE, spent many hours working with me on the electoral data.

Also during the fieldwork stage of this endeavor, the two institutions with which I was affiliated provided indispensable institutional support. Luis Miranda (at PAN) and Peter Marchetti (at UCA) maintained their interest in this study through thick and thin, the former making it possible for this errant "Asesora Extranjera" to undertake a task which was far removed from the usual realm of work at the PAN.

As the results of the study were being transformed into something I could share with others, a number of people provided me with valuable comments. These included Michael Burawoy, Peter Evans, Miguel Gómez, Jon Jonakin, Nancy Jurik, Marlen Llanes, Rose Spalding, Richard Stahler-Sholk, and Peter Utting. Several colleagues in the Department of Sociology at the University of California at Berkeley also gave me important input as I prepared this book. Among these, Michael Burawoy deserves special thanks, as he followed the meanderings of my writing on various pieces of this study—constantly challenging me to refine my thinking—until something resembling a book finally came out of the computer. I often wonder how I would have achieved that goal without the benefit of all his wisdom. The anonymous reviewers for the University Press of Florida were also key in strengthening the manuscript in countless ways.

A few institutions provided the funding that made the completion of my study possible. The Ford Foundation and the Organization of American States financed the first phase of research, and the President's Post-Doctoral Fellowship Program of the University of California enabled me to return to Nicaragua on several occasions to carry out follow-up work.

On a more personal note, my parents—Jean and Eduardo Enríquez—never ceased to give encouragement and support throughout the years in which this study consumed me, despite the fact that it meant my visits with them were less than frequent and I was often quite distracted during them.

Finally, Maurizio Leonelli smoothed the way through the many potholes that interrupt research in a Third World country. He endured endless conversations about the nuts and bolts, as well as the overarching theoretical questions, that lay behind this study. He also weathered the storms caused by my frustration about the innumerable difficulties involved in the project, while continually helping to remind me what it is about fieldwork in the countryside that moves me.

Abbreviations

AMNLAE	Asociación de Mujeres Nicaragüenses Luisa Amanda Espinoza (Luisa Amanda Espinoza Association of Nicaraguan Women)
ATC	Asociación de Trabajadores del Campo (Agricultural Workers' Association)
APP	Area Propiedad del Pueblo (Area of People's Property)
BND	Banco Nacional del Desarrollo (National Development Bank)
CAS	Cooperativas Agrícolas Sandinistas (Sandinista Agricultural Cooperatives)
CCS	Cooperativas de Crédito y Servicio (Credit and Service Cooperatives)
CDS	Comités de Defensa Sandinista (Sandinista Defense Committees)
CONARCA	Comisión Nacional de Renovación de Cafetales (National Commission of Coffee Plantation Renovation)
COSEP	Consejo Superior de la Empresa Privada (Superior Council of Private Enterprise)
CSM	Cooperativas de Surco Muerto (Dead Furrow Cooperatives)
CT	Colectivos de Trabajo (Workers' Collectives)
ECODEPA	Empresa Cooperativa de Productores Agropecuarios (Cooperative Enterprise of Agricultural Producers)
ENABAS	Empresa Nicaragüense de Alimentos Básicos (Nicaraguan Enterprise of Basic Foodstuffs)
FLSN	Frente Sandinista de Liberación Nacional (Sandinista National Liberation Front)
MICOIN	Ministerio de Comercio Interior (Ministry of Internal Commerce)
MIDINRA	Ministerio de Desarrollo Agropecuario y Reforma Agraria (Ministry of Agricultural Development and Agrarian Reform)
PATD	Programa de Asistencia Técnica Dirigida (Program of Directed Technical Assistance)
PCD	Partido Conservador Democrático (Democratic Conservative Party)

SAIMSA	Sistemas Agro-Industriales de Masaya, S.A. (Agro-Industrial Systems of Masaya, Inc.)
SMP	Servicio Militar Patriótico (Patriotic Military Service)
UNAG	Unión Nacional de Agricultores y Ganaderos (National Union of Farmers and Ranchers)
UNO	Unión Nacional Opositora (National Opposition Union)

Introduction

The results of Nicaragua's 1990 general election surprised the country's populace, as well as the multitude of those observing the elections around the world. The electoral defeat of the Sandinista National Liberation Front (FSLN) symbolized the termination of the process of social transformation its government had initiated in 1979. It was also probable that the country's international relations, particularly with the United States, would subsequently undergo major changes. The most likely change was that the Contra war would come to an end. The importance of the election results extended beyond their national and geopolitical significance, however. In addition, they underlined the difficulties inherent in efforts to shift from a capitalist development model to one of socialist development for countries in the periphery of the world capitalist economy. Moreover, the election results pointed especially to the extremely complex nature of politics during the transition to socialism.[1]

Most of those awaiting the election results on the evening of February 25, 1990, assumed that despite the hardship that had been borne by the population as a consequence of the economic crisis and the war, voters would still support the incumbent government. After all, it was the FSLN that had opened a new era in Nicaraguan history, in contrast to the opposition coalition which represented (to a greater or lesser degree) a return to the past. The Sandinista government, irrespective of its many shortcomings, had set the country on a different course of development. This new course was based on a shift in priorities: away from the promotion of private capital accumulation, to that of improving the general population's social welfare while also fostering a more balanced model of economic development.

The agrarian reform was a central component of the Sandinistas' development model. The expressed goals of the reform were to facilitate economic development and redistribute the country's agricultural resources. In addition to turning over land to landless and land-poor peasants, it also sought to provide them with other productive resources and shift their production from individual to collective farming. The changes that the reform was supposed to bring about in the countryside would lay the groundwork for the transition to socialism.

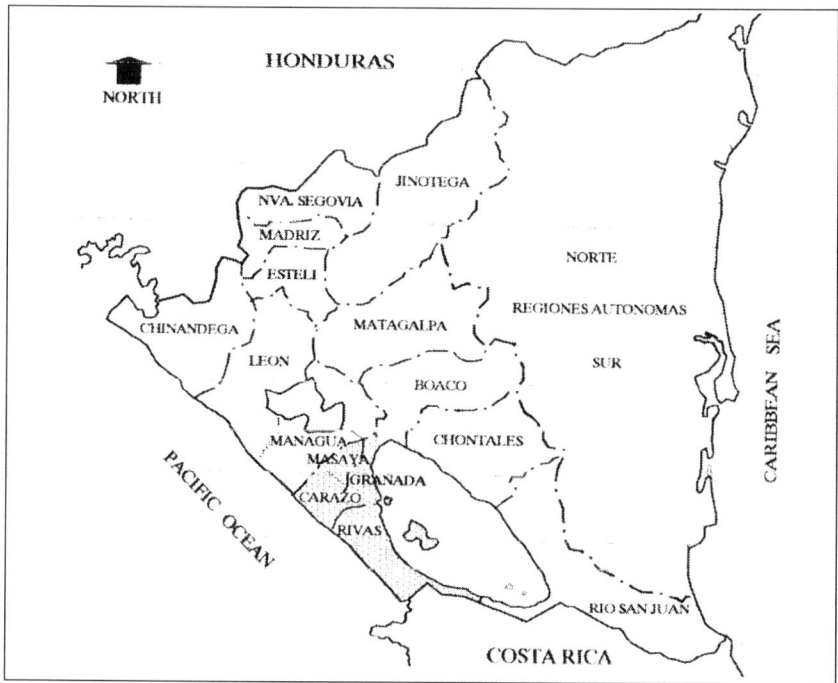

Map 1. Region IV within Nicaragua

In an effort to assess the impact of the agrarian reform on the peasantry, I initiated a study of two specific agrarian reform projects in 1987, Los Patios and Plan Masaya (see the Brief Discussion of Methodology). These projects had been implemented in prime agricultural areas in the region south to southeast of Managua (Region IV) (see map 1).[2] The population they targeted was that of the *minifundistas*, the poorest of the peasantry, with parcels of land so small in size that they were insufficient to maintain those who lived on them.[3] My study revealed the positive socioeconomic impact of these agrarian reform projects.

Nonetheless, in addition to the socioeconomic goals of the agrarian reform projects, they had political goals. In designing the projects, Sandinista policymakers assumed that the socioeconomic benefits they would produce for these peasant families would result in the latter's increased support for the government. Moreover, they took for granted that with this redistribution of productive resources would come a recognition within the peasantry that the government represented its interests. This, in turn, would contribute to the Sandinistas' overall political project of "consolidat[ing] the hegemony of the popular classes" in the new regime (Stahler-Sholk 1990b, 15). The consolidation of the popular classes' hegemony was seen to be essential for the eventual construction of socialism.

The first clear opportunity to assess the degree of support that had been generated by the projects presented itself in the 1990 elections. The FSLN's loss of those elections in the agrarian reform projects' areas of influence suggested that they had failed to produce the desired results. Although it was reasonable to suppose that the beneficiaries' enthusiasm for the Sandinista government might have been dampened by the difficult circumstances that characterized the lives of most of the country's poorer sectors by 1990, it was also within reason to believe that the special treatment they had received through the reform should have ameliorated somewhat the hardship that they suffered along with much of the rest of the population. After all, it was the salaried workers, based in urban areas, who had been most strongly affected by the hyperinflation and other economic ills that had plagued the country since the mid-1980s. So where had this reasoning gone awry? Did the reform produce no political results whatsoever? Was there, then, no relationship between socioeconomic improvement, or development, and political support for a regime which brought it about?

The search for answers to these questions led me back to the countryside, where I could become acquainted with the agrarian reform beneficiaries' world once again.[4] There, it became evident that a number of factors had influenced the peasants' attitudes toward the Sandinista government.[5] Some of these had been important for the entire population, such as the fact that almost everyone was anxious for the war to come to an end. They were also skeptical that the Sandinistas could resolve the economic crisis, given their inability to do so previously. In addition, however, the beneficiaries were opposed to several of the government's policies that had particularly affected them as agricultural producers. Moreover, even though many who had benefited from the agrarian reform had initially experienced economic gains, at least some of these gains had been undercut by 1990. And, they had given up hope that the Sandinista government could fulfill their aspirations in other areas.

Yet, notable differences existed between specific subgroups of peasants with regard to their support, or lack thereof, for the Sandinista regime. That is to say, the peasantry did not vote in a uniform fashion against the FSLN. The varied voting patterns reveal that other factors came into play as the beneficiaries of the agrarian reform projects under study prepared to go to the polls. A few characteristics served to distinguish each subgroup among the beneficiary population, the most significant of which were their class origins, the form of organization their agricultural production assumed after their entry into one or the other of these projects, and the type of agrarian reform strategy that had been benefited them. To be specific, my interviews with the projects' beneficiaries pointed to the fact that those peasants who were most closely tied to the land prior to their inclusion in the reform, who remained organized as individual farmers, and whose incorporation into the reform did not entail being part of a fundamental restructuring of agrarian social relations in their rural communities, tended to express very strong opposition to the FSLN and its goal of social transformation. In contrast, those beneficiaries who had experienced greater marginalization from the land, who participated in collective forms of production after receiving land through the agrarian reform, and whose receipt of land brought them into a thoroughgoing process of reshaping agrarian social relations, voiced significantly more support for the government that had made this dramatic change in their lives possible. Although my interview data illuminated these crucial differences between the agrarian reform's beneficiary populations, an explanation of them must be sought elsewhere.

In essence, my study of the agrarian reform points to two puzzles. The first puzzle is represented in the larger question of why the agrarian reform did not produce the expected political results given its economic achievements. The second puzzle lies in the nuanced responses of the rural population to Sandinista agrarian policy. At the same time, these two puzzles reflect the broader phenomenon which underlies them, this being the relationship between politics and economic development.

At this point, a brief exploration of the relationship between agrarian reform and development is in order. The term agrarian reform commonly refers to efforts made to restructure the agrarian sector of society. In the Nicaraguan case, these efforts were directed at the structure of ownership of agricultural property, the organization of production, and, to some extent, production priorities within agriculture. For Sandinista policymakers these changes were preconditions for making progress toward the larger goal of development, particularly agricultural development. Thus, agrarian reform formed part of the more comprehensive process of development.

Development itself is typically assumed to consist, in its core, of increased economic diversification, advances in the level of the productive forces, and economic growth, which is usually measured in terms of expanded production. This definition will be broadened here to also include improvements in the standard of living of the population. Given that this latter characteristic represented a fundamental goal of policymaking under the Sandinistas, and that it is traditionally one of the, if not the, most important objectives of those who promote the transition to a socialist model of development, it will form an integral part of the definition of this concept used herein.

I employed several complementary research methods in the study that provided the "raw material" for this book (see the Brief Discussion of Methodology). During the first phase of research, 1987–89, my team of research assistants (who were junior faculty and students from the Central American University—UCA—in Managua) and I interviewed representatives from the institutions and organizations that were involved in planning and implementing the Los Patios and Plan Masaya agrarian reform projects, as well as those who had elaborated the short-, medium-, and long-term development strategies for Region IV. In the process we obtained access to existing documentation about the projects and the region, as well as entree into the countryside where the projects had been implemented. We then conducted surveys of the beneficiary populations to assess the degree of change the projects had brought about in production patterns, distribution of productive resources, levels of technology employed in production, familial labor arrangements, and standards of living.

After the 1990 general elections I initiated the second phase of research, which entailed carrying out follow-up interviews with part of the population that we had surveyed earlier. I also completed an analysis of the 1990 electoral results for the projects' areas of influence. Both information sources, but most especially the interview data, pointed to the attitude of this population regarding the type of regime they preferred to have governing Nicaragua.

The present inquiry into how it is that the intersection of politics and economic development might produce results such as those witnessed in Nicaragua's 1990 general election will begin with a perusal of the theories of development and peasant politics that speak, at least to some degree, to the issues raised by this perplexing case. Subsequently, we will return once again to the Nicaraguan agrarian reform, in an attempt to address the first puzzle, that of the Sandinistas' electoral loss in the countryside. We will then narrow our focus to the Los Patios and Plan Masaya projects themselves, in an effort to explore the second puzzle, the reasons for variations within the beneficiary population of its support for the Sandinista government. In-depth analyses of the projects, as well as a subsequent comparison of them, will illuminate the factors that influenced the political orientation of their participants. Examination of these two cases should offer us insight with regard to the dilemmas that form part of the transition to socialism. They will suggest the concrete material obstacles that confront development policies and projects, especially where the goal is that of breaking away from capitalist production relations. In addition, by focusing on these two cases, the political tensions that emerge within the popular classes during the transition to socialism will be revealed. It will become apparent that even when socioeconomic benefits are experienced by these classes, their acceptance of and support for the project of social transformation cannot be taken for granted. In sum, the study that follows will highlight the complex nature of efforts to push forth a democratic transition to socialism.

1

The Theoretical Debates Concerning
The Impact of Development on Politics

Following President Daniel Ortega's early morning concession speech on February 26, 1990, a heavy silence seemed to descend upon Nicaragua's population. An awareness of the magnitude of the decision its voters had made the previous day began to sink in on the country. The silence expressed both astonishment about the election's outcome, as well as consternation as to what would follow. Even the victors were relatively subdued, also appearing to be stunned to learn of the Sandinistas' defeat.

Analyses of the causes of the Sandinista government's loss of the 1990 elections began to flow forth almost immediately. Yet the profound nature of the enigma represented by the elections would only become clear as the dust began to settle. The questions raised by this singular political phenomenon point in many directions. My study will focus only on a few of these questions, using the agrarian reform that lay at the center of the Sandinistas' social program—especially as epitomized in the Los Patios and Plan Masaya projects—as a means of addressing them. Thus, I will examine the complex of reasons that led to the loss of support for the Sandinista government among one of the populations that was supposed to have been a key protagonist of the process of change that was initiated in Nicaragua in 1979, the beneficiaries of the agrarian reform. Even more important, I will explore the differences within this population, which led to the adoption of varying postures between beneficiary groups toward the project of socialist transformation.

In addition to providing insight into the specific questions posed by the lack of support for the FSLN and its social project in the countryside, this exploration of the economic and political impact of the Los Patios and Plan Masaya projects should also facilitate a reevaluation of several bodies of theory, those of development and peasant politics. That is to say, the case studies should suggest the areas in which the two bodies of thought might be strengthened in order to be of greater explanatory value.[1] My particular avenue of entry into these theoretical traditions will be to search for answers to the following questions: What is the relationship between economic development and politics, most especially in the context of the transition to socialism? and, Under what conditions will the peasantry support a social project that is aimed at fundamentally transforming life in the countryside? The search for answers to these comprehensive theoretical questions, however, must of necessity begin with an assessment of the analytical tools that have emerged from several decades of debate about development and the politics of the peasantry.[2]

THE RELATIONSHIP BETWEEN POLITICS AND DEVELOPMENT

Within the theoretical field of development, the area of study that is directed at the relationship between economic development and political development offers a number of important hypotheses, the close examination of which provides a reasonable starting point for approaching the questions raised by the Nicaraguan elections of 1990. Samuel Huntington (see esp. 1965) was one of the earlier theorists to address this issue. Huntington's seminal work on this topic represented a response to several studies (particularly Johnson 1958 and Lipset 1963) that argued that political development, especially taking the form of democracy, would evolve alongside economic development. Huntington did not share their optimism about the prospects for stable, democratic governments to come into existence with economic development.

Instead, Huntington (1965) postulated that economic development would most likely lead to great instability. The cause of this sequence of events was the multiplication of political factors produced by economic development, which resulted in an excess of demands being placed on the system. This, in turn, produced social conflict that eventually became difficult to contain. What was required if modernization was to proceed successfully was a strengthening of authoritative government institutions. As Roxborough (1979, 113) succinctly asserts, "the implication is that there exists a single, unilinear dimension of political modernization, measured by the adequacy of institutions to meet the challenges of mobilization at any given time."

While I would agree with Huntington that Lipset, Johnson, and some of the other modernization theorists who assumed a positive relationship between these two phenomena were incorrect in their analyses, the pessimistic current of thought concerning political development that Huntington represents also evidences limitations in its explanatory power. Given the fact that Huntington (1965) refers to countries of both capitalist and communist orientation, we can test the power of his hypotheses by assessing their applicability to Nicaragua during the period in which the Sandinistas attempted to initiate a transition toward socialism in that country. The Sandinista era certainly demonstrates the fact that economic development gives rise to increasing demands on the part of the populace, as Huntington asserts. I would argue, however, that his concern with mobilization outstripping the government institutions' capacities for containment is only warranted in those countries where the state's economic project is opposed by the better part of the population. Thus, his thesis is probably accurate for many Third World countries where the low salaries and the marginal standard of living of the poor majority subsidize the cost of dependent capitalist development. In contrast, mobilizing the population was at the core of the Sandinista model of development in its early years of implementation. Between 1979 and 1985 the level of mobilization of the population far exceeded that which had characterized it at any previous time (excluding during the civil war against Somoza).[3] Without a doubt, the massive mobilizations surpassed the ability of the newly formed government, and the still-small FSLN, to constrain them.

Huntington (1965, 248) does refer to the impressive capacity of communist parties to mobilize their populations. But in the Nicaraguan case, the mobilization of the population did not have only political objectives. Popular mobilization was essential in the campaign to increase literacy (Barndt 1985 and Hirshon 1983), to expand health services (Bossert 1985 and Donahue 1983), to guarantee the completion of the cotton and coffee harvests (Enríquez 1991), and so forth.[4] Hence, in a situation of limited resources, social and economic development can be facilitated by mobilizing the population, at the same time as its active involvement in the development process increases its understanding and support for the regime's social project.

In a later study, Huntington (1968) contradicts his economic development/mobilization/social instability thesis somewhat by calling for peasant organizing to promote the implementation of agrarian reform (to be described at greater length below). But, even taking into account this exception to his earlier argument, Huntington fails to recognize that the massive incorporation of the population into such an effort, and into development efforts more generally, is only a possibility where those who are being thus mobilized identify with the regime that is promoting it. That is, the issue of whether the mobilization of the population poses a threat to the regime depends on the (class) interests represented by the regime and the degree to which the population considers those interests to coincide with its own.

To turn Huntington on his head, I would contend that the mobilization of the population is actually indispensable for development during the transition to socialism. In fact, it has been strongly argued that the demobilization of Nicaraguan society that accompanied the growing institutionalization of the revolution in the mid-1980s had a direct bearing on the subsequent decrease in support for the regime (Stahler-Sholk 1990b). As the hardship that had to be borne by the Nicaraguan population increased, due to the economic crisis and the war, its lack of involvement with the political and economic development process became an Achilles heel. Thus, contrary to what might be expected given Huntington's thesis, the shift to traditional party politics and authoritative institutions proved to be the undoing of the Sandinista regime.

In contrast, a number of theorists, whose focus of study has been the transition to a socialist model of development, have emphasized the crucial role played by politics—and political participation more specifically—in socioeconomic development. Clive Thomas's 1974 analysis of the economics of socialist transition in Third World countries was among the first general works within this field.[5] Thomas's study highlights the fact that the underdeveloped nature of these countries' economies sets parameters for socialist development efforts. Yet, in a brief detour from his almost exclusive focus on the economic aspects of the transition to socialism, Thomas makes a strong case for the importance of popular participation in this societal project. He asserts (1974, 132) that with such participation, there will be greater willingness on the part of the population to absorb the social costs entailed in accumulating capital in order to raise the level of the productive forces, a key aspect of development. Touching on this issue, nevertheless, is as far as Thomas explores the politics of the transition to socialism.

Richard Fagen (1986), however, takes the "politics of transition" as his starting point for analyzing the dilemmas encountered by countries following this alternative course of development. He argues that it is precisely because these countries' heritage of underdevelopment delimits the possibilities for the new model of economic development that is unfolding that politics become so important. That is to say, a very intimate relationship exists between politics and economics in these societies "in transition" (see also Coraggio 1986). Fagen (1986, 250) goes so far as to say that "since the material conditions are impossible to overcome in the short or even medium run, politics are (and ought to be) in command during the transitional period." Moreover, in addition to the obstacles presented by the inherited social and economic structures, most of these countries will have to contend with armed opposition that is organized by those representing the old regime (cf. Burbach 1986 and Marchetti 1986). Within this context, it is probable that the standard of living of the population will not only prove difficult to increase, but will actually drop. Thus, politics are critical in facilitating an understanding within the popular consciousness of the constraints confronting the government. Without this understanding, the legitimacy granted to the revolutionary government at the moment that the old regime is overthrown will be quickly eroded.

Nonetheless, Fagen goes on to suggest that not all kinds of participation will have the same salutary effects for the revolutionary project. Although he is referring specifically to political participation, his analysis is still relevant to the present discussion. Fagen is interested in the means available to a revolutionary regime to maintain its legitimacy. He argues that some loss of legitimacy is inevitable because of the class nature of the project it undertakes, as well as the predictable economic difficulties which will arise. Hence, Fagen is concerned with the forms and channels that are established for popular opinion (particularly dissent) to be expressed. Among other issues raised within this discussion, he questions the degree to which opposing sectors of the society should be permitted to contest state power, thereby contesting the implementation of the revolutionary project.

Michael Lowy (1986), another observer of transitional regimes, also underlines the importance of political participation for the success of the socialist project. He, too, explores the forms this participation should take. Lowy (1986, 276) states quite emphatically that "periodic elections . . . are insufficient to assure the people's effective participation in decisionmaking and economic political management." Thus, Lowy points to the need for "ongoing participation," especially as epitomized in functioning mass organizations, to make that possible. These mass organizations should be structured to reach into all sectors of the popular classes, so as to facilitate the incorporation of their members into them. Without this kind of ongoing, active engagement in the various mass organizations, in addition to participation in elections, it is not possible to ensure the emergence of democracy. And, for Lowy (1986, 265), "democracy . . . is an essential characteristic of the process of the construction of socialism." In sum, instead of representing a threat to socioeconomic development, for Lowy, political participation is an essential ingredient in its realization.

Rather than attempting to be exhaustive in scope, this discussion of the theoretical work addressing the political impact of economic development—including that focused on the transition to socialism—was designed to draw on the studies that are most relevant for the task at hand. Nonetheless, it suggests that work in this area has only just begun to bear fruit. It is hoped that the present study will contribute to efforts to remedy this theoretical weakness. The following exploration of this social phenomenon will be assisted by the conceptual backdrop offered by the studies that Fagen (1986) and a number of others have completed of socialist transformation in the Third World. This body of work should facilitate comprehension of the obstacles that were confronted by, and the alternatives which were open to, Nicaragua's policymakers as they inaugurated their new model of development geared toward achieving balanced economic development with social equality.[6] We must, however, look to another body of literature to find the elements that will provide an understanding of the responses that this process of change might illicit in one of the sectors most affected by it, the peasantry.

PEASANT POLITICS

Theorizing about the peasantry has focused on attaining a definition of the peasantry, understanding its political propensities, and determining its potential for participation in the development process—whether that process be of a capitalist or socialist orientation. Rather than review this entire literature, the following discussion will concentrate on the latter two areas, especially as they relate to the present study.

The wave of revolutions that have occurred in the Third World during the past thirty to forty years has given rise to much debate about peasant politics. This debate has yielded widely varying positions on the issue of the revolutionary potential of peasants. Several of the earliest of those to participate in this round of debate—particularly Eric Wolf (1969) and Hamza Alavi (1965)—argued that it is the middle peasantry who will be most receptive to revolutionary organizing.[7] The grounds on which this argument was made are that it is this fraction of the peasantry that is most vulnerable to the consequences—including land expropriations, market fluctuations, high interest rates—of the expansion of capitalism into agriculture. And, this sector has a sufficiently independent economic base, as well as other tactical resources (in contrast to the poorer peasantry) to be able to support a revolutionary movement. What this peasantry seeks is economic stability and a renewal of political order.[8]

Despite sharing some common ground with Wolf, however, Alavi distinguishes himself from the middle-peasant thesis in several important senses. Harking back to some of the more classical studies of the peasantry (e.g. Lenin 1966), he emphasizes that it is crucial to recognize distinctions within the peasantry. That is, not all fractions of the peasantry have the same political or economic orientation.[9] Hence, while sharing Wolf's optimism about the potential for political organizing within the middle peasantry, Alavi (1965) also argued that once the revolutionary movement had been set into motion, it would be the poorer peasantry who would see it through to the overthrow of capitalism.[10] His reasoning was that there was, ultimately, a limit beyond which the middle peasantry would not be willing to go, due to its own class interests. As a landowning class, it would have qualms about the redistribution of land and the calling into question of private property that are often part and parcel of revolutionary transformations.

It is at this point that Alavi's work echoes the hypotheses set forth by Lenin (1966) and Mao Tse-tung (1967) in response to the earliest socialist revolutions. It is also with respect to this argument that he is joined by a host of others who participated in the debate of the 1970s and 1980s concerning peasant politics. Paige (1975), Saul (1974), and Wickham-Crowley (1989) are several theorists from this latter generation who have given new emphasis to Lenin and Mao's line of thinking on the poor and middle peasantry. They, like their predecessors, see the greatest potential for revolutionary organizing among the most marginalized sectors of the rural population, especially the poor peasantry, sharecroppers, and migratory laborers.

In a series of hypotheses, Paige (1975) develops an argument as to why this is the case. In the process he provides us with a characterization of the political tendencies of both the poorer and middle peasantries. His typology is based on a strict definition of class that finds its dividing lines in the relationship each sector has to agricultural land. The key points in his thesis are as follows: the middle peasantry tends toward conservatism because the better part of its income is derived from the land. That is, this fraction of the peasantry will tend to be risk-averse and to be very resistant to revolutionary organizing. At the core of this peasantry's position lies an inclination to identify itself with the agrarian upper classes and their interests, instead of with its poorer counterparts. This is especially true where "productive technology is sufficiently advanced to convert the peasant into a small commercial farmer . . . [because] . . . as the small holder or former peasant becomes more affluent . . . he [sic] . . . becomes fearful of movements which threaten property rights or draw too heavily on the support of the landless peasants or laborers" (Paige 1975, 27). Thus, at heart, what we find in the middle peasantry is an aspiration to become rich peasants or capitalist producers, not to transform the structure of social relations in a way that will redress these distinctions.

On the other hand, Paige's poorer rural dwellers, be they poor peasants, sharecroppers, or migratory laborers, do have the potential for partaking in a movement that will have this as its goal. Here the crucial measure for Paige is the degree of dependency each of these sectors has on wages. The logic is as follows: the more important that wages are as a source of income, the more structural interdependence there will be among the individuals who compose the work force, and consequently the greater degree of pressure that will exist for political solidarity among them (Paige 1975, 34). This situation will also lead to an increased willingness to risk one's life and livelihood and participate in a revolutionary movement.[11]

The theses set forth by Paige, and the others mentioned above who share his general perspective, will find a resonance in this examination of the Nicaraguan peasantry and its varied responses to agrarian reform and economic development. Moreover, my examination of these two case studies will show that the position which the literature would lead one to expect each sector of the peasantry to assume in the initial stages of a revolutionary movement suggests the posture it will adopt once a process of thoroughgoing reform gets under way.

At this point a small detour is required, and that is to address briefly the research that has been done focusing on the impact of agrarian reform on the peasantry. The better part of this literature, and almost all of that which has looked at Latin America, has examined the nature and goals of agrarian reform in nonrevolutionary settings. Much of it has sought to shed light on the succession of agrarian reform programs that were implemented in the region in the 1960s and 1970s.

At the outset of the 1960s, agrarian reform was set forth as the key to resolving Latin America's economic stagnation, as well as to ameliorating the social inequality that threatened to provoke the spread of rural unrest if left untended. Yet the reforms that were actually implemented reflected the principal objective of their designers. Unoccupied areas and public domain land were utilized for colonization schemes, and property titles were extended to squatters on undisputed land. Consequently, the *latifundios* (large agricultural estates), which had ostensibly been the target of the reforms, were left intact (cf. Grindle 1986 and Feder 1970). The reforms typically incorporated land-poor peasants as individual farmers, thus transforming them into peasant capitalists or rural petty bourgeoisie. With this change, as Paige (1975) had theorized, the interests of the reform beneficiaries shifted from aspiring to the goal of radically transforming the rural social structure to maintaining their newly won property rights.[12] These minor reform efforts thus succeeded in establishing resistance against further revolutionary organizing.

Although not having Latin America as his area of inquiry, Huntington (1968) draws on a number of historical examples to hypothesize the same probable outcome from agrarian reform that ensures land ownership for the peasantry. In fact, Huntington (1968) states that "no social group is more conservative than a landowning peasantry, and none is more revolutionary than a peasantry which owns too little land or pays too high a rental" (375). Like Latin America's reformers of the 1960s and 1970s, Huntington's principal concern with land reform is its usage as a means of bringing about social stability. For Huntington, this is a key means for governments, in societies undergoing modernization, to avert the outbreak of revolution.

Interestingly, in apparent contradiction to the preoccupation with popular mobilization as a source of instability during the process of modernization that he expressed in earlier writings (1965), with regard to land reform Huntington (1968) argues that organizing the peasantry is crucial for its success.[13] Yet, the actors that he designates as being the most appropriate for taking on this organizing effort are the existing political parties. In essence, what he is suggesting is that any tensions that might arise in the countryside as a result of economic development can be channeled through political-party organizing into "safe" forms of political action that bring these potential revolutionaries into the fold as peasant capitalists.

The real contradiction in Huntington's thesis, however, lies in the fact that agricultural capitalism in most Third World countries is ultimately incapable of accommodating the existence of a large, thriving peasant-capitalist sector. As has been amply demonstrated elsewhere, the spread of capitalism into agriculture has, in most cases, resulted in increased marginalization for the bulk of the peasantry (cf. de Janvry 1981 and Murdoch 1980). Even though specific agrarian reform programs may succeed in creating a pampered minority group within the peasantry, the concentration of productive resources that typically goes hand-in-hand with agricultural capitalism does not allow for their ample redistribution. Therefore, mobilizing the peasantry under these circumstances may, indeed, prove to be a threat to the status quo. Once the peasantry becomes organized, it may not be possible to control the direction of its demands.

Thus, even when Huntington suggests that select cases of popular mobilizing may further development efforts, the basic weakness in his argument remains. That is, he fails to recognize that the possible outcomes of popular mobilization, in terms of its being beneficial or destabilizing for governments fostering economic development, depend on the extent to which the population being mobilized identifies with the larger social project the government is promoting. Once Huntington's mobilized peasantry realizes that limits exist in the extent to which agrarian reform under a capitalist regime can guarantee its livelihood, it may very well use its newly acquired organizational skills to struggle for more fundamental change.

Moving beyond Huntington and agrarian reform in capitalist settings, the process of agrarian reform that unfolds in those countries where more fundamental change has been initiated has also been a focus of study.[14] The two goals that usually characterize the reforms implemented under revolutionary regimes are the modernization of the productive forces and the achievement of social equity through the redistribution of resources. Yet, in order to avoid the pitfalls of creating a new class of small-scale capitalists, the redistribution of resources commonly occurs through the organization of peasant cooperatives or the formation of state farms. The objective then becomes the collectivization or proletarianization of the peasantry, respectively. This shift within the peasantry, in addition to that of raising the level of the productive forces, is seen as being essential for the advancement of the development process.

In sum, whether it be in the literature addressing the nature and impact of agrarian reform, or that focusing on peasant politics, the political tendencies of this sector of the rural population have received great attention. The present study will draw on various of the hypotheses set forth in these fields of literature to analyze the political impact of the development process begun by Nicaragua's agrarian reform. It is my hope that the examination of the two case studies of agrarian reform that follows will contribute to our understanding of the larger questions that have been highlighted above within each one of these bodies of thought.

THE NICARAGUAN CASE

Even prior to its assumption of power in 1979, the provisional government led by the FSLN had publicly articulated a social project that was notably distinct from the project that the government of Anastasio Somoza Debayle had represented. Whereas Somoza's government had prioritized the concerns of Nicaragua's large, private industrialists and agricultural producers—and most especially those of his own economic group—the government that was formed upon his ouster represented a different grouping of class interests. That grouping initially consisted of a sector of more liberal-minded, national-oriented capitalists and professionals; students; workers; peasants; and much of the urban marginal sector. The force unifying this unlikely coalition of interests was its constituencies' opposition to Somoza. They also agreed, however, on the need for major changes in the economy, polity, and society in general, so as to improve the standard of living of the poorer sectors and set the country on a new, more balanced course of development.

The social project they drew up would gradually be reshaped, as a consequence of both the tensions and conflicts that emerged within this coalition as the process of social change progressed,[15] and the dismal economic situation it encountered upon assuming power (cf. CEPAL 1979). Nonetheless, by 1981 the Sandinista government had initiated the reactivation of the economy, the implementation of a major investment program, and the formation of a social agenda that would move the country toward a socialist course of development. The reorganization of production and the productive structure was considered to be a fundamental component of each of these efforts. Thus, the country's productive structure was broadened to include state and cooperative sectors.[16] The logic behind the establishment of the state sector was that it would allow for the social use of the surplus generated by its agricultural enterprises and industries.[17] The cooperatives, on the other hand, represented the most efficient manner in which to redistribute scarce productive resources to the popular classes, while also avoiding the emergence of a small-scale capitalist class.

The agrarian reform that the Sandinista government initiated was to play a major role in restructuring production and in promoting agricultural development more generally. In fact, Sandinista policymakers were convinced that agricultural development was not possible without agrarian reform. As was true of the government's social project as a whole, agrarian reform policies reflected a mixture of sectoral interests. These included giving priority to the recently formed state sector—with its growing population of workers—and the peasantry.[18]

The Sandinistas implemented their agrarian reform program in several stages.[19] The first, which took place between 1979 and 1981, was characterized by the formation of state farms, massive extension of agricultural loans or credit, and limited redistribution of agricultural land to collectively organized peasants (see table 6.1). It was not until after ratification of the agrarian reform law in mid-1981 that the land redistribution process began in earnest, thus representing the second stage of the agrarian reform.[20] Even then, only those who had formed production cooperatives were provided with land. However, in the mid-1980s the agrarian reform underwent a decisive shift, thereby entering its third stage. At that time, both the quantity of land distributed and the variety of forms in which it was distributed increased notably.

The Plan Masaya and Los Patios agrarian reform projects were products of this last shift in policy. They were designed to respond to the problem of landlessness and land poorness that characterized the regions where they were implemented. Although one of the projects (Plan Masaya) was more explicitly political than the other, they both had political as well as economic goals.[21] Yet they varied in terms of the elements that composed them, the forms in which they organized their beneficiaries, and the precise class origins of those beneficiaries.

The first project, Los Patios, was implemented in the coffee-growing area of the Carazo plateau region (see map 2). Its target population was that of the minifundistas, who had failed to be reached thus far by the agrarian reform. Although the implementation of Los Patios did not involve the redistribution of land, other key agricultural resources were redistributed through it. These resources included agricultural loans, technical assistance, and inputs.[22]

The project's objective was to increase the economic potential of its beneficiaries through the introduction of new crops (fruits and vegetables) that could be produced in large quantities on their tiny pieces of land. A by-product of this effort would be an improvement in the level of the productive forces employed by this sector of the agrarian population. It would also bring about an increase in production for the domestic market, thus contributing to the attempt to alter the historic imbalance between export and food crop production.[23]

The vast majority of its participants were organized in Credit and Service Cooperatives (CCS), but they continued to carry out their agricultural production on an individual basis. It was assumed that the special attention the producers would receive through their incorporation into the project would convince them that the Sandinista regime represented their class interests.

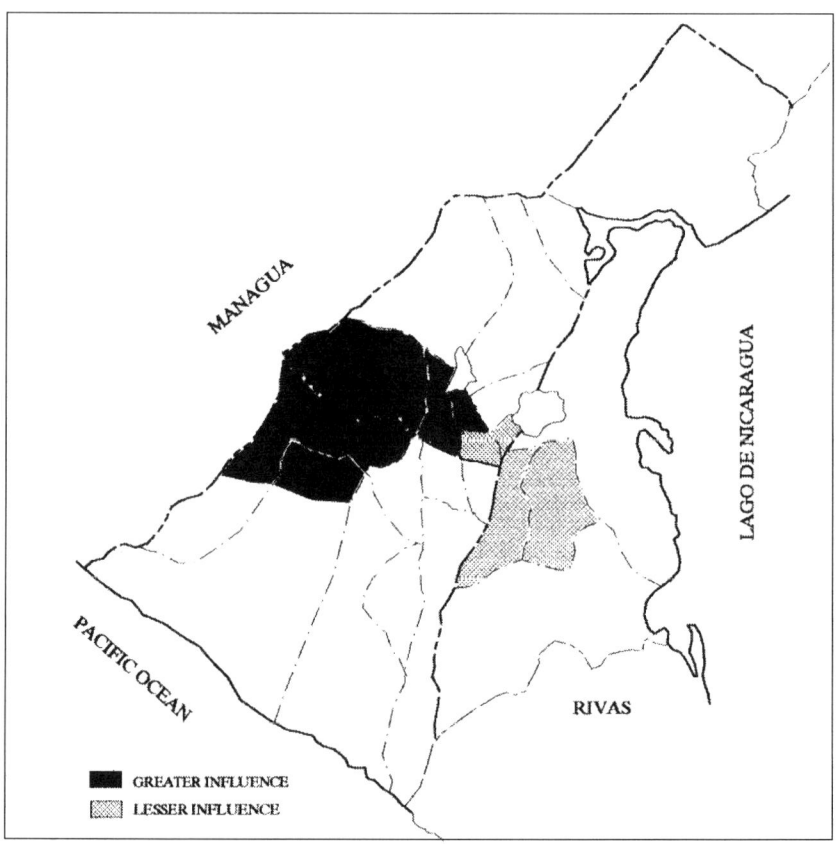

Map 2. Los Patios areas of influence.

This conviction, reinforced by the improvement in economic status experienced by Los Patios beneficiaries, should have led to an increase in their support for the Sandinistas.

The second project, Plan Masaya, was carried out on the plains of Masaya and Diriomo (see map 3). The project involved the massive redistribution of land to minifundistas from the surrounding areas, thereby representing a different strategy of addressing the same problem of landlessness and insufficient land that had motivated the implementation of Los Patios.[24] At the same time, Plan Masaya also brought about a shift from export production (cotton in Masaya and cattle in Diriomo) to food crop production (basic grains) in its areas of influence. In addition, Plan Masaya and a complementary project—the Program of Directed Technical Assistance (PATD)—introduced new, significantly higher levels of technology, thus distinguishing production in this area from traditional basic grain production. Finally, the vast majority of the project's beneficiary population was organized into cooperatives of various

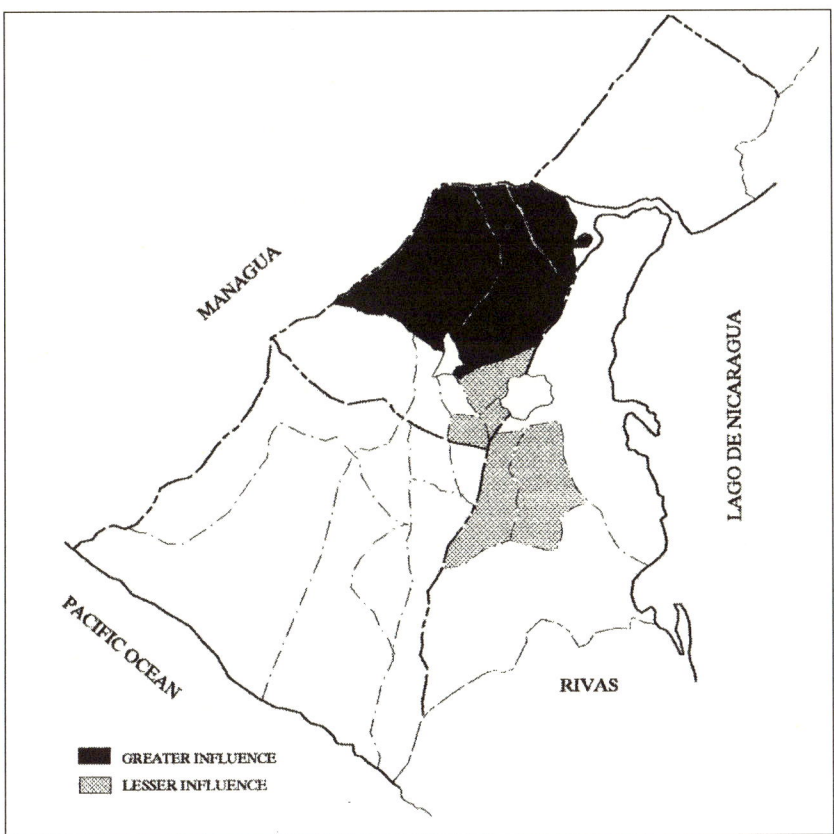

Map 3. Plan Masaya areas of influence

kinds. Although not all of them composed Sandinista Agricultural Cooperatives (CAS) or Workers' Collectives (CT), in which the entire production process was carried out collectively, even in the CCS formed by the project, collective production relations were quite common. All of these changes were designed to contribute to attaining the goal of a better balance between production for the export and domestic sectors of the economy. They also symbolized a rupturing of the social relations and productive structure that had come to characterize Nicaragua's agroexport economy (cf. FitzGerald 1986).

Through a series of surveys that I coordinated in 1988 and 1989 of Los Patios and Plan Masaya beneficiary populations, I was able to document a dramatic increase in their access to essential productive resources. In addition, the interviews with beneficiaries highlighted the improved standard of living they had experienced in the period following their entry into the respective agrarian reform projects. This sector of the agricultural population historically had very limited access to the key productive resources employed in agriculture.

Although neither Los Patios nor Plan Masaya transformed them into medium- or large-scale farmers, the economic benefit the participants received through their inclusion in the projects was tangible.

What, then, motivated a significant number of the beneficiaries to vote against the government that had made this change in their lives possible? Why were they willing to reject the Sandinista development project in favor of a traditional, capitalist economic model? Some of the reasons that led to the loss of their support for the FSLN were also important for the rest of Nicaragua's population—especially that dwelling in rural areas—and others were specific to them in their capacity as small-scale agricultural producers. The following chapter will address the first of these two phenomena. Here I will briefly present the argument with regard to the second that will unfold in the remaining chapters of this book.

Although the multiple reasons for discontent that influenced Nicaragua's general voting population clearly also described the Los Patios and Plan Masaya beneficiaries' position in early 1990 and would seem to more than adequately explain their attitude toward the Sandinista government, they are revealed to be insufficient when it is taken into consideration that not all of those who participated in the agrarian reform voted in the same fashion. Important differences in voting patterns exist between the projects' areas of influence, which can only be accounted for by the divergences between the type of production arrangements that were adopted within each project, the impact that each of these projects had on the nature of agrarian social relations in their areas of influence, and variations in the participants' class backgrounds (see figure 1). That is, these factors mediated the extent to which the overall socioeconomic crisis turned them away from the revolutionary project.

Los Patios beneficiaries were the group most anxious to see a change in government. This group comprised poor peasant farmers who, although falling into the category of minifundista because of the size of their landholdings, were generally more economically secure than many other minifundistas. Their economic security stemmed from their *relatively* greater access to land through ownership, especially deriving from inheritance, and it was most clearly expressed in their *comparatively* limited experience in the wage labor market.

Furthermore, the Los Patios beneficiaries continued to carry out their agricultural production in an individual fashion in spite of their participation in the project. In fact, the nature of the project was such that not only did it not change the organizational form of their production, but it also did not in any significant way alter agrarian social relations in the rural communities where it was implemented. That is, given that the project did not include the redistribution of land as one of its facets, it basically served to strengthen the economic position of its beneficiaries (one of its principal goals), while leaving

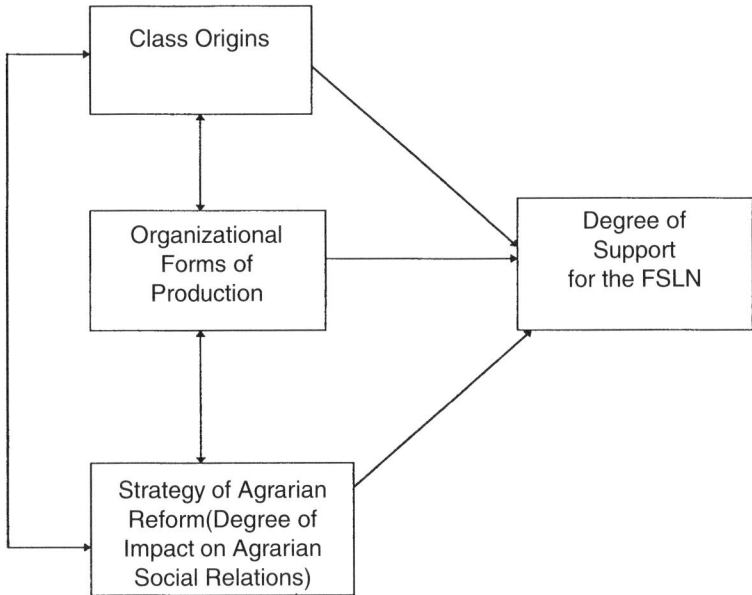

Figure 1. General model of the projects' political impact.

the existing landholding patterns in these areas intact. The end result was an increase in social differentiation between the project's beneficiaries and their (non-beneficiary) neighbors, as well as, in all likelihood, within the population of beneficiaries itself. As a consequence, the benefits that Los Patios participants received only served to reinforce their position as small-scale capitalist farmers or petty bourgeoisie.

Given their social origins, their individual production orientation, and the fortification of their relatively higher social status vis-à-vis others in their communities that resulted from the implementation of Los Patios, it should not have been surprising that the project's beneficiaries would prefer a candidate who had a clear capitalist orientation, evidenced among other things by a loud promotion of free market economics. Moreover, the agrarian reform made them fear for their property rights. This was especially the case because, by and large, they had not partaken in land redistribution and, therefore, could not identify with the process. At the same time, having their own land to farm—land which they had either received from their relatives or purchased themselves—they *could* identify with property owners whose land was being affected by the agrarian reform. In addition, the Sandinistas' pro-proletarian rhetoric and their general tendency in policymaking to favor urban over rural dwellers in terms of social services and so on did little to endear them to this sector of the population. Taking into account the beneficiaries' lack of identification with the social project represented by the Sandinistas, it becomes more comprehensible that the electoral option that suggested a way out of the years-old economic crisis and war was an easy choice for them.

The conservative reaction of Los Patios beneficiaries to the Sandinista government points to a fundamental dilemma encountered by those attempting to promote social transformation in the Third World. One of the basic characteristics of these countries' economies is that they rely on the continued existence of petty-commodity producers in order to subsidize export production (see esp. FitzGerald 1986). In the agrarian sector, this typically means that the peasantry still has an important presence in the social structure. The agrarian policies of the governments that seek to embark upon the transition to socialism are then confronted with the problem of responding to this population's very legitimate needs, while also somehow avoiding the political minefield represented by the creation or fortification of the rural petty bourgeoisie.

The theoretical literature on the logic of agrarian reform in both capitalist and socialist settings, as well as that which addresses peasant politics, points to the consequences of a strengthening of the economic potential of individual peasant farmers (cf. Grindle 1986, Feder 1970, Paige 1975, and Wolf 1969). While policymakers in capitalist regimes, in all likelihood, have the resultant commitment to the status quo on the part of the peasantry as the goal of their agrarian reforms, this is not the case for those in socialist regimes. The history of agrarian revolution and agrarian reform in the latter regime type highlights the distinctly counterrevolutionary position that is quickly adopted by this sector as its interests begin to merge with those of other parts of the capitalist sector. The changes the Los Patios project brought about for its beneficiary population clearly demonstrate this dynamic at work. The Sandinista government's efforts to incorporate this sector of the rural population into the process of social transformation ultimately had the opposite effect: it converted its members into vociferous opponents of the revolution, or, in Huntington's words, "bulwark[s] of the status quo" (1968, 375).

One means available to a socialist government in its efforts to address this dilemma is the promotion of collective production arrangements, especially when it is made possible by a significant restructuring of agrarian social relations. The Sandinistas successfully adopted this alternative in the case of Plan Masaya, whose beneficiaries had a close relationship with the socialist project through their participation in agricultural cooperatives. These farmers had previously been even more marginalized from the agricultural resources they needed to gain their livelihood than their Los Patios counterparts. Only a tiny minority of them had, through inheritance or other means, achieved the economic security derived from owning a piece of land.

Just as the fortification of a sector of small-holding capitalist farmers has political implications for the regime that makes this possible, the fact that Plan Masaya beneficiaries came from a fraction of the peasantry that was heavily proletarianized also had implications. As Paige's (1975) hypotheses about the political tendencies of those who depend to a significant degree on wages suggest, it is among this fraction of the rural poor—be they rural proletariat or poor peasants—that the greatest potential exists for the organization of revolutionary movements. I would extend this hypothesis to argue that it is also here that one is most likely to find support for revolutionary transformation of the countryside once the old regime is overthrown. It was this sector that experienced the greatest losses with the spread of agricultural capitalism, and it was this sector that stood to gain the most from the profound changes that are typically the goal of a socialist regime.

Thus the incorporation of these heavily proletarianized *campesinos* into Plan Masaya provided the project with a beneficiary population that would be strongly inclined to favor its overall impact. Plan Masaya brought about profound change in the regions where it was implemented. It accomplished this by taking land away from medium- and large-sized capitalist producers and turning it over to the formerly landless and land-poor. In the process, it reshaped the nature of agrarian social relations in its areas of influence.

However, although the land they received through Plan Masaya changed their status in the labor market, the collective form of organization their production took prevented them from developing the consciousness of individual capitalist farmers. In fact, their collective production would have reinforced the solidarity toward others in their position that their proletarian origins had instilled in them. Just as structural interdependence characterizes wage labor (Paige 1975), it describes labor relations within a cooperative as well. In the specific case of Plan Masaya, it also served to integrate them more fully into the Sandinista project. As a consequence, they tended to maintain their support for the party that had made Plan Masaya possible, in the midst of economic decline and the continuing war.

These two cases, drawn from Nicaragua's agrarian reform, confirm the assertion made above that popular participation is crucial during the transition to socialism in Third World countries. Although most of the examples upon which this thesis is based do not refer to simply partaking in collective production, I would argue that it is another instance of participation-integration in the revolutionary project. This same assertion was made by Serra (1991, 237) following an extensive study of peasant political participation during the

Sandinista regime. From that study, he concludes that cooperatives—especially CAS—played a central role in facilitating participation. He highlights the fact that, for many campesinos, membership in a cooperative represented their first opportunity to interact in an ongoing fashion in a group outside of their immediate families. It was in this environment that they learned how to express their opinions, vote on issues, and essentially become political beings. Serra (1991, 251) emphasizes that despite limitations that might have existed in the degree of democracy within cooperatives, they were a crucial initial step in the direction of incorporating this sector into the political life of the country—a step that was distinguished in a fundamental way from the virtually complete political exclusion that had characterized their members' lives previously.

Collective production arrangements, whether in agriculture or industry, symbolize a break with the past. In addition to providing a forum for learning how to participate politically, they reflect the recognition that, by uniting forces, those who compose the collectivity will advance further than each one of them could do on his or her own. This is a major step away from the individuality that is the essence of capitalist production relations. At the same time, collective production relations represent progress toward the social orientation that forms the basis of socialist production relations.

It is my contention that participation in a revolutionary form of production arrangement has the potential of causing as significant an impact on its members' thinking about their society as does their participation in other aspects of the revolutionary project. Burawoy (1985, 7), in fact, makes a convincing case for the preeminent role production relations play in the formation of political consciousness.[25] He succinctly states that "as men and women transform raw materials into useful things, they also reproduce particular social relations as well as an experience of those relations." Although Burawoy's discussion of production relations is based upon examples quite different from those of the Nicaraguan case, the dynamics that he analyzes are certainly relevant to the subject at hand, even if only in terms of recognizing general societal patterns. Thus in the Nicaraguan context, membership in a production cooperative was, in principle, quite likely to strengthen people's identification with the socialist project.

In essence, popular participation, whether it be in the form of collective production arrangements or otherwise, plays a critical complementary role for efforts made by a revolutionary government to improve living standards.[26] That is to say, given the virtual impossibility of sustaining, in the short to medium term, any economic advances that are successfully brought about (cf. Fagen 1986), participation raises the population's consciousness as to the reasons for the economic reversals that are bound to occur. Moreover, in a context like that of Los Patios, in which economic improvements may actually be politically counterproductive for the socialist project, popular participation can potentially modify such tendencies.

In addition, participation can also be crucial if it leads the popular sectors to have a genuine impact upon policymaking. In these circumstances, to some extent regardless of the outcome of policymaking, the popular sectors will identify the project promoted by the government as their own. Clearly, developing this degree of participation and identification will require time and a high level of creativity in opening up avenues for its realization. Nonetheless, mass organizations, collective production relations, and many other kinds of organizations have the potential of contributing to this process.

Yet, although this kind of participation may be related to the mobilizing efforts of the regime—oriented to fostering development projects, as well as garnering political support—the two phenomena are not synonymous. On the one hand, participation implies the incorporation, from the ground up, of people (in this context, particularly members of the popular classes) into decisionmaking related to production, distribution, development, and so forth. On the other hand, mobilization implies the active effort—potentially and frequently, from the top down—to organize this participation. However, the state or dominant political party can "mobilize" its citizenry into projects that the latter may or may not have played a role in designing. In order for mobilization not to revert to mere manipulation of the population aimed at creating an unreal image of its participation in politics, constant attention must be paid to ensuring the openness and functioning of those avenues of participation (cf. Harris 1992 and Friedland 1982). In sum, although closely related, it is important to bear in mind that these two concepts are not identical.

Thus, in reflecting on the case of the Los Patios agrarian reform project, what I am suggesting might have ameliorated the potential inherent to the project to produce a conservatizing effect, was the organization of its beneficiaries into associations or organizations that would have brought about their genuine involvement in its implementation and in the resolution of any problems that might have characterized that process. Nevertheless, the major shortcoming represented by the lack of a comprehensive organizational element within the Los Patios project was not the only instance in which the active participation of a sector of Nicaragua's population failed to take place. In fact, Los Patios beneficiaries came to form part of the growing pool of Nicaraguans whose participation in the process of societal change was becoming increasingly limited by the mid-1980s. At that point in time, a reversion toward exclusive reliance on traditional avenues of political participation was beginning to occur.

The results of the reversion highlight the problematic nature of this approach to politics during the transition to socialism. As Fagen (1986) had theorized, the continuing class conflict, growing economic difficulties, and military threat had begun to produce a drop in support for the regime. Yet, instead of attempting to maintain the level of popular mobilization and participation that had existed within the general population during the early 1980s (Serra 1985 and Vilas 1986a and 1986b), the Sandinistas moved to institutionalize the revolutionary process and channel popular opinion almost solely through the electoral ballot box. The process of institutionalization began in the mid-1980s and was symbolized in the fact that the political parties replaced the mass organizations in the newly elected legislature (the National Assembly).[27] This change signaled a shift to more traditional forms of governing.

The other side of the process of institutionalization was a process of demobilization of the Nicaraguan population. This was especially true of the mass organizations that had formed in the period preceding and immediately after the overthrow of Somoza in 1979. These organizations had served many functions, including political organizing in opposition to the regime and assisting with civilian defense against Somoza's National Guard, when the latter reacted with violent repression to the popular uprising against the dictatorship (cf. Booth 1985 and Serra 1985). Once the Sandinista government was in power, the mass organizations facilitated the provision of government services, such as vaccination campaigns and the sale of rationed goods. In addition, the population was organized into brigades that formed the "teacher corps" for the literacy campaign, and militia forces and neighborhood defense groups that complemented the work of the army and the police. In sum, the mass organizations played a key role in raising political consciousness, carrying out development projects, and assisting the defense effort. Moreover, they were the primary means open to the majority of Nicaragua's population to participate in the country's process of social transformation.

Yet the wave of popular organizing that had fueled the activities of these organizations in the late 1970s and early 1980s was receding, even by the time the elections were held in 1984. The elections, however, represented a definite turning point in that they clarified that the government recognized the organizations' weakened status and sanctioned their decreasing importance in ensuring their members' continuing participation in decisionmaking.[28] The organization most clearly affected by this process of change was the Sandinista Defense Committee (CDS). This organization had been established at the neighborhood level, especially in urban areas. It was designed to be the widest-reaching of the mass organizations and to tend to some of the basic needs of every household, while also serving as a transmission belt for demands from the base level up to government policymakers.

Nonetheless, by the mid-1980s the CDS had come to find that many of its functions had gradually been taken over or eliminated by the government.[29] Moreover, the CDS was likewise affected by the escalating war and the deepening economic crisis. This was expressed, on the one hand, in the government's use of the CDS to assist its draft-recruitment drives and to notify families of the death or injuries of draftees. These tasks are not typically popular in any country at war. Even more important, they made the delicate balance that needed to characterize this organization if it was to be all that it was set out to be—an extension of the government and a representative for the population's interests—tip in favor of the former. On the other hand, the urban development projects that the CDS had earlier helped to shape, through voicing neighborhoods' needs, were severely cut back as a consequence of the expansion in defense-related spending and the simultaneous reduction of investments in other areas. Thus, the influence it had been able to exert earlier over governmental decisionmaking—which varied somewhat between communities depending on their degree of organization and capacity for voicing demands—had clearly dropped off as its activities, and the government's resources, became restricted. Finally, the increasingly difficult nature of everyday life limited the amount of time people had to devote to activities outside of work and family maintenance. With a growing scarcity of energy and diminishing returns from that expended, people instead chose to direct their attention elsewhere. The end result was that, by the mid-1980s the CDS was largely inactive. Although efforts were made to resurrect it starting in 1985, it never recovered the dynamism that it had acquired in the early 1980s.

Several of the other mass organizations also experienced changes during this period that led to a reduction in the level of mobilization characterizing their memberships. The Luisa Amanda Espinoza Association of Nicaraguan Women (AMNLAE) was one of these. AMNLAE had originally been founded as a means for middle-class housewives to decry the repression of the Somoza regime, and it had gone on to become an advocate of women's rights. Even though the organization was still able to raise certain key feminist issues for debate into the latter half of the 1980s, such as that of legalizing abortion, frustration over its general inability to maintain a consistent struggle on behalf of women's concerns had led to a major desertion of its ranks by 1987–88. The organization's submission to the FSLN's position, that other issues must be secondary to that of the revolution's defense, meant that there were a restricted number of areas in which it could work and a limit beyond which it would not push the state in its efforts to better the lives of Nicaraguan women.

The one notable (and only partial) exception to the pattern of demobilization that described the various mass organizations was the case of the National Union of Farmers and Ranchers (UNAG). Over the course of the 1980s, the UNAG assumed an ever-greater autonomy from the government and the

FSLN.³⁰ It played a crucial role in pushing through the shift in agrarian policies of the mid-1980s and in promoting the improvements that occurred during this period in producer prices for basic grains.³¹ In addition to functioning as a pressure group from outside the government, the UNAG continued to make its presence felt from inside the policymaking process even after the changes occurred in the structure of the National Assembly in 1984–85. That is, nine of the sixty-one seats (and seventeen of the alternates' positions) won by the FSLN in the National Assembly in the 1984 elections—of the total of ninety-six seats in the Assembly—were occupied by UNAG members who had run on the FSLN ticket (Luciak 1995, 106). Seventeen of these twenty-six representatives were also members of the FSLN, but the rest belonged to other parties. In contrast to the other mass organizations, the UNAG's strong presence in the legislature permitted it to exert considerably more influence over policymaking than it would have if it had not had its own representatives in the Assembly.

Yet the UNAG was distinguished from the other mass organizations in another sense as well. This difference stemmed from the fact that its membership was largely composed of agrarian reform beneficiaries organized into cooperatives, which represented a special "pocket" of mobilization and participation. Collective production arrangements—a key form of participation in Nicaragua's ongoing process of social transformation—remained significant in the countryside. They were, nonetheless, an exception to the norm in terms of the demobilization of the country's population. Thus, where popular organizing and mobilization continued to be strong, the sectors involved were able to remain important actors in the country's political process. That is to say, an interactive relationship existed between the level of popular organizing and government recognition of the group's demands and rights to actively participate in decisionmaking.

In sum, although many were surprised by the results of the 1990 elections, after calm reflection it is easier to understand them. In essence, permitting an opposition group to fully contest the power of the state in the context of a generalized demobilization of the popular classes, who were exhausted and pessimistic after years of economic deterioration and military threat, was tantamount to surrendering the socialist project.

Conclusion

The foregoing review of development theory revealed the relatively limited degree of understanding that prevails with regard to the complex relationship between politics and economic development. This theoretical weakness characterizes the work of those whose focus has been on capitalist development, as well as those who have studied socialist development in the Third World. Nonetheless, the latter subgroup has initiated a line of analysis that offers a framework for the study of specific aspects of this process.

In contrast, the field of peasant politics, while not devoid of differing viewpoints, presents a much more advanced analysis of the political tendencies of the peasantry and the political impact of agrarian reform. An essential component of the theses that have been set forth about the peasantry's political inclinations is the effect that the expansion of capitalism into agriculture has on the peasantry—and, as a consequence, on its political outlook. However, the literature addressing the impact of socialist development on the peasantry is less abundant, particularly with regard to that which occurs in the Third World.

The following discussion attempts to bridge the literature of development and that of peasant studies, drawing on ideas that have emerged from each, to contribute to filling in the gaps still existing in both. Thus, this analysis of the Nicaraguan case, as seen through its agrarian reform, provides some corollaries to the theses that have been elaborated to explain the dilemmas of the politics of the transition. Nicaragua's heritage of dependent capitalism created the need for agrarian reform, if balanced, equitable development was to be achieved. It also set the parameters within which such reform could be implemented. The reform, as evidenced through the study of two specific projects, did succeed in bringing social and economic benefits to its participants. It introduced new levels of technology to food crop production and food crop producers (i.e., the peasants). It also opened up key areas of the fertile Pacific coast to domestic crop production, where export crop production had prevailed since the latter's adoption. Yet these changes were not sufficient to ensure continuing support for the Sandinista regime in the context of growing economic deterioration and an almost decade-old war. When provided with the option, a majority of the agrarian reform's beneficiaries joined forces with the rest of the population in voting for a candidate that represented a reorientation of the society toward the capitalist world. Armed with the theoretical tools provided by those who study socialist development, this outcome becomes more comprehensible. However, our analysis of Nicaragua's agrarian reform will demonstrate that there were nuances in this political dynamic. In essence, it will highlight the mediating effects that class origins, the social organization of production, and the strategy of reform pursued have on popular support for a socialist project.

In sum, states attempting to bring about a socialist transformation of their societies are confronted by many of the same structural impediments to economic development that their counterparts in capitalist regimes face. The former have the additional responsibility of trying to meet the needs of the social sectors in whose name their efforts are being waged. Moreover, the establishment of a socialist regime, in and of itself, will almost automatically stimulate an escalation in the population's demands, for dependent capitalism had permitted no illusions of equality. The transformation process will also typically encounter growing opposition, of both a military and political nature, as class conflict deepens. The challenge then becomes to maintain the loyalty of the popular classes, even as economic hardship is intensified. Their participation, in a multitude of forms, is crucial in this effort. For if they are closed off from participation, they will probably question what they are getting for all of their sacrifices. Within such a context, the opening up of the political arena to a genuine contestation of power through such traditional political forms as elections, contains within it the potential of producing an overthrow of the socialist project.

2

How the FSLN Lost the Hearts and Minds of the Peasantry

The agrarian reform process that was initiated in Nicaragua in 1979 had both economic and political goals. In the economic sphere, Sandinista policymakers sought to raise the level of the productive forces characterizing agricultural production, achieve a better balance between production for export and that oriented toward domestic consumption, and improve the standard of living of the rural poor. All of these achievements, but especially the last, were supposed to contribute to the goal of consolidating political support for the new government among the rural population. In addition, the overall process of democratization, in both economic and political terms, that was set in motion by the agrarian reform was seen as a further means of strengthening the legitimacy of the Sandinista regime.

Nonetheless, by the mid-1980s, Sandinista policymakers had come to recognize that their initial model of agricultural transformation had yielded limited results in both economic and political terms. That is, the strategy of developing major agroindustrial projects as a means of making the country's interchange with the international economy more advantageous to Nicaragua required massive ongoing investments. These investments were more and more difficult to maintain in the face of diminishing foreign assistance and the need for greater expenditures on defense as the Contra war deepened. In addition, the state farm sector had still not, as yet, begun to generate the surplus that had been envisioned early on, despite continuing subsidization by the state. On the political terrain, it was becoming increasingly clear that a significant part of the peasantry did not share the policymakers' vision that the road to raising its standard of living lay in its proletarianization (i.e., through employment on state farms). Moreover, the offer of land through participation in a cooperative proved lacking in attractiveness to those who had any resources whatsoever.

The adoption of this initial strategy of agricultural transformation had been based on a number of factors. These included a concern that if the land that had been held in the state farm sector was redistributed to the peasantry, a very serious shortage of labor for agroexport production would occur because the new reform beneficiaries would opt to work their own land instead of selling their labor to the export crop growers.[1] In addition, the argument was made that if the land was redistributed—especially in the form of individual plots—it would be almost impossible to achieve higher levels of cooperation in agriculture later on. Also, the goal of maintaining a modus vivendi with the larger members of the private sector—i.e., keeping "national unity" alive—was also at play. That is, the strategy's designers feared that unless the state tightly controlled the redistribution of land, and unless it remained relatively limited in scope, the peasantry would push the process at a pace and in directions that would threaten the agrarian bourgeoisie and weaken national unity.

But there was more at issue in the agrarian reform and development strategy than these three concerns. Furthermore, support for this strategy was not forthcoming from all of the sectors that were involved in policymaking with regard to agriculture and the rural population. At heart, two quite distinct visions of an appropriate strategy of rural development existed within policymaking circles—one a more technocratic vision and one a more propeasant vision. The technocratic vision was primarily represented by high level officials at the Ministry of Agricultural Development and Agrarian Reform (MIDINRA)—led by the minister himself, Cmdt. Jaime Wheelock. Its adherents succeeded in prevailing in policy decisions during the first half of the 1980s. In contrast, the propeasant (or *campesinista*) vision was promoted by some middle-level MIDINRA officials and some local FSLN representatives, but most importantly by the UNAG. By the mid-1980s the latter vision had begun to gain ground over the former.

A number of elements underlay the differences between the two visions. On the one hand, according to the the technocrats' vision, Nicaragua's transition to socialism—and socialist agriculture—depended on closely following the model of development that had been pursued by the more advanced socialist countries. The key aspects of this model included the push to raise the country's productive forces at a rapid pace; the nationalization of agrarian reform property and its management in state enterprises; and a reduced emphasis on reaching an accommodation with the various fractions of the peasantry, as its proletarianization was seen to be inevitable and preferable.[2]

On the other hand, the propeasant vision argued for a gradualist approach to raising the level of the productive forces—one based on appropriate levels of technology that could be utilized by the various sectors of the rural population, including the peasantry. This vision's proponents sought the incorporation of all sectors of the rural population—but most especially the distinct fractions of the peasantry and the *chapiollo* (domestically oriented) bourgeoisie—into the process of agricultural development and transformation. And, the propeasant sector also promoted a deepening of the agrarian reform—which would dramatically expand the pool of beneficiaries and broaden it to include individual peasants.[3]

Those who held this latter vision remained relatively marginalized until the above-mentioned shortcomings of the first had become abundantly apparent. Even then, what emerged as the predominant strategy in the second half of the 1980s was something of a hybrid of the two approaches. Within this hybrid the state sector lost ground—as exemplified by the drop of 44 percent in the area/properties it controlled between 1983 and 1988—but was not eliminated (calculated from Wheelock 1984a, table 5, and CIERA 1989a, table 1). Likewise, while the agrarian reform was deepened—and individual peasant households also began to be benefited by it (as described below), cooperatives were still emphasized, and, by and large, the land of productive medium and large growers remained untouched by it (i.e., after the confiscation of Somoza and his close associates' holdings in the 1979–81 period).[4] Despite the fact that this hybrid approach to policymaking indicated that the technocrats had yet to be completely defeated,[5] the shift signaled a real advance for the propeasant vision of agrarian development.

The shift in agrarian policymaking also reflected the redefinition that was underway at this point in time of the concept of "mixed economy," a process that was not unrelated to the larger ideological shift between the technocratic and propeasant visions. Earlier, while in theory the concept had referred to the coexistence of the state and private (including small, medium, and large producers) sectors,[6] it was commonly used to describe the state and the large, capitalist-producer sectors. But as this latter relationship experienced growing difficulties, the state began to turn to the cooperative and medium and small producer sectors as increasingly important allies in the mixed economy.[7]

The concept of mixed economy, however, was not only used to refer to the political alliance whose common project was national reconstruction. In addition, it referred to the economic weight each sector was understood to have within the national economy. Thus, by 1986 the government's perception of the potential economic importance of small- and medium-sized producers and the cooperative sector had grown in inverse proportion to its perception of that of the large, capitalist-producer sector.[8] That is to say, during the first few years of Sandinista policymaking, the gradual elimination of the peasantry as a participant in the nation's economy was the dominant vision. Its members were to be incorporated as workers in a simplified class structure. By the mid-1980s this vision of the peasantry's role in Nicaragua's economic development had been replaced by one that considered it an important economic actor in its own right. The goal then became to fortify its production or initiate a process of repeasantization.

The policy shift this changed orientation was embodied in took a variety of forms, including the implementation of a number of region-specific agrarian reform projects that were propeasant in nature. Los Patios and Plan Masaya were two such projects. These projects shared the agrarian reform's dual goals of economic development and political consolidation. Both Los Patios and Plan Masaya set in motion a process of strengthening the economic potential of the campesino population in the regions where they were implemented. They also broadened the reach of the agrarian reform to include peasants that were collectively *and* individually organized. In the process, the projects concretized the more propeasant orientation emerging in Sandinista policy making at this time, toward greater flexibility in the form of organization that agrarian reform beneficiaries might adopt. Yet the success of Los Patios and Plan Masaya at increasing the government's legitimacy among this sector of the population remained to be determined.

Several indicators had been employed by the Sandinista government prior to the policy shift to determine that the legitimacy of the regime was becoming strained, and that some changes would be necessary to counter that process. One such indicator was the high level of membership rotation that characterized the cooperatives. That is, many people joined cooperatives in order to receive land, but dropped out shortly thereafter. It became apparent that collective forms of production were a last resort to many, and that their full acceptance as an alternative to *minifundio* production had not yet been achieved. At the same time, low recruitment levels for the military draft—or Patriotic Military Service (SMP)—and a lack of response to FSLN organizing efforts served as additional cues that support for the government and the FSLN was waning.

The results of the 1984 General Election were an additional indication that a new strategy for addressing the problems of the countryside had to be adopted by the government. At the national level, the elections were a tremendous success for the Sandinistas: with 75 percent of the registered voters casting ballots, the incumbent party won 67 percent of the valid votes, or 63 percent of the total votes cast (LASA 1984, 17).[9] The next party in line in terms of votes received, the Democratic Conservative Party (PCD), won a mere 14 percent of the valid votes, or 13 percent of the total votes cast. Furthermore, the FSLN only lost the election in one of the country's one-hundred and thirty-nine municipalities.[10] Yet, the close results in a number of the municipalities indicated that policy shifts would be required in order to increase support for the governing party.

Electoral results from certain of the country's rural areas pointed to the

Table 2.1. Electoral support for the FSLN, 1984 and 1990 (percentages)

	1984	1990	Drop
National	62.9	40.8	22.1
Urban[a]	61.9	38.5	23.4
Rural[b]	62.7	35.9	26.8
Agrarian reform projects' areas of influence (precinct-level)			
Los Patios	—	34.5[c]	
Plan Masaya	—	39.8[c]	

Sources: IHCA (1985a); Supreme Electoral Council (CSE 1990); CSE (unpublished data, 1990).
[a]Nicaragua's twenty-six most urbanized municipalities, as defined by IHCA (1985a).
[b]The rural figures for 1984 were calculated from data for 99 of Nicaragua's 139 municipalities; the figures for 1990 were calculated from data for 103 municipalities. In 1985 the total number of municipalities grew to 143 and several of those included in the figure for 1984 were divided in two.
[c]Dividing lines between precincts were altered throughout the country between 1985 and 1990, making a comparison of the electoral results at this level impossible.

need to respond more directly to the concerns of the peasantry, if it was to be enlisted in efforts to consolidate the regime. The provision of land was seen as being the key to reaching the peasantry. The government reacted to this show of weakened support by initiating a number of land redistribution projects (epitomized by Plan Masaya). Where land redistribution was not possible, the redistribution of other productive resources and the promotion of schemes that would benefit the peasantry even without increasing their access to land (with programs like Los Patios) were seen as alternative solutions.

Given the weight placed on the results of the 1984 General Election in assessing the success of the agrarian reform after five years of implementation, the results of the 1990 General Election would appear to be a reasonable indicator of the achievements and limitations of the policy shift that occurred in the agrarian reform in the mid-1980s. Moreover, analyzing the 1990 elections is arguably a valid means by which to evaluate the political impact that the agrarian reform had produced following more than a decade of implementation. Thus, we will use this indicator as a starting point in our exploration of the response of the peasantry to the process of transformation that was initiated by the reform.

The outcome of the 1990 General Election came as a surprise to most Nicaraguan voters and international observers.[11] Contrary to many predictions, the FSLN lost the election by a striking margin: the National Opposition Union (UNO) won 54.7 percent of the vote, in contrast with the FSLN's 40.8 percent (see table 2.1). Support for the FSLN had dropped markedly in the five and one-half years that had passed since the last general election. And this was especially the case for Nicaragua's rural areas.

Beyond stating the obvious, that the majority of Nicaraguan voters were clearly dissatisfied with the FSLN's tenure of governing, it is important to examine the election results to see what further conclusions can be drawn. Two principal means have been employed in the present study to do that: (1) an assessment of voting patterns in the precincts that were in the areas of influence of Plan Masaya and Los Patios; and (2) in-depth interviews conducted several months after the election with the projects' beneficiaries concerning their attitudes about the Sandinista and UNO governments.

My review of the data gleaned from these two sources will begin with the former. It is important to note, however, that what these data provide is a general picture of the level of support for the FSLN in these rural areas, rather than clear evidence as to how the projects' participants voted. This is so because the number of beneficiaries who might have voted in any one precinct represented a relatively small percentage of the total voting population there (this issue will be discussed at greater length below). Nonetheless, the electoral data offer a starting point for addressing the issue of the political impact of the projects by describing the common sentiment of the adult population in these two regions.

A detailed, precinct-level assessment of the election results for the whole country is beyond the scope of the present study.[12] Yet, it is possible to obtain an initial impression by analyzing voting patterns at the precinct level for the areas in which Los Patios and Plan Masaya had an influence. As can be seen in table 2.1, the voting population in the Los Patios areas of influence supported the FSLN even less than the rural population in the nation as a whole in 1990. In contrast, voters in the Plan Masaya areas of influence were slightly more inclined toward the FSLN than either the rural voting population at the national level or voters in the Los Patios areas of influence. Regardless, in neither of the two projects' areas did the voting population as a whole (as opposed to certain specific precincts) reelect the FSLN.

In order to assess the reasons for the low level of support for the FSLN among the voters in the areas of influence of Los Patios and Plan Masaya, I returned to the countryside to converse with members of each project's beneficiary population in mid-1990.[13] The in-depth interviews I conducted with them revealed that support for the incumbent party among this more select population appeared to have varied slightly from that of the rural population as a whole in the precincts included in their areas of influence. That is, support for the FSLN was significantly stronger among Plan Masaya beneficiaries than in the rest of the rural population, while Los Patios beneficiaries voted in a fashion similar to most of their rural counterparts.

The differences between the two projects' populations in the vote, and their political perspectives more generally, will be addressed in subsequent chapters. Prior to this, however, it is important to understand the broader reasons for the FSLN's defeat in the countryside. The interviews I conducted with both projects' beneficiaries highlighted many of these factors. For, even though my interviews suggested that Plan Masaya participants supported the FSLN more than either the rural population as a whole in the municipalities in which they lived or the country's entire voting population, a significant number of them did vote for a change in government. Thus, what follows is a description of the specific issues that had alienated a sector of the beneficiaries from the Sandinista government. Given the influence that these issues had for the rural population in general, it is assumed that this description should also shed light on the political impact of the agrarian reform in the country as a whole.

What Went Wrong?

What many observers, both national and international, concluded in the aftermath of the UNO electoral victory over the incumbent FSLN party, was that a variety of factors had contributed to produce this unexpected outcome. The most important factors were the drastically deteriorated economic situation, the Contra war, and a desire for improved relations with the U.S. Several other factors probably also swayed some voters away from the FSLN, such as certain campaign errors, a fear of FSLN *continuismo* (the tendency to maintain oneself in power indefinitely), and a history of problematic relations between the incumbent party and the Catholic church hierarchy.

This combination of issues represented concerns held by most Nicaraguans. The specific emphasis they were given in determining the vote for UNO might have varied slightly by region and sector. Thus, in those areas most directly affected by the war, the desire for peace, and the perception that with the Sandinistas in power it would prove unattainable, may have outweighed all of the other factors. Nonetheless, peace and economic improvement were clearly priorities for the vast majority of those who voted for UNO, including those among the rural population in Masaya, Carazo, and Diriomo.

The Economic Crisis

Los Patios and Plan Masaya beneficiaries pointed to the tremendous economic decline of the previous few years as being especially important in determining their vote against the FSLN. These farmers were hurt by the general economic deterioration experienced by the country as a whole, as well as by economic policies specifically directed at agricultural producers.[14]

An idea of the dimension of Nicaragua's economic crisis can be grasped by reviewing a few key indicators. One such indicator was the inflation rate. From an average of 32 percent annually between 1980 and 1984, it rose to 747 percent in 1986, 1,347 percent in 1987, and 33,603 percent in 1988, before dropping to 1,690 percent in 1989.[15] Both the monetary reform that was implemented in February of 1988 and the destruction caused by Hurricane Joan, which struck Nicaragua in October of that year, contributed to the extraordinary rate of inflation in 1988.[16] By late 1989, though, there was a clear, consistent trend toward improvement in the inflation rate.

The positive effects of this trend, however, were undercut for the popular classes by other economic factors. For example, wages had not kept pace with price rises throughout the period of hyperinflation. It was not until 1989, after six years of wage increases being undermined by inflation, that an increase in real wages occurred (CEPAL 1990, 23). Yet this increase was of a mere 25 percent, which did little to ameliorate the accumulated effects of the previous years' slippage.

At the same time, unemployment was on the rise. From the low point of 16.0 percent in 1981, un- and underemployment had grown steadily to 32.1 percent in 1989 (CEPAL 1990, 32). Moreover, what had been an incremental annual increase in unemployment was accelerated when, in the few months following the monetary reform in February 1988, the government carried out a campaign to streamline its bureaucracy. The objective of the campaign was to reduce the government's budget deficit. Known as the "*compactación*," it resulted in the loss of employment for more than 10,000 people (with the goal of total government lay offs being 30,000 by 1989) (Stahler-Sholk 1990b, 211).

In addition, the stabilization program that was initiated with the monetary reform entailed reductions in what had come to be known as the "social wage." The social wage consisted of social services and subsidized goods, with several of the most important being the free provision of health care and education, and low-cost public transportation and basic foodstuffs. The social wage had served as a buffer to rising prices, and guaranteed access to services that had previously been out of reach for much of the population. Although government subsidization had begun dropping in 1985, the significant reduction that occurred in 1988 made palpable the full effect of the country's economic crisis for the popular classes.[17]

Several other economic indicators also suggest the depth of the crisis. For example, the real Gross Domestic Product per capita in 1989 was 65 percent of what it had been in 1980, even falling below what it had been nearly three decades earlier, in 1960 (CEPAL 1990, 23, and Conroy 1990, 6). The trade deficit, although showing an improvement over the previous six years, was still $418 million (U.S.) in 1989 (CEPAL 1990, 38). The accumulation of this notable a yearly shortfall over more than a decade severely strained the economy and limited the range of goods that could be imported. Finally, the foreign debt had reached $7.6 billion (U.S.) by the end of 1989, almost five times what it had been in 1979 (CEPAL 1990, 40, and 1981, 39).

Toward the end of 1989, however, clear signs had emerged that the economic reform had produced some positive results. In addition to a significantly reduced inflation rate, agricultural exports had increased 13 percent over what they had been in 1988 (CEPAL 1990, 35). Nonetheless, though a number of macroeconomic indicators pointed to an improvement in Nicaragua's economic situation, most of the population did not perceive any changes for the better in its household economy during this period.

Nicaragua's peasant farmers were seriously affected by the economic crisis, but they experienced it in a different manner from salaried workers. In general, most were able to guarantee their basic food requirements with their own production, in contrast to salaried workers who only saw the purchasing power of their wages decline. Yet, given the cyclical pattern of agricultural production, many campesinos found themselves having to survive from one year to the next on harvest earnings that were worth significantly less several months after the harvest than when they had been received. Moreover, price increases during the few months lapse between the harvest and the next planting made these earnings meaningless vis-à-vis the inputs purchases that were required to begin the following agricultural cycle. Consequently, most peasants were unable to plant and cultivate their crops without 100 percent of the costs being assumed by the state through agricultural credit.

The economic reform, however, brought about changes in many key policy areas related to agricultural production.[18] One of the first measures to affect agricultural producers was a policy directed at the population as a whole, the temporary freezing of assets over the specified limit considered normal for an average family. That is, during the three-day period in which the national currency was replaced by a new currency, those who had more than $10 million old *córdobas* (equivalent to 10,000 new córdobas or $1,000 (U.S.) at the official exchange rate established by the reform) in their possession were given a certificate for the amount above this quantity. The certificate was not redeemable in the recently introduced currency until 12-24 months later. The logic behind this measure was that of reducing the currency in circulation and nullifying the large sums of money presumed to be held by the Contras and speculators.

Among agricultural producers, those most affected by the temporary limitation on currency conversion were the larger growers. Nonetheless, some of the bigger cooperatives, including several of those participating in Los Patios, also had their bank accounts frozen. Serious cash flow problems resulted for these cooperatives. Members of their administrative staffs had to be laid off, and working capital for inputs purchases for the coming planting season was unavailable. Although the rationale behind this measure was reasonable, and it did serve to decapitalize the Contras and many speculators, the cooperatives that had been able to accumulate some capital were unintended victims.

At the same time, agricultural producers were also hit by the major currency devaluation that formed part of the monetary reform. Even though the devaluation affected the population as a whole, farmers were especially hard hit because their income does not come in regular installments. Many of them had only just received their year's income from the sale of their harvest when the reform was implemented on 15 February. Thus, these producers' annual earnings were instantly and massively devalued.

Shortly thereafter agricultural producers throughout the country were confronted by the government's new credit policy. The implementation of the monetary reform brought with it the announcement that there would be a reduction in short-term agricultural financing of 10 percent and one of 30 percent for long-term loans. Ultimately, short-term financing was not cut to this extent. The percentage of production costs officially covered by credit, however, dropped from 100 percent to 70 percent. It could certainly be argued that agricultural financing of 100 percent was beyond what could reasonably be expected from state financial institutions. Moreover, such financing did nothing to encourage reinvestment of earnings in productive activities. For the newly formed cooperatives, the absence of a need to reinvest did little to stimulate a conception of their farms as financial enterprises that would have to be economically efficient and solvent to survive. Yet, coming on the heels of the devaluation of their harvest earnings, and an eight-year-old tradition of extensive financing, the more restricted credit policy represented a financial burden the peasantry was not prepared for.

In June of 1988, follow-up measures were implemented to correct some of the weaknesses of the policies initiated four months earlier. Among these measures was a restructuring of the government's credit policies. One of the primary changes made at this time was the pegging of loan interest rates to changes in cost-of-living indices. Interest rates had, in real terms, been negative since 1980 because the rate of inflation had consistently surpassed the low, fixed rates set on credit each year. The end result was that producers were, in essence, not required to invest any of their own resources in production, and they could actually make a profit off the loans provided to them. This policy proved to be a tremendous drain on state resources, given that the bank was never able to recover in full what it lent to producers.[19] Thus, in an effort to increase the level of recuperation and promote more efficient production, the transfer of resources that was implied in fixed interest rates was eliminated. As a consequence, agricultural credit suddenly became more expensive for producers.

In addition, the purchase of many agricultural inputs had heretofore been subsidized. This was especially the case for imported inputs. Some of these were basic supplies for agricultural production, even for farmers employing traditional levels of technology (e.g., rubber boots). The subsidization had been made possible by the existence of multiple exchange rates that lowered the price of these goods in an effort to stimulate production.[20] With the implementation of the monetary reform in February 1988, however, the exchange rate was made uniform. The outcome was the elimination of previous subsidies, immediately making inputs more costly.

This policy change was oriented toward furthering the larger goal of reducing the government's huge fiscal deficit and financial losses that had been caused by subsidization in a number of areas of the economy. The new exchange rate policies also sought to make "prices for imports and exports . . . more closely reflect the acute scarcity of foreign exchange" (Stahler-Sholk 1990b, 411). Another hoped-for side effect was that of encouraging increased efficiency in the use of imported inputs.

The producers that were hardest hit by the exchange rate unification were those who were heavily dependent on imported technologies.[21] This general pattern was evidenced in the case of Los Patios and Plan Masaya beneficiaries. As briefly mentioned in chapter 1, a significant percentage of Plan Masaya beneficiaries had been included in a second agrarian reform project, the PATD. One of the PATD's primary objectives was to raise the level of technology characterizing their basic grain production. Between 1986 and 1987 these producers shifted from a reliance upon animal traction and manual labor to cultivate their corn crop to a reliance upon mechanical means of carrying out most stages of the production process. The state sold tractors at favorable prices to the cooperatives that participated in both Plan Masaya and the PATD. Participating cooperatives that were not sold tractors started paying state enterprises, cooperatives, or private producers with tractors for assistance with their production. They also began to depend upon aerial spraying of the pesticides employed in the cultivation of their crop, which implied an additional service charge. Thus, these producers were affected by the purchase of the imported inputs they had adopted as part of the PATD's technological package, as well as the increased cost of mechanization caused by rising fuel prices.

In contrast, Los Patios beneficiaries, and those of Plan Masaya who were not included in the PATD, were less affected by the exchange rate unification. Although both of these groups did employ some imported inputs, their dependence on them was not nearly as great as was that of the PATD participants.

The entire beneficiary populations of Los Patios and Plan Masaya were, however, affected by the increase in transportation costs that resulted from the reform. A system of periodic adjustments to the price of fuel had prevailed until then, which had served to keep prices low because of the high levels of inflation. It was altered with the reform's implementation so that fuel price adjustments became pegged to the exchange rate. Once again, the rationale behind this policy measure was twofold: to reduce government subsidization of fuel use and to encourage more efficient use of this imported input.

For Los Patios beneficiaries the new fuel pricing policy translated into a significant increase in the cost of getting their produce to the market. They were consequently forced to raise the price at which they sold their produce once there. At the same time, the opening up to market economics implied in the reform, and the removal of most subsidies, meant that many of those who had previously been able to purchase the "non-essential" food items produced by Los Patios beneficiaries were no longer able to do so. That is, fruits and vegetables had gone back to being "luxury" items accessible only to the middle and upper classes. Those among the popular classes who were unable to produce their own fruits and vegetables typically had to limit their diet to indispensable food products such as basic grains.

Many Plan Masaya beneficiaries were also negatively affected by growing transportation costs because of their dependence on public transportation to go back and forth from their homes to the farms where their cooperatives were located. Given the process of marginalization of the peasantry that had accompanied the expansion of export crop production, most of Masaya and Diriomo's campesinos did not reside close to the export estates that were included in the project. They lived in the hills and other less-fertile areas surrounding the prime export land. When Plan Masaya turned this land over to these campesinos, building materials, which would make possible a move from their traditional communities to the cooperatives, were not provided. In addition, most of the beneficiaries were strongly attached to the rural hamlets where their families had resided for generations. Thus, the norm was for them to travel by bus, on a daily basis, to their cooperatives. However, with significantly greater transportation costs, and credit reductions, it quickly became impossible to make this regular commute. Thus, they resorted to alternating work on the farm among the cooperative members, so that no one would have to pay for transportation more than a few days a week.

Finally, after managing to cultivate and harvest their crop, the country's agricultural producers were confronted by prices for their produce that bore no relation to the costly credits and inputs with which they had been forced to work. Basic grains producers were among the hardest hit by this situation, a population which included Plan Masaya beneficiaries. The basic grain prices established at the time of the monetary reform by the state's grain purchasing agency, the Nicaraguan Enterprise of Basic Foodstuffs (ENABAS), were raised over their previous value. However, they were still much less than the increases experienced by other factors of production. According to Gutiérrez (1989, 101), then director of Campesino Programs for MIDINRA: "the prices for basic grains rose 400 percent during these months . . . [in contrast] . . . basic inputs rose 700 percent, and manufactured consumer goods, 1,200 percent." And, while interest rates and input prices were indexed, producer prices were only sporadically boosted upward. The end result was that most grain production was not profitable. Moreover, although in some senses the implementation of the monetary reform symbolized the adoption of a new, free market strategy, the prices established by ENABAS still served to set the market price for grains.[22]

In sum, prior to 1988, many Los Patios and Plan Masaya beneficiaries had been shielded from feeling the full effect of the country's economic crisis. Certain elements of the social wage had protected them. They had also been cushioned by the subsidization implicit in credit and input pricing policies. In addition, in the previous few years most of the beneficiaries had received access to productive resources that had heretofore been unavailable to them. By early 1988, however, government planners considered these subsidies to be unsustainable given the fiscal deficit, financial imbalances, and hyperinflation. Regardless of the objective need for such major policy changes, and the (then) apparently reasonable expectation that the economic reform would bring about an overall improvement in the economy in the near future, many Los Patios and Plan Masaya beneficiaries focused their attention on how these measures had hurt them. They reflected on how, slowly but surely, the gains they had experienced through the agrarian reform were reversed, as the economy deteriorated and the economic reform widened its reach.

The Contra War

During the campaign period leading up to the 1990 elections, most observers and political analysts assumed that Violeta Barrios de Chamorro's (the presidential candidate for the UNO) close links to the U.S. government and the Nicaraguan Contras would prove to be a tremendous liability when voters went to the polls. The U.S. government had openly supported Chamorro, both politically and economically. In addition, several members of her political inner circle had been members of the Contra leadership, and the Contras publicly backed her. In the wake of the election, however, Chamorro's relationship with the U.S. was reinterpreted to have been seen by Nicaraguan voters as offering the only road to peace. That is, from the voters' point of view, the U.S. government would continue supporting the Contras as long as the Sandinistas remained in power.

For those living in the central mountain region, peace meant the possibility of returning to a normal life. It meant being able to live and work without the daily threat of becoming victims of the war. But achieving peace was also extremely important to people living in areas not immediately affected by the war. For them peace represented an end to the almost constant state of tension that had been endured by the population as a whole since the early 1980s, given the specter of an even more direct intervention by the U.S. With peace, the potential also existed that the dismal economic situation might be ameliorated by increased production and, although seeming to be only remotely likely, by the normalization of economic relations with the U.S. Finally, and perhaps most crucially, peace symbolized the bringing to an end of the military draft.

Implementation of the SMP had been suspended in September of 1989, as part of the political agreements between the government and the opposition parties reached in early August of that year. Those agreements had been designed to insure the participation of all of the latter groups in the elections.[23] Violeta Chamorro had, however, promised to eliminate permanently the draft as part of her program for governing. In contrast, the FSLN had only pledged to consider ending the draft if it won the elections.[24]

When the election results became known, many concluded that the FSLN's position vis-à-vis the draft had cost them the elections. Others argued that it was among the most critical of a number of factors that had produced the Sandinistas' electoral defeat.[25] My interviews with Los Patios and Plan Masaya beneficiaries suggested that the draft was *perhaps* only rivaled by the economic crisis, in terms of the rural population's reasons for opposing the FSLN's candidacy.

The military draft was unpopular among much of the population as a whole. In addition to concern for the draftee's life, family members were dismayed with the interruption it imposed in the secondary and university educations of those drafted. Even more importantly, in many cases the removal of their relatives from the household implied a loss of the income they typically generated. As the economic crisis deepened, the earnings of each member of the household, however little, were what made survival possible (see, e.g., Alemán et al. 1986).

In the countryside, the draft may have been still more unpopular than in urban areas because of the key role played by sons and daughters in agricultural production. Their participation in the myriad of tasks that composed daily life on the farm began early. Daughters often accompanied parents when the harvest was taken to the market, until they were old enough to assume the responsibility themselves. Sons assisted in the production process of the crops cultivated by the family. Their absence implied that someone had to be found to replace them, resulting in an increased expenditure of either labor or money for the household.[26] The families of draftees who provided the primary source of sustenance were supposed to receive a stipend to help substitute for their lost income. These stipends, however, were small and frequently arrived only after much delay because of bureaucratic bottlenecks and logistical difficulties.

They also usually fell far short of replacing the earnings normally brought home by the draftee. I became acquainted with one beneficiary of Plan Masaya who supported herself and her six children, after her spouse had been drafted, by farming the two *manzanas* that she had received through the project.[27] When her children were ill, she was forced to hire a laborer to work the farm. In the face of the extreme hardship implied in sustaining her household alone, it would not have been surprising had this *campesina* voted "to bring her husband back from the front."

El Puño de Hierro

El "puño de hierro" (iron fist) was the informal name given to the Sandinista government's clampdown on black-market grain sales in the mid-1980s. The name, which was coined by officials from the Ministry of Internal Commerce (MICOIN), came to represent government efforts to control various aspects of the agricultural production and marketing process. Regardless of the well-intentioned rationale that may have led to the implementation of each of these efforts, they were almost universally opposed in the countryside. Even several years after the elimination of a number of the key measures regulating produce marketing, campesinos still referred with resentment to the government interference epitomized by the *puño de hierro*.

ENABAS was founded within a few months of the establishment of the Sandinista government in July 1979. One of ENABAS's primary objectives was to capture enough (estimated at 40 percent) of the grains destined for the market to enable it to "set" the price that private intermediaries would have to match (MIPLAN 1980, 94–95). State policymakers believed that by controlling the grain market they would be able to guarantee reasonable prices to producers, as well as insure that a certain minimum quantity (to be distributed through "safe channels") of these goods would be accessible to the entire population. Nonetheless, the war, the deepening economic crisis, and earlier mistakes in setting prices that would stimulate production began to take their toll in diminishing grain supplies.[28] In response, the government looked for new mechanisms to eliminate the multitude of private intermediaries who engaged in speculation with these crucial and scarce foodstuffs.

The puño de hierro policy, which was initiated in early 1986, was one such mechanism. It essentially consisted of increased enforcement of grain marketing regulations through the use of roadblocks where vehicles were searched for grains that were being illegally transported for sale outside the rural area where they had been produced. Although the policy of impeding basic grain commercialization by private intermediaries had begun several years earlier (in 1984–85), it was seriously tightened up at this time. The primary attraction for producers of selling to intermediaries and/or taking their crop to urban markets was the substantial price difference between that offered by ENABAS and that offered outside of official channels.[29] If found, however, the produce would be confiscated by MICOIN officials. Its confiscation represented the loss of income that would have been derived from its sale.

The *tranques*, or roadblock inspections, were so deeply feared that even after grain marketing had become liberalized, farmers often preferred to continue selling their produce to ENABAS rather than risk its confiscation. This fear was reinforced by bureaucratic structures that made repayment of bank loans easier when produce was sold to ENABAS. Moreover, MIDINRA officials, and FSLN and UNAG organizers, encouraged cooperative members to continue selling their grains to ENABAS.[30]

Don Domingo, a member of a CCS that had received land through Plan Masaya, responded "to ENABAS," when I asked him in 1990 where his CCS sold the corn they produced.[31] I then asked him why they had opted to sell their crop to ENABAS (given that they were no longer legally required to do so), and his reply was: "They said we had to sell it there"; the "they" being representatives of ENABAS. Thus, despite the legal change with regard to who crops could be sold to, many producers continued to feel that they had little or no choice in this regard.

Yet the cooperatives' compliance with government grain marketing did not translate into agreement with that policy. General resentment toward the implicit requirement of selling to ENABAS was compounded in some cases by perceived anomalies in the institution's purchasing practices. For example, the fact that municipal and other taxes were automatically subtracted from the total payment made to producers did nothing to convince them of ENABAS' merits. They had only to speak with neighbors who sold to private intermediaries and did not have taxes subtracted from their payment in order to conclude that selling to ENABAS had distinct disadvantages.[32] In addition, grain prices varied from the "guaranteed price" according to the produce's quality (particularly in terms of the grain's humidity level). Thus, if a producer received less than expected because of deductions for poor quality, ENABAS (i.e., the state) was often seen as depriving him/her of the payment s/he deserved.

Don Luis, a CAS member from Diriomo who was a Plan Masaya beneficiary, complained at length about having to deal with ENABAS: "Yes, we have had problems with produce prices this year. In ENABAS in Diriomo the man [the person responsible for purchasing their grain]—that Sandinista—always reduced our payment a lot, saying that the grain was very humid. Every year he reduced our payment, but it was even worse this past year."[33] Interestingly, Don Luis was president of his CAS at the time of this interview. From many of the comments he made as we spoke, it was clear that he had a strong sense of class consciousness and was in favor of many of the goals of the Sandinista government. Nonetheless, the vehemence with which he mentioned the "Sandinista" who had, for him, effectively cheated his cooperative of part of the payment it deserved for its crop, put in evidence how widely opposed ENABAS had become by 1990.

ENABAS was not, however, the only government agency established with the mandate of purchasing produce from farmers. Two other such agencies were the National Perishables Enterprise (ENAPER) and the Perishables Marketing Promoter (PROCOMER), both of which were set up to market perishables.[34] Nonetheless, government planners never assumed that these two agencies would control the perishables market. Instead, ENAPER and PROCOMER took responsibility for specific projects developed by their respective ministries. One such project was Los Patios.

Government commercialization of the produce generated by the implementation of Los Patios had not been part of the original conception of the project. It was not until concern developed about some of the problems caused by uncontrolled commercialization that this possibility was considered. Among these problems was the fact that because the peak of the harvest was roughly simultaneous in all of the project's areas of influence, the beneficiaries' produce arrived at the market at generally the same time. Prices dropped as a consequence. In addition, most beneficiaries lacked vehicles of their own and were, therefore, forced to pay for transporting their goods to the market. Given the perishable nature of their harvest, they were at the mercy of the *transportistas* vis-à-vis the price they had to pay for this crucial service. In the interest of insuring that producers would receive a "fair price" (that would cover their production costs and provide them with a reasonable margin of profit), the government began to experiment with different forms of facilitating the commercialization process.[35]

The establishment of purchasing agreements between PROCOMER or ENAPER and perishables producers was one means employed by the state in its attempts to ameliorate the effects of the free market. Due to the nature of these crops, time is of the essence in getting them from the tree, vine, or bush to the market. Unfortunately, PROCOMER's and ENAPER's organizational capacities were not of the level required to insure consistent, successful marketing of the perishables produced by Los Patios beneficiaries. On a number of occasions, purchasing contracts were signed. But later, when the crop had been harvested, the purchasing agents simply failed to arrive at the appointed time to pick up the produce. Thus, it was left to decompose on the producer's or cooperative's property.[36] Following these fiascos (in 1986), several of the larger CCSs assumed responsibility for controlling some aspects of the commercialization process. By issuing a limited number of permits (which cost a small fee) for produce bound for urban centers, these cooperatives sought to keep the markets from being flooded. The rationale was that by this means it would be possible to keep prices fairly stable. Yet, over the next few years even this minimal control system was dismantled and the commercialization of perishables reverted to being unrestricted.

Although state control over perishable marketing never approximated ENABAS's pervasiveness in the commercialization of basic grains, in mid-1990 fruit and vegetable producers still spoke with animosity about this form of interference in their affairs.[37] Rather than interpret it as an attempt by the government to insure them a decent income, these farmers perceived it as one more example of the Sandinistas' efforts to control their lives.

Produce marketing was, however, only one area where they felt that the Sandinista government interfered too much. Many also expressed, in one form or another, that the degree of independence they had with respect to production of their crops was less than what they would have preferred. This began with the selection of what crops they would grow. For example, all of the cooperatives that formed part of Plan Masaya were required to develop an annual "production plan" prior to receiving agricultural credit. These plans were supposed to be prepared "with assistance" from MIDINRA's agricultural technicians. Yet, it was not uncommon for the technicians simply to elaborate the plan and only later review it with cooperative members. Because the relationship between the state and the cooperative sector was closest with the CAS, this tendency was clearest there.

Planners in MIDINRA's local offices were responding to a variety of factors when they encouraged cooperative members to produce certain crops. These factors included what types of crops would be most appropriate given the area's ecosystem, what crops the producers had prior experience with, and so forth. Although MIDINRA's crop selection was normally made in a reasonable fashion,[38] most of the beneficiaries who had been farmers prior to entering the project had previously been accustomed to choose the crops they would grow themselves and therefore did not necessarily see this as welcome assistance.

Moreover, it was not uncommon for the technicians who had day-to-day contact with cooperative members to perceive of themselves as more knowledgeable than the campesinos and to communicate this sense of intellectual superiority in the form of top-down advising.[39] In addition, low wages and difficult working conditions did not stimulate the technicians to seek new, innovative ways of carrying out their work with the *campesinado*. And, the centuries-old conception of the peasantry as the most backward sector of society—which the process of social change had only begun to erode—inhibited efforts to make the administration of technical assistance a joint endeavor.

Los Patios beneficiaries also resented interference vis-à-vis the "technological package" that they employed in their production.[40] The package of inputs they were encouraged to utilize was an integral part of their participation in the project. Thus, it could be argued that their willingness to participate in the project implied their agreement with the use of the technological package it promoted. But, as the economic situation worsened, and the price of inputs rose—while the market for their crops disappeared—they demonstrated a growing reluctance to invest in administering the prescribed inputs. The words of one project beneficiary, Doña Socorro, who grew *pitahaya* (a cactus fruit used to make juice) on her minifundio, convey this sentiment quite poignantly: "the cooperative ... took responsibility for buying inputs for all of the members [in fact, they even delivered her quota to her house]. But they sold them as a package—with an overall price. When I didn't want to buy the fungicide that came with the package in 1989, he [the person who brought it to her] told me that I was irresponsible—so I had to buy it and I still have it stored away here ... and they wouldn't even tell me what it was worth so that, at least, I could sell it."[41] Several informants went so far as to drop their cooperative membership so as not to have to follow the instructions of the cooperative technician with regard to inputs.[42]

In sum, much of MIDINRA's involvement in the production and marketing of the agrarian reform beneficiaries was well-intentioned and sought to protect the interests of both the rural and urban poor. Yet, the independent nature of the peasantry, and problems in the implementation of such efforts, conspired to produce interpretations of the government's actions as interference in its affairs. Resentment grew as the economic situation made survival more difficult. And nonegalitarian treatment by some of MIDINRA's agricultural technicians only served to increase antagonism toward the government.

A Persisting Resistance to Collective Agriculture

By the mid-1980s government agrarian planners and FSLN party officials were aware that the agrarian reform was not proceeding with the hoped-for success in the entirety of its facets. One particularly problematic area was that of efforts to foment cooperative development among agrarian reform beneficiaries.[43] It was concluded that the policy of collective distribution of land had not been well-received by all, and that future agrarian reform projects would have to be more flexible in this sense. But, in the wake of the 1990 elections, it was clear that many agrarian reform beneficiaries who were organized in cooperatives (especially CAS) remained discontented with this production arrangement. Some of them expressed hope that the change in government would open up the possibility of farming individually.

The interviews I conducted in mid-1990 provided a chance to "follow" the path taken by these agrarian reform beneficiaries over the few years since our earlier interview. Several of those interviewed in 1990 had left the cooperatives they had belonged to two years earlier; the cooperative of one had been transformed from a CAS into a CCS and another's cooperative had undergone the opposite transition; and one had shifted from individual farming to CCS membership. In addition, in the CAS I visited there was a strong trend toward setting aside a section of the cooperatives' property for individual farming by their members. Thus, I had the opportunity of exploring the reasons for these various changes in the cooperatives in this region.

One cause of resistance to collective farming mentioned on numerous occasions was that members were required to act as part of a group, rather than being able to operate as individuals. In essence, the source of tension was their having to abide by the collective's decisions. These involved issues ranging from work schedules, to what they would produce, to what they would sell.

The shift from generating one's livelihood as an individual to working collectively does not always take place easily. Without a doubt, farming is one of the sectors of production in which the transition is most fraught with difficulties. Agricultural production, particularly as carried out by campesino households, entails a level of independence found almost no where else in the economy (cf. Paige 1975 and Foster 1960–61). The process of collectivization was also complicated by the problems that developed with government efforts to control certain aspects of production and commercialization. As long as the cooperative functioned well, and its members could see tangible benefits resulting from their joint labor, they were likely to accept less than their ideal in terms of work organization. As the economic situation became more difficult, however, maintaining this kind of cooperation would require an increasing effort.

Fending for oneself was seen by some as an attractive alternative when faced with growing economic hardship. On almost any cooperative one could encounter a concern that at least some members did not do their part to insure that the production and commercialization processes would be completed successfully. Whether based in fact or not, circumstances such as these would become more and more onerous to accept when the well-being of the cooperative was being undermined by the economic crisis. The general reluctance on the part of the campesinado to work collectively was also probably influenced by the attitude held by some who had participated in cooperatives that the cooperative's land and resources were not really theirs. That is, they thought of themselves almost like salaried workers who collected their salary during the harvest, but who had no ongoing relationship with the land. Clearly, this identification with the land would take time to develop. Moreover, its resolution, and that of the other problems associated with the formation of cooperatives, would require a major organizational and educational effort.

The implementation of Plan Masaya in 1985 represented an acknowledgement on the part of the government and the FSLN that not all campesinos were accepting of the idea of joining a cooperative. Throughout the early 1980s, an implicit condition for receiving land was a willingness to join a CAS. CCSs were almost always formed on land that already belonged to those who joined them. Thus, CCS members organized themselves into cooperatives in order to receive benefits other than land. The implementation of Plan Masaya, however, embodied the shift that was underway in land redistribution policy (see table 6.1). Through this project, land was turned over to CAS, CCS, and individual farmers, although the number of beneficiaries in the last category was not large.

The policymakers, as well as regional UNAG officials, who brought about this shift argued that forcing campesinos to collectivize their production had serious drawbacks.[44] Rather than creating satisfied agrarian reform beneficiaries, it led to discontent among some of those who joined CAS in order to receive land, and produced an unwillingness among many *minifundistas* to consider the reform as a means of resolving their problem of landlessness. Yet, although these national and regional level planners and organizers articulated a need for flexibility vis-à-vis cooperative formation, in some instances their counterparts at the local level were more rigid in outlook.

As a consequence, some local UNAG and FSLN organizers, and MIDINRA officials, continued to exert pressure on CCS members to make the transition from this "lower form" of social organization to the CAS.[45] Given that most contact between agrarian reform beneficiaries, on the one hand, and FSLN and UNAG organizers and government officials, on the other, was restricted to the local level, pressure from these sources could weigh heavily on the former. The end result was that many campesinos in the late 1980s still perceived that their only avenue for access to land was through cooperative membership, whether or not that option was agreeable to them.

In sum, it must be recognized that the FSLN, and the mass organizations closely allied with it, had fallen short of their goal of creating a more collective mentality among the rural poor. Nonetheless, the profound economic crisis, and the tremendous shortages of resources, had also clearly conspired against them in their effort. Moreover, a mere half decade was little time in which to transform an independent campesino into one firmly convinced of the benefits of collective organization. The process of overcoming centuries of tradition and developing this new consciousness had only just begun. And, this endeavor was taking place in far less than ideal circumstances.

"Nos Han Prestado Estas Tierras"

A key ingredient in achieving a positive outcome, in political terms, from the implementation of these agrarian reform projects was the emergence of a sense of identification on the part of the beneficiaries with the resources they had received.⁴⁶ That is to say, those who had received land had to come gradually to see it as their own. They had to begin to make plans for how they might develop the cooperative in the future and, with economic circumstances permitting, start to set aside some income after each harvest for investments that would facilitate it. This process of identification-building should have been fostered by government officials and technicians, and by FSLN and UNAG organizers. Yet, cooperatives whose members demonstrated this level of identification with the land they had received were the exception, rather than the rule, in the late 1980s.

Only a minority of the cooperatives formed through land distribution in the Los Patios and Plan Masaya areas of influence had gradually begun to reinvest their yearly harvest income in inputs for the following agricultural cycle.⁴⁷ Instead, most chose to distribute all of their earnings among the membership and rely entirely upon credit for the subsequent year's production-related expenditures. The majority also continued to depend on bank credit to provide a stipend to their members throughout the agricultural cycle, which was repaid with harvest earnings. Thus, nothing was being reinvested in the cooperative.

This disregard for the cooperative's future resulted from a variety of factors. Perhaps foremost among them was their members' lack of training in management and entrepreneurial skills. MIDINRA and UNAG provided the cooperatives with abundant resources. Nonetheless, technical assistance was typically limited to pest-management techniques and, in some cases, basic bookkeeping (often the latter skill was sorely lacking). It was not until the late 1980s that this weakness in the cooperative movement was even recognized, and discussion began about how to address it.⁴⁸ But by then, the depth of the economic crisis had converted the issue of investments into a mute point and economic survival became the primary concern.

Several other factors, however, also contributed to the agrarian reform beneficiaries' weak identification with their newly formed cooperatives. Among them were some of the issues described above that were related to the state's efforts to control certain aspects of the cooperatives' production and commercialization practices. Thus, cooperative members perceived that: the choice of what crops they would produce was not their's to make, but instead was determined by MIDINRA planners; they were not free to sell their produce whenever and to whomever they chose; and even selection of the inputs they were to employ in their production was handed down to them from above.

An additional area of concern for the region's land reform beneficiaries was that the legal titles for the property they had received were held collectively, not by each individual.⁴⁹ Consequently, if for whatever reason they chose to leave the cooperative, they would be forced to leave behind the land they had been granted.[50] Moreover, until April of 1990 the agrarian reform law specified that land distributed through the reform could not be sold or subdivided and passed on to offspring.[51] The rationale behind these legal specifications was sound. On the one hand, perhaps the key means traditionally employed to reverse the redistributive effects of agrarian reform has been that of large producers purchasing beneficiaries' land. Economic hardship and other forms of pressure have typically forced beneficiaries to accept the landed class's offers to rescue them from their quandary through buying them out. On the other hand, the subdivision of agrarian reform land to provide an inheritance to offspring would, over several generations, lead to a resurgence of the problem of *minifundismo*. Thus, it was hoped that by effectively guaranteeing the beneficiaries' use rights over the land, the possibility of land reconcentration in the reformed sector of agriculture would be eliminated.

With the change of regimes that occurred in April of 1990, Violeta Chamorro's campaign promise to provide individual land titles to all agrarian reform beneficiaries became a subject of debate in Nicaragua's countryside. She had promised to replace the collective title given to every cooperative with a title for each member.[52] As of this writing, however, Chamorro's government has yet to establish a new form of land titling for agrarian reform beneficiaries. Nonetheless, when I conducted follow-up interviews in mid-1990 I took the opportunity of discussing this issue with those Los Patios and Plan Masaya beneficiaries who had received land. Interestingly, the majority of those who had remained in cooperatives were opposed to the conversion of their collective land titles into individual ones. They argued that it would weaken their position if they were confronted with an effort to take the land away from them. They reasoned that it would be easier to accomplish the agrarian reform's reversal if each of them had to fend for him/herself. In addition, several informants stated that maintaining a collective form of organization would facilitate their cooperative's socioeconomic development. Thus, although in other respects many of these agrarian reform beneficiaries had expressed a lack of identification with their cooperative and its land, when faced with the possibility of loosing it, they showed concern about their right to continue farming it.

Yet, a significant minority of those I interviewed were strongly in favor of replacing the cooperative's collective land title with an individual one. Some simply stated that they preferred not to be involved with a cooperative, but feared the loss of their land were they to leave the cooperative. Others' concerns were more specifically related to their preference for making their own choices (i.e. as opposed to having to acquiesce to the group's [or MIDINRA's] choice) about various aspects of the production process. For example, Don Carlos stated matter of factly, "I would prefer to have an individual title, because then I could plant what I want to . . . and I could even build a house there if I wanted to."[53] An extension of this latter position was that members would then be able to elect for themselves whether or not to rely on agricultural credit (as taking out a loan became very risky following the establishment of the Chamorro government, because of its new tougher credit policies). Ironically, Don Eugenio, a CAS member from Masaya and very strong Sandinista supporter, preferred to receive an individual title: "it would be convenient because then everyone could decide [for themselves] what they want to plant, and perhaps even do so without taking out credit . . . even though it would be difficult to work without credit."[54] Finally, several people also expressed the opinion that each beneficiary would work harder at tending an individual parcel.

In keeping with this argument, the informants who had chosen to leave their cooperatives between 1988 and 1990 and were no longer participants in Los Patios or Plan Masaya stated that this decision had been made because they preferred to work as individuals, even if it meant having a more marginal existence. For example, Don Santos had chosen to leave his CAS, and thus his access to the cooperative's land, during this interval. He was an extremely poor farmer who had no land of his own and was, subsequent to leaving the cooperative, forced to shift from year to year the small plot he worked with his father and brother according to where they could find land to rent or use on loan. Clearly, there was less security—if in no other sense than in terms of his access to land—in having chosen this option than in staying in his CAS. When I asked him why he had left the cooperative, he said several things: "I have been better off since I left the cooperative . . . perhaps I harvest the same amount of produce, but I can keep what I harvest [as opposed to being obliged to sell it.] Its possible that I bring home the same amount [at the end of the harvest], but you know that when you work with a group of people, perhaps you want to eat and yet you have to wait until everyone is ready to eat."[55] Basically the issue was not being one's own boss, but, instead, having to cooperate with the group.

A final means I employed to assess the degree of identification Plan Masaya and Los Patios beneficiaries had with their land was to discuss with them a scenario that was quite real in the early months of Chamorro's government; that the former owner of their land would attempt to take it back from them.[56] For the majority, the land they had received through the agrarian reform was theirs and they were unwilling to give it up without a struggle. The form that struggle might take varied from physically defending what they considered to be theirs, to appealing to all possible authorities to confirm their legal right to the land. The responses given by these informants seemed to contradict much of the other evidence vis-à-vis their identification level. What their reactions might very well have revealed was an understanding of the existing threat to their land ownership. That is, they might still have resented the "interference" of the Sandinista government in their productive activities, and they might still have preferred to farm as individuals, but they did not want to loose their access to land once they were confronted with that possibility.

Nonetheless, a minority of the beneficiaries expressed a distinct lack of confidence with regard to their legal ownership of the land.[57] Instead these beneficiaries' answers reflected a genuine fear of the power the former landowners were capable of wielding. They spoke of asking the landowner to allow them to complete the year's agricultural cycle (1990–91), thereby enabling them to reap the earnings from the harvest. Assuming that the landowner's response to this request might be negative, one informant responded, "I'm not going to fight for this land, [but] I would ask him [the former owner] to pay us for the work we've done this year."[58] Their extreme lack of identification with the land they had been granted was captured in their spontaneous statements about the former landowners: "We will have to give it [the land] to him, it isn't ours . . . it has only been loaned to us"; "It's he [the former landowner] who runs things . . . " [so it will be he who decides].[59] Interestingly enough, both of these statements were made by cooperative presidents who were among those I interviewed. Clearly, the dominant social relations that emerged with Nicaragua's rural class structure in the pre-1979 period had not been completely transformed in the five to eight year period since these projects had been initiated. When faced with a situation in which the new government was seen to represent the interests of the former landed classes, these campesinos opted for the safest course. That course was to take as given the supreme power of the *patrón*, or landlord, and to seek a means of survival in the paternalistic relationship that had traditionally characterized relations between landowners and peasants.

Conclusion: What UNO Could Do For Them

Why did people in the countryside support the UNO ticket in the 1990 General Election? What did people, including the population of agrarian reform beneficiaries who voted for Violeta Chamorro, expect from an UNO government? The answer to these questions can be summed up by saying they expected UNO to bring an end to their economic hardship and to the war.

One of the central elements of the UNO campaign was that of eliminating the military draft. It also emphasized bringing peace back to the "Nicaraguan family." Moreover, given that Violeta Chamorro was clearly the favorite candidate of the U.S., a majority of voters assumed that her presidency would pave the road to peace and bring their loved ones back from the war.

Most of the rural poor also saw an UNO victory as the way out of the economic misery they had been suffering and the crisis that the country as a whole was experiencing. The U.S. government had held out the carrot of eliminating its economic embargo against Nicaragua if Chamorro was to win. In addition, UNO campaign organizers painted images of U.S. aid flooding into the country in the form of food and supplies. They described a situation of abundance in their rural campaigning that contrasted starkly with the reality of extreme scarcity characterizing most campesinos' lives. Doña Concepción, a single mother of four who had made ends meet in the past by having a *tiny* store in her home (which she had lost to bankruptcy a year earlier), in addition to working on her 2 manzana farm, recounted the UNO campaign in the following way: "When those from the UNO campaigned, they promised many things. Many boats were going to arrive [from the U.S.]; it was as if they were just about to arrive in Nicaragua—with food—with everything for everyone. There wouldn't be little neighborhood stores anymore [i.e., those with few items in stock—where people had purchased rationed goods in the mid-1980s], because there would be mountains of things in the markets."[60] Another Los Patios participant, Don Gregorio, who was a very strong critic of the Sandinistas told me, "the U.S. is sending boats filled with medicine," when I interviewed him a few months after the elections.[61]

The FSLN's campaign also forecast economic improvement for the country, with concrete benefits for Nicaragua's poor. But rural voters looked at their economic decline of the previous years as indicative of what the incumbent party was capable of accomplishing. Washington's candidate could obviously do more to ease their economic hardship with the U.S. aid that would follow Chamorro's election than the FSLN would be able to, given its antagonistic relationship with Nicaragua's historic ally.

Finally, for many in the countryside an UNO victory represented the end of government interference in marketing and production. The UNO championed free marketing of agricultural products destined for both the domestic and international markets.[62] The title UNO leaders chose for their economic program, "The Social Economy of the Market," highlighted the alliance's free market orientation.

In sum, what most voters saw in the UNO ticket was a way out of the extremely difficult circumstances that characterized their lives. Rather than being a vote in favor of a new program, their support for UNO represented a rejection of the adversities they had come to associate with the Sandinista government.

Nonetheless, not all of Nicaragua's voting population voiced opposition to the FSLN. This was also true of those in the countryside, many of whom had benefited from the agrarian reform. Slightly more than 36 percent of the voters in the country's heavily rural municipalities maintained their support for the Sandinista government in the 1990 elections (see table 2.1). But this vote evidenced some notable variations from area to area. One such variation—especially as revealed in my in-depth interviews with agrarian reform project beneficiaries—can be found between the populations that participated in Los Patios and Plan Masaya.

Given the overwhelming nature of the general reasons that the rural population's support for the incumbent party had worn away, instances in which voters demonstrated decidedly less interest in a change of government merit some attention. This situation describes what I found to be true of Plan Masaya beneficiaries. The beneficiaries' attitude vis-à-vis the FSLN raises the question of what distinguished this subgroup from the rural population as a whole to make those that composed it more tolerant of the many difficulties that had come to characterize their lives, and still anxious to see the process of social transformation continue. Yet deviation from the national pattern in the opposite direction also suggests that further explanation is required. Los Patios beneficiaries—and particularly those from the area that represented the heart of the project (as will be seen in chapter 4)—expressed more opposition to the FSLN remaining in power than rural voters in general. What might have led them to be so resistant to the revolutionary process and desirous of a return to capitalist-oriented governing?

Examining the sources of these notable differences is essential if we are to understand the varied political outcomes that agrarian reform can have. Only in this way will it be possible to further our knowledge concerning the impact of economic development on politics. Thus, in the chapters that follow, we will take a closer look at each of these projects, exploring their roots, the social origins of their beneficiaries, and their political and economic impact.

3

Los Patios
Its Roots

The liberalization in agrarian reform policy that characterized the mid-1980s was expressed in a variety of forms. On the one hand, it was reflected in the escalation in land redistribution that occurred at the national level during this period. On the other hand, for areas where land redistribution on a major scale was not feasible, it led to the designing of development projects that would strengthen peasant production under existing land-tenure conditions.

The goal of both of these policies was to facilitate a transition within the peasantry from engaging in mere subsistence production to engaging in production that would also be geared for the domestic market. Thus, the country's food situation would be improved, while the need for imports would be reduced, using a low-cost investment strategy that would also generate social benefits for the campesino population. Moreover, it was expected that such efforts would lead the new agrarian reform beneficiaries to experience an increase in identification with the government that had made it all possible. Finally, the rise in living standards resulting from the receipt of these social benefits, and the advancement beyond subsistence production stemming from the adoption of higher levels of technology in the peasantry's production, would foster development in the regions where such projects were implemented.

The Los Patios project was an agrarian reform scheme that was carried out during the initial stages of the *campesinista*, or propeasant, era. The project was developed, in large part, in response to the limitations that had resulted from an overreliance on nationalization as the solution to the numerous problems affecting the rural population (particularly that of minifundismo and the resulting rural poverty). Its objectives were several, including that of fortifying the economic potential of its beneficiaries' minifundio production and thereby raising their standard of living. In addition, the implementation of Los Patios implementation represented an attempt to extend the process of redistributing Nicaragua's agricultural resources to a sector of the rural population that had not before been incorporated into the agrarian reform. The minifundistas' inclusion in the beneficiary pool of the reform was implicitly expected to generate increased support for the government within this sector. Policymakers also hoped that the project would contribute to the ongoing *recampesinización* effort. Recampesinización was one of the underlying goals of the propeasant policy orientation in that it sought to reinforce this sector's ties to the land and facilitate its assumption of a heightened role in agricultural production, and thereby in the economy more generally. Although it was hoped that project participants, who were primarily individual peasant farmers, would eventually organize themselves into CCS to receive these resources, collectivization of production was not a prerequisite for joining the project.

During its first five years of implementation (1983–88), the Los Patios project was relatively successful in moving toward the objectives set forth when it was being designed.[1] Its greatest accomplishment was in extending the distribution of productive resources to a new sector of the population. It also raised the farm-generated earnings of many of its beneficiaries, thereby playing a role in furthering the process of recampesinización. Both of these achievements implied that progress had been made toward promoting an overall process of economic and social development in the Los Patios areas of influence. Nonetheless, my interviews with project participants in 1990 revealed that the underlying goal of increasing support for the government went unmet.

Given the widely held assumption that agrarian reform will produce political support for the government that implements it, and that the socioeconomic development that may result from such reform should do the same, it seems essential to find an explanation for this unexpected outcome. This chapter, and that which follows, will be dedicated to an exploration of the dynamics underlying the failure of Los Patios to have the political consequences that were anticipated when it was implemented. Prior to focusing on the project's impact, however, I will describe the socioeconomic, as well as political, context out of which it emerged and the development strategy of which it formed a part. This chapter addresses these two phenomena. In addition, the social origins of those who became beneficiaries of the Los Patios project will also be examined herein. This will set the stage for the more detailed analysis of the socioeconomic and political effects that the implementations of Los Patios generated, which will be presented in chapter 4.

Los Patios: The Context Out of Which the Project Arose

The Los Patios project was carried out in the plateau region that stretches from Carazo to Diriomo (see map 2). Historically speaking, this area's economic development mirrored, in many respects, that of the nation as a whole. Agroexport production was first introduced to this region in a serious way during the mid- to late 1800s. By the time of Somoza's overthrow it had come to predominate the Carazo plateau region's economy.

In fact, southwest Nicaragua (also known as Region IV), where the Carazo plateau region is located, was the first area in Nicaragua where agroexport production was introduced.[2] Granada-based *latifundistas* (i.e., latifundio owners) were the principal protagonists of Region IV's early agroexport efforts—in cattle raising and cacao and indigo production. They were also responsible for the expansion of coffee production in the Carazo plateau region after its introduction there between 1840 and 1850. Carazo was the only area in Nicaragua where coffee was grown until late in the century, when its cultivation began to spread into the country's central mountain region.

The first coffee boom in Carazo took place between 1870 and 1926. During this time, the infrastructure that was crucial for the expansion of coffee production was developed, and European processing equipment began to arrive. By the turn of the century, Carazo's coffee producers began to apply chemical pesticides and plant higher-yielding varieties of trees. Thus, in the fifty years following the initiation of widespread cultivation in the region, a tangible process of modernization in its production practices occurred.

Alongside these technological changes, a transformation of the region's social structure was also under way. The expansion in areas cultivated with coffee gave rise to a dramatic increase in the concentration of Carazo's prime agricultural land. Legal and extralegal mechanisms were relied upon to make this possible.[3] The expulsion of campesinos from land that was consumed by coffee gave rise to a minifundio population that was increasingly forced to offer its labor services on the coffee estates during the seasonal surge in demand for harvest workers.

With the downturn in the international price for coffee in 1926, which was shortly followed by the Great Depression, Carazo's producers expanded their coffee acreage to counterbalance their falling incomes. Later, as coffee prices experienced another swing upward in the 1940s and 1950s, its production stimulated the development of related economic activities. Several banks, such as the Banco Nacional de Nicaragua (BNN) and the Banco Nicaragüense de Industria y Comercio (BANIC), established branch offices in Carazo, offering financial assistance for the continuing growth in this sector. At the same time, new transportation and commercial enterprises sprang up, especially those geared toward agricultural activities.

Despite Carazo's expansions in coffee acreage, this region was soon surpassed by the central mountain region in absolute production terms (cf. MIDINRA 1983). Yet, even though the central mountain region had the room for expansion that expedited its replacement of Carazo in national production quotas, the latter's superior infrastructure and its relative proximity to the country's principal port, Corinto, assured its continued participation in the cultivation of this crucial crop. In the mid-1970s, approximately 13 percent of Nicaragua's coffee acreage was located in this region (calculated from CIERA 1980a, 145–47; 1980b, 121; and 1980c, 138).[4] But as a consequence of its lower yields, only 6 percent of the actual coffee crop was produced there. Nonetheless, within the Carazo plateau region, coffee production remained the predominant agricultural activity.

Another export crop that was produced in the Carazo plateau region was sugarcane. It had been cultivated in various parts of Region IV since the colonial era, including Rivas (which would later become a key cane-growing area), Nandaime, and the Carazo plateau region. After experiencing some new growth in the late 1800s, sugarcane underwent a real boom in the 1940s when the price of sugar rose significantly in the international market. At that time, several industrial cane-processing facilities (*ingenios*) succeeded in consolidating virtual control over whole territories of sugarcane production. The two principal ingenios were located in Rivas and Nandaime. A few wealthy families, including the Somozas, were responsible for the crop's processing. Likewise, most of the area planted with sugarcane was located on the farms of medium- and large-scale capitalist producers (calculated from Ministerio de Economía 1966, table 31). The ingenio and cane land became capitalist development poles for Region IV.

In the 1960s, sugarcane production underwent another upsurge, as a result of the U.S. embargo on sugar imports from Cuba following the establishment of the revolutionary government there. The Nicaraguan state facilitated this expansion, reflecting its interest in the economic benefits to be reaped from agroexport production. Some modernization of sugarcane production practices occurred at this time, with acreage under irrigation experiencing a notable increase. In fact, by the late 1970s approximately 50 percent of national sugarcane acreage was irrigated, with cane being among the most irrigation-intensive crops (Biderman 1982, 119).

Given the predominance of medium- and large-sized capitalist producers in the production of these export products (see table 3.1),[5] the products' rising importance had serious implications for the campesino sector and the crops it cultivated. The most significant such implication was this sector's growing difficulty in obtaining access to land. As agroexport production expanded, it began a deepening process of land concentration.

This was very clearly illustrated in the wake of the most recent major boom in agroexport production, which characterized the expansion of cotton cultivation in the 1950s and 1960s (this boom will be described in greater detail in

Table 3.1. Land concentration in agroexport production, Region IV (percentages)

Size of farm	Cotton	Coffee	Sugarcane	Pastures
<5 mz	0.38	6.49	0.86	0.93
5–<10 mz	0.75	6.52	2.89	1.77
10–<50 mz	3.75	28.52	17.01	8.06
50–<500 mz	51.31	52.82	40.10	26.58
≥500 mz	43.81	5.65	39.14	62.66

Source: Calculated from Ministerio de Economía (1966).

chapter 5). In just the first thirteen years following the widespread adoption of cotton production in 1950, a dramatic increase in the number of farmers who fell into the category of minifundista (i.e., with farms 5 manzanas or smaller in size) occurred, while access to land for this sector remained extremely limited. Between 1952 and 1963 the number of minifundios grew by 21.7 percent and, when combined with the small farm category (6 to 10 manzanas), this sector made up the vast majority (73.6 percent) of farms (see table 3.2). Yet these same farms only controlled 7.1 percent of the agricultural land. On the other hand, those with farms larger than 500 manzanas in size were small in number but controlled a growing percentage of Region IV's land: this sector's farms represented only 1.2 percent of the farms in the region, but they controlled 53.2 percent of the farmland. As table 3.2 demonstrates, the level of land concentration was not reduced during the succeeding ten years. In fact, by 1971 the area held by the minifundio and small farmer sector had dropped still further, while that of the latifundio sector had expanded.

In contrast to the large producers, the peasant sector had traditionally specialized in food crop cultivation. Except for rice and sorghum, which had been adopted for high-technology production by the capitalist sector, the peasantry was largely responsible for producing the country's basic foodstuffs. Corn and beans were the key crops grown by this sector, which supplied its subsistence needs and provided cash income if any surplus production was available to be marketed. When the campesinado experienced growing marginalization with the expansion of agroexport production, so too did its cultivation of basic grains. Corn and beans were pushed into the less fertile areas in the region—if not out of the region entirely.[6] Yields and overall production levels dropped accordingly.

Because land was the principal means of generating a livelihood, the concentration of this crucial productive resource translated into a concentration in the income derived from agriculture. Thus, the campesinos' decreasing access to land implied increasingly restricted income levels. According to na-

Table 3.2. Changes in Region IV land tenancy following the agroexport boom

Farm size[a]	1952		1963		1971	
	% farms	% area	% farms	% area	% farms	% area
Minifundio (0–5 mz)	34.8	2.3	56.5	3.6	70.4[b]	5.0[b]
Small farm (6–10 mz)	19.3	3.2	17.1	3.5		
Medium farm (11–50 mz)	30.3	13.8	18.2	11.0	19.5	10.2
Large farm (51–500 mz)	13.8	34.7	7.1	28.8	8.5	28.2
Latifundio (>500 mz)	1.8	46.1	1.2	53.2	1.6	56.6

Sources: Blandón (1962); Ministerio de Economía (1966); CIERA (1980a, 1980b, 1980c, and 1980d).
[a]These size distinctions are taken from the 1952 census (cited in Blandón 1962).
[b]Combined figure for minifundios and small farms. A more refined breakdown of this data is unavailable.

tional data, the income level of the majority of the rural population was not even sufficiently high enough to meet minimum nutritional requirements (see Bider-man 1982).

In order to supplement its farm-generated income, some of the rural poor turned to the wage labor market. The possibilities for permanent employment in the agricultural sector, however, were extremely limited. Deere et al. (1985, 78) found that only 19.8 percent of the rural Economically Active Population (EAP) had permanent wage employment in 1978. The alternative that many of these minifundistas resorted to was participating in the agroexport harvests during a few months each year. Coincidentally, employment opportunities in the harvest had become abundant with the expansion of agroexport production. In addition to the ever more circumscribed income-generating potential of the small farms and the restricted possibilities for obtaining ongoing employment in the countryside, the rudimentary social services in rural areas served to compound the plight of its dwellers. The growing impoverishment was expressed in higher-than-average levels of illiteracy: the illiteracy level for the population as a whole in Region IV was 44.8 percent at the end of the 1970s, but that of the rural population there was 65.4 percent (calculated from CIERA 1980a, 179). In some of the region's rural areas the figure reached as high as 74.3 percent, as in the case of the rural population of the municipality of La Concepción, which lay at the center of the Los Patios area of influence (CIERA 1980c, 173). It was also expressed in a life expectancy of only 49 years and an infant mortality rate of 126.8 per thousand births (CIERA 1980d, 178).

In response to the growing discontent that these social conditions produced in the countryside, and the opposition party's efforts to organize the discontent on its behalf, the Somoza regime made several gestures at implementing "agrarian reform" in the region. A small number of peasants in this area were beneficiaries of the Rural Credit Program set up by the Somoza government in 1959, as well as the credit programs sponsored by INVIERNO in the mid-1970s.[7] Yet the programs did not address the crucial issue of land distribution. Thus, they were doomed to failure in terms of resolving the basic problem of rural poverty and quelling unrest in the countryside, the latter being the primary objective of their implementation.

THE SANDINISTA AGRARIAN REFORM IN REGION IV

When the Government of National Reconstruction was established in 1979, one of its primary commitments was to implement an agrarian reform that would fundamentally restructure agriculture. The goals of its agrarian reform were twofold: to increase agricultural production (both for export and domestic consumption) and to raise the standard of living of the rural poor (see CEPAL 1981a and MIPLAN 1980). In addition, the reform was supposed to steer the country toward a new, more equal balance between production geared toward the export market and that destined for internal consumption (FIDA 1980). This goal was based on the assumption that the dramatic imbalance between these two sectors had contributed to the country's developmental difficulties and the deepening of rural poverty.

Multiple elements of agricultural policy were to be employed in the reform's implementation. They included the promotion of land redistribution; the formation of state farms and agricultural cooperatives on the redistributed land; the reallocation of agricultural credit, specifically targeting the campesino sector; the provision of technical assistance and training programs; the dissemination of improved technologies; the setting of price ceilings on agricultural land that was rented during the growing season; and the establishment of a system of guaranteed prices for agricultural producers. These policy elements formed the core of the agrarian reform program. However, varying constellations of these policies were adopted to meet the particular characteristics of each area.

In Region IV a strategy of agricultural development was elaborated that was designed to work toward achieving the fundamental goals of the agrarian reform, while taking into account the nature of agricultural production there and the class relations to which it had given rise. Nonetheless, early on policymakers concluded that in those areas where agroexport production had predominated in the past, the aim of giving an equal emphasis to food crop and export production would have to be a medium- to long-term one. Given the importance of agroexport production to the reactivation and future stability of the national economy, it would have to continue to receive high priority in development planning. Instead, the agrarian reform's focus there would have to be placed on modifying the social relations of production. This national-level orientation conditioned the model of agricultural development and agrarian reform elaborated for Region IV. Yet food crop production was not to be totally marginalized as it had been during the Somoza regime.[8]

Within the model of development that was prepared for Region IV, several "development poles" were designated for government attention. One of these development poles was located in the Carazo plateau region, and the principal focus of its efforts was that of renovating the area's coffee production. This was to be carried out under the auspices of the National Commission of Coffee Plantation Renovation (CONARCA).

CONARCA's program had several objectives, which were: to slow the spread of the plant disease *la Roya*, which had affected Nicaragua's coffee production since 1976; to modernize the region's coffee cultivation through the introduction of higher-yielding varieties, greater use of fertilizers and pest control, and so forth; to concentrate coffee production in ecologically appropriate areas; and to create employment opportunities in the program's area of influence. The renovation program did not include farms smaller than five manzanas in size or those in "marginal zones." Thus most of the farms in the minifundio sector were excluded from participation in CONARCA. However, the program generated jobs for many from this sector: at its peak, CONARCA provided 15,000 people with employment (Gariazzo 1984, 86).[9]

CONARCA reflected MIDINRA's national-level focus on large-scale, capital-intensive projects (see further Wheelock Román 1984a and 1984b), although it was somewhat more modest in nature than most of the rest of the projects that formed the basis of the regional development plan. These projects were seen as being crucial for the country's economic development. That is, they were supposed to move the country up a step in the international economy, from being an exporter of raw primary products to being an exporter of processed primary products.

At the national level, the ministry was also especially inclined to have the state sector at the center of these development efforts, with it gradually replacing the formerly dominant large, capitalist-producer sector. The campesino sector was to be absorbed into this modernization process through its employment on the state farms. That is, its members were to be transformed from independent peasant producers into a proletarian class, following the traditional course of development.

Beginning in the 1981–82 period, another nationwide policy measure was implemented in this region: the promotion of agricultural cooperatives (especially CAS) through land redistribution. Production in the better part of Nicaragua's cooperatives was geared toward the domestic market (particularly basic grains) during the first few years of the agrarian reform. Yet a very limited amount of land planted with export crops was turned over to the cooperative sector beginning in 1982.[10] In Carazo, the cooperative sector began to produce a small part of the region's coffee crop at this time.

While the cooperative movement in the Carazo plateau region did grow during the early 1980s,[11] some resistance to collective production was encountered within the campesino population (interview no. 16, FSLN, Region IV, San Marcos Zonal Office, August 19, 1986). This resistance was evidenced in both the high membership turnover rate of many cooperatives and the fact that those who had even a tiny parcel of land were not attracted to the movement. As was described in chapter 2, however, the problem was not limited to peasants in this region.

In addition to all of the factors that contributed to this phenomenon at a national level, a characteristic specific to the Carazo plateau region further confounded efforts to develop a collective orientation toward agricultural production. That is, the rural population as a whole in this region was politically conservative. The right-wing orientation of Nicaragua's Catholic church hierarchy held great sway in the region. And, the historically strong—and growing—mercantile relationship between this area and the capital also reinforced the more conservative conception of society that prevailed there. Because the idea of cooperative production relations was new, gaining its acceptance in this more traditional population was not an easy task.

Moreover, the development strategy designed for the Carazo plateau region, as well as that of Region IV as a whole, shared with the program elaborated for all of Nicaragua the major weakness of essentially ignoring the unorganized campesino sector. Campesino producers (ranging from poor to rich peasants) represented approximately 90 percent of all producers in Region IV in 1971 (calculated from CIERA 1980a, 75; 1980b, 66; 1980c, 66; and 1980d, 66). Thus, the needs of an overwhelming majority of the region's rural population were not to be addressed or would only be addressed if they chose to pursue the proletarian or cooperativization options.

In 1982 CONARCA's renovation program began to near its completion, and its labor requirements diminished dramatically. The number of those employed by the program dropped from 15,000 in 1980 to 8,000 in 1981 and to 3,000 in 1982 (Gariazzo 1984, 86). The workforce CONARCA had succeeded in absorbing was suddenly, once again, unemployed. At the same time, employment on state farms had stabilized. Consequently, both of these avenues of recourse had become restricted.

Besides all of the factors described above, which fueled government policymakers' concern about addressing the needs of the peasants, an additional element came into play. While the population in the Carazo plateau region had developed many links with Managua prior to 1979, the links increased rapidly after 1979. This phenomenon was part of the dramatic escalation in rural-urban migration that occurred throughout the country following the establishment of the Sandinista government. Although the expansion of agroexport production had accelerated rural-urban migration (especially to Managua) between 1950 and 1980,[12] movement to the cities exploded after 1979. The causes were multiple and included the military conflict that Nicaragua was enduring, a degree of urban bias in the distribution of social services, and the widening gap in living standards between rural and urban low-income groups (in favor of the latter).[13]

By 1982–83, government policymakers had begun to realize the seriousness of the growth boom that Managua, in particular, had experienced. Part of this recognition entailed the acknowledgement that the capital's infrastructural base simply could not support a continually expanding population. Moreover, the exodus of people from the countryside implied for most a shift in their participation in the economy from being engaged in production to being engaged in informal and service sector activities, while resolution of the country's economic crisis depended on expansions in the former type of participation. Consequently, a search began for options that might slow the urban-bound flow of people. Los Patios offered the possibility of stalling, if not reversing, emigration from its areas of influence by providing the region's poor with an economically attractive, farm-based livelihood. Thus, migration pressure, at least from this area, would be reduced.

Given the minifundistas' relative lack of interest in becoming wage laborers or in collectivizing their production, another alternative had to be found to address the problem of the landless and land-poor. The issue was further complicated by the limited possibility of redistributing significant quantities of land in this area. Most of the farms that were subject to confiscation there were designated for inclusion in the state sector because of their larger, capital-intensive nature. Furthermore, even though the cooperative sector had begun to play a role in the region's coffee production, it had yet to be completely accepted by government planners as an equal within the export sector of the economy. Therefore land redistribution in export crop areas, such as the Carazo plateau region, would remain restricted for the following few years. This region's problem of minifundismo would require another solution. The Los Patios agrarian reform project became that solution.

THE SOCIAL ORIGINS OF LOS PATIOS BENEFICIARIES

The Los Patios project was designed to strengthen the economic position of minifundistas in the Carazo plateau region by giving them a means of supporting themselves on their own tiny parcels of land (i.e., their "patios"). In order to gauge the distance between the plans leading to the implementation

Table 3.3. Economic activity of two generations of Los Patios campesinos (AP = agricultural producer; AW = agricultural worker; FP = family plot; SE = self-employed; UW = urban worker)

	Parents	Informants
One economic activity	62.8	13.6
AP	41.9	—
SE	11.6	4.6
UW	7.0	2.3
AW	2.3	4.6
FP	—	2.3
Two economic activities	34.9	43.2
AW/AP	30.2	9.1
FP/AP	—	15.9
SE/AP	4.7	9.1
UW/AP	—	2.3
FP/AW	—	4.6
AW/SE	—	2.3
Three economic activities	2.3	34.1
FP/UW/AP	—	9.1
FP/AW/AP	—	9.1
SE/AW/AP	2.3	4.6
AW/UW/AP	—	4.6
SE/UW/AP	—	4.6
FP/AP/SE	—	2.3
Four or more economic activities	—	9.1
FP/UW/AP/SE/AW/other	—	2.3
AW/UW/AP/SE	—	2.3
FP/AW/AP/SE	—	2.3
AW/UW/SE/other	—	2.3

Source: Author's survey data, 1988 (N = 44).

of Los Patios and the reality of its impact, a small survey of the project's beneficiaries was undertaken in 1988 (see the Brief Discussion of Methodology). The results of the survey show that the project succeeded in reaching the population it had targeted.

In fact, the life histories of Los Patios beneficiaries poignantly recount the gradual breakdown in subsistence production that coincided with the expansion of agroexport production in the Carazo plateau region. Their ties to the land had been a family tradition passed down through the generations.[14] The survey revealed that the majority (79 percent) of the informants' parents had worked in agriculture at some point in their lives (see table 3.3).[15] Most had access to a small parcel of land, with more than half (55 percent) owning that which they farmed. The rest farmed on rented land or land made available to them through the myriad of precapitalist relations that existed prior to 1979. Within the group of informants' parents who had been landowners, several had been medium-sized capitalist producers (i.e., with between 10 and 50 manzanas).[16] However, most had only a very small parcel of land. Their limited access to land resulted in their encountering growing difficulty in sustaining themselves and their families with their own agricultural production. Not surprisingly, only 42 percent of the parents of Los Patios beneficiaries were able to do so. A minority of the beneficiaries' parents had such restricted access to land that they were forced to supplement their income with wage labor (within agriculture). Yet only a few of this generation had left the countryside in search of other opportunities.

The fact that the informants' parents had only limited access to agricultural land had significant implications for the next generation. Among the implications was the short-lived nature of the childhoods of the interviewees. As was customary in minifundio production in pre-1979 Nicaragua, these families were often forced to send their children into the workforce at an early age: 23 percent of the informants had begun to work before the age of ten; 73 percent before the age of fourteen; and 89 percent by the age of sixteen. Participation in the agroexport harvest was the typical means children used to contribute to family income at this stage of their lives. Notably, 50 percent of those interviewed had worked in the agroexport harvests as children or young adults. While most had participated in the local coffee harvest, nearly two-thirds of those who joined this massive labor force had also, at some point, worked picking cotton. For the majority, picking cotton implied traveling as far as León and Chinandega. In contrast, those who had never sold their labor in the agroexport harvests were from families whose resource base was more extensive than the rest (e.g. they had more sizable parcels of land).

Participation in the agroexport harvests was an indication of the future that lay ahead for this next generation. Given the tradition of having large families, when land was passed on from parents to offspring the parcels became smaller and smaller.[17] Moreover, the fact that the farms were not big to begin with meant that the inheritance for each child was minuscule. Thus, it was not surprising that the generation to which the informants belonged had even less access than their parents to the resources required (principally land) to eke out a living on the minifundio. Although 36 percent of the informants inherited land from their parents, the parcels were almost all insufficient in size to maintain a family (the norm was approximately one manzana). Even more important, the majority did not inherit any land.

As a result of this pattern of shrinking resources, there were no informants who were able to work as agricultural producers in their own right, without having to seek employment off of the farm. Even though 55 percent of the sample were involved in agricultural production on either their own or rented land *just prior* to becoming beneficiaries of the Los Patios project, and 91 percent had been agricultural producers at some point before their entry into the project, all of them had to resort to at least one additional economic activity in order to provide for their own and their family's survival.[18] The other economic activities in which the informants had participated over the years included agricultural wage labor (46 percent) and the operation of cottage industries (34 percent). (See table 3.3 for a summary of their labor histories.) Necessity also pushed them into surrounding urban areas in search of employment. Thirty percent of the informants had participated in the urban wage labor force at some point in their lives.[19] This panorama contrasted strikingly with the labor histories of their parents, whose experience as wage laborers was limited and as urban wage laborers, almost nonexistent.

What is illustrated by these labor histories is the extent to which, with each new generation, the peasantry was being pushed out of agricultural production. Their ties to the land remained alive, in the sense that they were loath to move permanently away from their places of origin. But their ability to sustain themselves from their own production was becoming a dream of bygone days. Although a revival of independent peasant production was not initially a goal of the Sandinistas' agricultural development strategy, by the time of the initiation of Los Patios it was being seriously considered as an alternative approach to agrarian reform by the country's policymakers. The informants represented precisely the sector of the peasantry that Sandinista planners thought to be the most appropriate candidates for recampesinización. And, as we will see in chapter 4, they did indeed prove themselves to be amenable to the possibility of "going back to the land."

Conclusion

The social problems to which the Los Patios project was designed to respond characterized much of Nicaragua's countryside. They had emerged along with the spread of agroexport production. The agrarian reform was envisioned as the principal means of resolving these social problems as well as of addressing the developmental imbalances that had been generated by agroexport capitalism. Yet the form of its implementation was constrained by the need to maintain the national economy's solvency. Therefore its actual application in each area reflected the Sandinistas' image of a reformed agriculture, the limitations imposed by the national economy, and the specific nature of production and class relations in the area.

The developmental history of the Carazo plateau region epitomized, in many senses, that of the nation as a whole. Agroexport production, particularly in the form of coffee cultivation, stimulated the growth of related infrastructure and commercial and financial institutions. But it also brought with it the marginalization of the peasantry. With its increasing exclusion from key productive resources that had been caused by the voraciousness of export agriculture, the peasantry's production dropped off. This affected both the general availability of basic food products as well as the livelihoods of the peasant farmers.

The agrarian reform was seen as the remedy for the peasantry's marginalization. Yet the initial opportunities that it offered them were not deemed by the peasants to be attractive. The first of these opportunities was that of proletarianization, through working as wage laborers on the newly established state farms. Several years later a new alternative was opened to the peasantry, that of receiving land in the form of a cooperative. But the fact that those who had access to any land at all rejected this alternative pointed to the lack of interest held by this sector in collective production arrangements.

The recognition by Sandinista policymakers that another answer would have to be found to respond to the needs of the minifundistas grew out of an understanding of the latter's reactions to the earlier efforts that had been directed at them. Concern was growing that the absence of a solution to the plight of the peasantry could lead to its political alienation from the Sandinista regime. Likewise, the culmination of CONARCA's renovation program accentuated the need for an alternative for the peasants, as those it had employed were thrown back into the pool of un- and underemployed campesinos.

The Los Patios project embodied the decision to address these problems on the minifundistas' terms. That is, the fact that it proposed to provide them with a number of key agricultural resources, without requiring their collective use, was an indication of the larger policy change that was in the offing. It also suggested that if land redistribution was perceived to be unfeasible for economic reasons, other means would be sought to ameliorate the socioeconomic consequences wrought by agroexport production. Sandinista policymakers were confident that the provision of benefits to this sector of the peasantry, and the larger context of social transformation within which the project was to take place, would undercut any tendencies toward conservatization that might have been implied by this kind of partial reform.

As my survey data illustrated, Los Patios did reach the sector of the peasantry toward which it was directed. The project did pull into its orbit those peasants who had been increasingly marginalized by the expansion of coffee production. The logic underlying the project's implementation, however, proved to be fundamentally flawed. The benefits Los Patios brought to its participants' lives did not succeed in weakening, much less reversing, the political outcome that is usually produced by the transition from minifundio to peasant capitalist production. In order to understand the nature of this transition, and the consequences it had for the Los Patios beneficiaries' relationship with the Sandinista regime, we need to examine more closely the impact the project had on this sector of the campesinado. It is to this that we turn in chapter 4.

4

Los Patios
Its Social and Political Impact

In the mid-1980s Sandinista policymakers adopted a new strategy within the agrarian reform. That strategy had recampesinización of the beneficiaries as a central goal. Its adoption was a consequence of the failure of the government's initial strategies of seeking a solution to the "peasant question" in the latter's proletarianization or collectivization.

The Los Patios agrarian reform project was one of the earlier experiments in the implementation of this new strategy. It sought to reach the campesinos who had yet to be touched by the agrarian reform, providing them with productive resources that they could employ on their own *individual* plots of land. It did not entail offering them additional land through a restructuring of land tenure, which was still a very radical initiative at the time the project was being designed. Nonetheless it did suggest that a departure from the formerly reigning strategies was being considered.

Implementation of the Los Patios project was motivated by the need to provide those in the minifundio sector with the means to improve their living standard. At the same time, it was aimed at expanding the production of food products that would be destined for local markets. But its goals were not strictly limited to social and economic achievements. Also underlying the project was the objective of increasing the level of identification of the campesinado with the Sandinista regime—and by extension with its social project of transforming Nicaraguan society in the direction of socialism.[1]

The Los Patios project was partially successful in attaining the goals that had stimulated its implementation. As we will see in the following pages, its achievements in the socioeconomic realm were notable. This was not true, however, of the political realm, a fact that contradicted the expectations of those who had designed the project, as well as of those contributing to the literature on peasant politics and development. The contradictory nature of this political phenomenon called for an exploration of its origins. This process of exploration, the results of which are presented below, led me to the conclusion that it was precisely the social and economic success of the project that undermined support for the Sandinista regime. That is, because its beneficiaries were almost entirely individual campesinos—and more specifically, relatively better-off campesinos—the project had the effect of transforming them into peasant capitalists or members of the petty bourgeoisie. Even those peasants who joined CCS maintained their individual form of production. Consequently, by 1990 Los Patios beneficiaries were anxious for a government that would represent their capitalist interests, rather than one that would continue to promote the transition to socialism. In essence, Sandinista agrarian policy in this region had sown the seeds for its own demise.

Los Patios

The Model

The design of the Los Patios project was a result of a combination of factors. First, the history of economic development in the Carazo plateau region delimited the possibilities for change that were open to the Sandinista policymakers who were charged with planning projects for this area. In addition, the nature of the specific sector of the peasantry that was targeted by the project placed constraints on what it might look like if it was to be successful. That is, its beneficiaries were to be minifundistas who were still quite tied to the land. They were not to be those who had been largely transformed into a rural proletariat. The makeup of this constituency required that an entirely new approach be taken in efforts to incorporate them into the agrarian reform.

The means by which Los Patios was supposed to benefit the minifundio sector was through the promotion of certain crops that would strengthen its economic position. The crops included in the project were avocado, squash, citrus, and several other fruits.[2] Farmers participating in Los Patios were to be encouraged to gradually replace their non-renovated (low-yield) coffee with high-yield varieties of the new crops. Given the potential for producing a large quantity of any of these crops on a small parcel of land, policymakers believed that the project would address the needs of the campesino sector without necessitating the redistribution of land from the region's capital-intensive coffee estates.

The proximity of the Carazo plateau region to the country's major urban centers (particularly Managua), and its more developed road system, would give these farmers a special advantage over fruit and vegetable producers in other areas of the country. Specifically, lower transportation costs and the reduction of losses due to shipping delays would translate into higher profit margins than those attained by producers located at a greater distance from the market. Further, while some citrus production had traditionally taken place in this region, Los Patios offered its beneficiaries higher-yielding varieties, with shorter time lags before the first harvest.

In addition, national demand for fruits and vegetables had grown during the early 1980s. At the same time, a gradual reduction in imports of perishables (and other nonessential items) had taken place, as the country's foreign exchange situation deteriorated. Consequently, it was an extremely favorable moment to enter into the production of these crops.

Project beneficiaries were to be drawn from both the individual producer and cooperative sectors. The designers of Los Patios envisioned the project as providing an impetus to the organizing effort directed at small- and medium-scale individual producers, because of the common interests that would naturally arise with the introduction of these new crops. The formation of CCS was to be encouraged. However, these CCS were to have a much broader base than had been the norm. That is, they would eventually service all of the small- and medium-scale producers in a given area, channeling credit and technical assistance to them. It was hoped that this strategy would help overcome resistance to cooperative formation by demonstrating the advantages to be gained through collectively organizing at least some aspects of production and commercialization. The project was also seen as a means of strengthening the existing cooperatives by improving their income-generating potential.

In order to attain its various objectives, Los Patios furnished its beneficiaries with the plants promoted by the project, significant amounts of agricultural credit, and extensive technical assistance. By late 1987, 720 manzanas had been incorporated into the project and approximately 650 campesinos were participating in it.[3]

The Reality

The description of Los Patios presented above is a sketch of this agrarian reform project as it appeared on the drawing board. The survey of its beneficiaries permitted an assessment of how closely the reality of the project matched the plans for its implementation. Initially I evaluated the extent to which the project facilitated the process of recampesinización that had been a key goal. Thus, I looked for shifts in the labor patterns of Los Patios beneficiaries and those of their family members, which would reflect this process. I also explored the degree to which their standard of living had been altered during their inclusion in the project, a factor that would shed further light on the socioeconomic impact of Los Patios.

Through the survey of Los Patios beneficiaries, I found that participation in this agrarian reform project had partially modified the effects of the grow-

Table 4.1. Agricultural production of two generations of Los Patios campesinos (percentages)

	Parents[a]	Informants	
		Before 1982[a]	After 1982
Coffee	28	30	59
Basic grains	70	55	59
Chayote	—	14	27
Citrus	2	27	50
Pitahaya	—	9	36
Avocado	—	2	30
Other[b]	30	30	36

Source: Author's survey data, 1988 (N = 44).
Note: Most of these farmers grew more than one crop. Thus these figures refer to the percentage of informants or informants' parents who grew each crop.
[a]Not all of those who were agricultural producers after 1982 had been prior to that time, nor were all of them children of agricultural producers.
[b]Additional crops that were grown in small quantities, such as yuca, tapioca, plantain, bananas, and various fruit trees.

ing marginalization that had been experienced by this sector of the rural population as a consequence of the spread of agroexport production. The project's policy mechanisms had succeeded in redistributing resources to its participants, thereby fortifying the economic potential of their tiny parcels of land. The result was, as planned, a retreat from the wage labor force into agricultural production, or the start of a process of recampesinización.

Among the changes brought about by Los Patios, perhaps the easiest to identify was that of the types of crops that the project's beneficiaries grew. The primary crops grown by the informants prior to the initiation of the project were corn and beans (see table 4.1). A minority of these campesinos had produced coffee and, to a lesser extent, citrus crops in addition to basic grains. Interestingly, although the Los Patios project had been designed to benefit the marginal coffee producers who had been excluded from CONARCA's renovation program, coffee was clearly a secondary crop for these campesinos. A number of project beneficiaries did, however, begin to grow coffee during the time that they were participants in Los Patios. Most of these producers were members of cooperatives that had also received land planted with renovated coffee through the agrarian reform (see discussion below). Moreover, even though traditional varieties of citrus crops were common in the region, 85 percent of the informants had no previous history of producing the specific crops and high-yield varieties introduced through the project.

Further, cultivation of the fruits and vegetables promoted by the project represented a change from the traditional production patterns of the informants' families (see table 4.1). While coffee had been the predominant crop grown in this region, only a minority (36 percent) of the informants' parents who had been farmers had cultivated it. Instead, almost all of them (91 percent) had opted to first guarantee their subsistence by producing basic grains and only after that, if sufficient land was available, did they cultivate this export crop.

What is significant about this change is that it implies the beginning of a transition from production geared primarily toward subsistence to production oriented toward the market. Although a key objective of the project was to reduce these campesinos' need to seek a livelihood away from the farm, the idea was not simply to reinforce subsistence production. Rather, the goal was to develop new kinds of links between production (and producers) in the countryside and life in the city. Despite the fact that the informants' experience shows that minifundio production in this region was not entirely of a subsistence nature before the introduction of Los Patios, interchange with the market increased following its implementation.[4]

The shift in crop production that stimulated this process of change was facilitated by the use of a number of policy instruments, the most important of which was the provision of agricultural credit. Credit is a critical input in agricultural production because it supplies the producer with working capital during the extended period of time before the crop is harvested and the returns begin to come in. However, the provision of credit was even more crucial for Los Patios beneficiaries than is usually the case, because of the several-year time lag between planting and harvesting that existed for many of the crops introduced by the project.

The survey results showed that almost all of those interviewed (93 percent) had relied on credit to begin cultivation of the new crops. A few of the informants later opted to self-finance their production, once the initial investments in plants and other inputs were made. This decision was motivated by two factors: the fear of being indebted that remained from the Somoza era, when a farmer's land could be taken away to pay his/her debt; and lack of know-how concerning the need to apply various inputs to the plants even before they began producing fruit (i.e., during the period in which they were developing). Still, the majority of the beneficiaries interviewed (84 percent) continued to use credit to finance their production throughout the agricultural cycle (see table 4.2).[5]

What was particularly notable about the project's extensive provision of credit was that for more than half of the informants (66 percent), this was the first time they had ever received agricultural credit. Peasant producers had traditionally been essentially excluded from the official credit system.[6] Most

Table 4.2. Reliance of Los Patios beneficiaries on agricultural credit (percentages)

	Before 1982	After 1982
Received credit	34	84
Did not receive credit	66	16
Total	100	100

Source: Author's survey data, 1988 (N = 44).

Note: This data refers to an ongoing reliance on credit as opposed to cases in which farmers may have used credit to finance initial investments made in crop production.

agricultural credit provided during the Somoza regime had been destined for export crop producers (BCN 1979), thus barring the participation of the better part of the minifundista sector, given its extremely strong subsistence orientation. Moreover, medium- and large-scale producers were the primary recipients regardless of the crop that was produced (see CEPAL 1966). Even after Somoza established a credit program that was heralded as a response to the minifundio sector's credit needs, the pool of recipients remained very small (cf. Enríquez and Spalding 1987). Thus, the project beneficiaries' newly acquired access to this productive input signified a step forward in the transition away from subsistence production and represented a major advance in the redistribution of Nicaragua's productive resources.

The special credit policy was complemented by two other policy instruments in the Los Patios project. The provision of technical assistance was one of these additional instruments. Technical assistance plays a key role in all agricultural production by supplying more information about each stage of a crop's development than the producer is typically familiar with. Access to this resource was particularly critical for Los Patios beneficiaries because they were being introduced to new crops and the crops were perennial in nature; consequently the initial few years of their development were especially important.

Through the interviews with project beneficiaries, I learned that approximately 64 percent of them had received technical assistance for the crops promoted by the project, and for most, the assistance had been provided on a regular basis. It was, however, more often directed to members of cooperatives than to individual producers. The BND, MIDINRA, and the cooperatives to which they belonged extended the assistance. Except for those beneficiaries who had participated in other agrarian reform projects previous to the implementation of Los Patios, it was probably the first time that they had access to this resource.

The provision of technical assistance to small- and medium-scale producers dates from the establishment of the Sandinista government, which conceived of it as an integral part of furthering agricultural development and agrarian reform. In contrast, before 1979, access to technical assistance was restricted to those who could pay for it (i.e., usually only the larger producers). Thus Los Patios contributed to expanding the pool of recipients of this fundamental service.

A final benefit received by Los Patios project participants was privileged access to agricultural inputs. The inputs employed by project beneficiaries included plants, fertilizers, pesticides, and a limited variety of agricultural implements and supplies. Although the majority of these producers (75 percent) had utilized various kinds of inputs prior to their entry into the project, they had frequently encountered difficulties in obtaining them in a timely fashion.[7] Many of the inputs employed in Nicaraguan agriculture were imported, and their availability had become constrained by the foreign exchange crisis that affected the country after 1979. Shortages developed as a consequence. Nonetheless, project beneficiaries were guaranteed access to the inputs required in their production.

Another policy instrument employed by MIDINRA in this region, the redistribution of agricultural land from the state sector to cooperatives formed by landless and land-poor campesino families, was used by Los Patios planners in concert with the mechanisms described above. Approximately one-third of the informants had received land through the agrarian reform. Most of this subgroup had first been land-reform beneficiaries who were only later incorporated into the project. Los Patios provided a means of complementing the coffee or basic grains these campesinos were already cultivating on the ceded land.

The Héroes y Mártires and Julio Buitrago cooperatives (both of which were CCS) were examples of the way in which several agrarian reform programs were, at times, combined to benefit the producer population. Both cooperatives received land where coffee production was already under way. Producers in the first cooperative planted avocado and citrus trees in the rows between the coffee plants on a 384 manzana coffee farm ceded to them prior to their incorporation into the project.[8] The project enabled these producers to make the best possible use of the land they had received through the agrarian reform. In the second cooperative, members had already begun cultivating pitahaya on the parcels of land where their homes were located when MIDINRA ceded them a 300 manzana coffee farm. Pitahaya had been the crop included in the project in this case.[9] The additional land was seen as a means of absorbing more family labor into their agricultural production.

In sum, participants in the Los Patios project benefited from the project's provision of key productive resources, such as agricultural credit, technical assistance, and inputs. I found that receipt of these resources had, in the majority of cases, translated into an increase in farm-generated income for the project's participants. This was clearly evidenced by the fact that the better part of its beneficiaries were no longer forced to seek supplementary sources of income away from the farm. Moreover, their agricultural production developed to such an extent that other household members were also employed on their parcels. Approximately 52 percent of the project beneficiaries surveyed incorporated other members of their immediate family into the cultivation and/or commercialization of fruits and vegetables on their minifundios. This represented a significant increase (from 27 percent) in their participation in work on the farm. Thus the survival strategies employed by these minifundistas and their families were dramatically altered following their inclusion in the Los Patios project. Whereas in the past the marginal production of their tiny plots of land typically forced one or more family members to seek other employment, the same farms came to absorb all of the project beneficiary's labor time and frequently that of his/her spouse.

Additional evidence of a positive change in the beneficiaries' income levels could be found in home improvements and the purchase of farm animals and agricultural implements that occurred after their entry into the project.[10] Thirty-seven percent of the informants had been able either to improve the condition of their already existing home or to construct a new one. And, most of those interviewed had been able to make some purchases of tools or livestock that would aid them in their agricultural production.

Yet, implementation of the Los Patios project also brought about a number of modifications that were of an even more far-reaching nature than those described above. Included in these was the fact that participation in the cooperative sector grew notably in the San Marcos–Masatepe area as a consequence of its implementation. By 1984–85 many minifundistas in this region were joining together in "Producers' Associations" in order to receive credit and technical assistance from the government. The Associations were strongly identified with production of the specific crops promoted by Los Patios and thus with the project itself. By 1986 the Associations had begun to redefine themselves as CCS and had swelled to massive proportions. As a result of this process, the better part of Los Patios beneficiaries had become cooperative members.

Cooperative development, however, underwent a reversal following the Sandinistas' implementation of the economic reform in February 1988. Many of the larger cooperatives had their assets temporarily frozen. In addition, the government's new credit policies, combined with other spin-off effects of the reform, greatly weakened the once-thriving cooperatives. As a result, cooperative membership diminished in the course of 1988.

The Los Patios project also changed the nature of the crops grown in this region, as renovated coffee trees came to share its agricultural land with citrus, avocado, and a number of other crops. A step was thus made toward the achievement of a better balance between production destined for export and that destined for the domestic market. Additionally, the introduction of these crops where export-oriented production had traditionally predominated initiated a process of transforming the region's social structure. That is, the campesino sector had been increasingly marginalized by the expansion of coffee production in the Carazo plateau region. Los Patios began to alter this situation; by promoting the adoption of fruit and vegetable production and redistributing some of the region's agricultural resources, the project's beneficiaries experienced an improvement in their living standards.

The Project's Political Impact

Given the positive socioeconomic results of the Los Patios project, it was logical to expect that its political results would be similarly sanguine, but the outcome of the 1990 general elections demonstrated that this had not been the case. By returning to the two sources of data mentioned in chapter 2—precinct-level electoral data from 1990 and post-election interviews with project beneficiaries—which point to the political attitudes of project beneficiaries, it is possible to identify the degree to which the project's political results diverged from the anticipated outcome. Beginning with the most general data, those describing the voting population as a whole in the areas of influence of Los Patios, it is evident that the vote went decidedly against the incumbent party in these precincts: only 34.5 percent of the voters there expressed support for the FSLN (see table 2.1).

It is also noteworthy that the vote against the FSLN in the municipality that had been at the heart of the Los Patios project, La Concepción, was particularly strong. It was in La Concepción that the project had been initiated and that the vast majority of its beneficiaries lived. Focusing on the polling stations designated for the project's beneficiaries within this municipality, I found that the Sandinistas received only 27.2 percent of the vote (CSE, unpublished data 1990).

Nonetheless, in spite of what at first glance appears to be relatively overwhelming evidence as to the lack of political benefits resulting from the Los Patios project, it is important to offer a cautionary note about relying exclusively on data from the 1990 elections to reach this conclusion. Even though the impact of Los Patios may have reached into numerous rural hamlets in each of the precincts whose vote has been described above, ultimately the absolute number of project participants was quite small compared to the entire voting population. For example, in the municipality of La Concepción alone (only taking into account the precincts where Los Patios beneficiaries voted), 9,310 voters cast ballots in 1990, in contrast with 650 campesinos who had

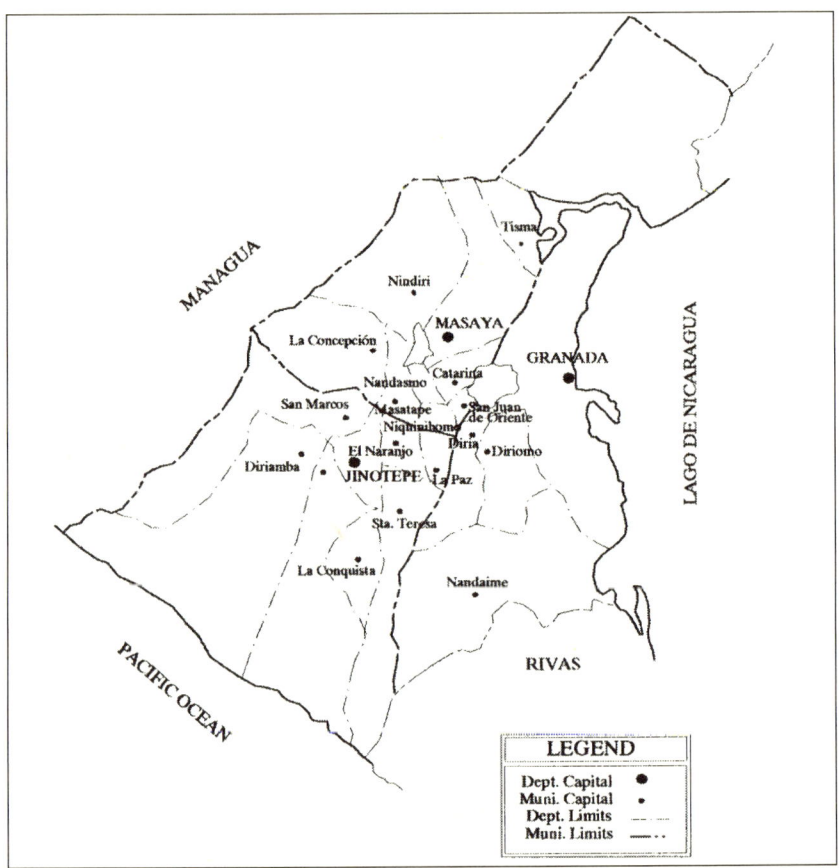

Map 4. Municipalities in Granada, Masaya, and Carazo

been incorporated into the project in all of its areas of implementation by 1988 (CSE, unpublished data 1990, and MIDINRA 1987, respectively).[11] Thus, the election data at best can only suggest the general direction that the beneficiary population might have voted, given the strong pattern set within their rural communities.

The information I gathered through follow-up interviews conducted after the elections—with a subsample of the original group—points more directly at the project's political impact by focusing specifically on its beneficiary population. While the opinions expressed in these interviews were not quite as lopsided in their opposition to the Sandinistas as the electoral data would lead us to anticipate, they did underline the strong dislike of the incumbent party held by the project's beneficiaries (see table 4.3). Only approximately 36 percent of those who participated in these interviews indicated that they were in

Table 4.3. Voting pattern of Los Patios beneficiaries

Organizational form	FSLN	UNO
CAS	—	1
CCS	2	3
Individual	2	3
Total	4	7

Source: Author's interview data, 1990 (N = 11).

favor of the FSLN in mid-1990. Of those participants who lived in La Concepción, support for the Sandinistas was even lower, 33 percent. That is to say, my interviews highlighted the fact that the project beneficiaries followed the pattern set by their communities in expressing their dissatisfaction with the Sandinista regime. Even more importantly, they also put in evidence that the implementation of Los Patios did nothing to counter this general tendency.

This surprising outcome not only contradicted the expectations of FSLN activists, it also refuted commonly held assumptions concerning the political benefits of agrarian reform. In addition to providing information as to how Los Patios beneficiaries voted, the follow-up interviews offered a means of exploring these enigmatic election results. As described in chapter 2, project beneficiaries were unhappy about the effect the economic crisis had on themselves and their families, as well as the fact that the Sandinista government had imposed a military draft which they considered oppressive. Furthermore, they expressed profound resentment against the government for what they perceived to have been excessive interference in their agricultural production, and in their lives more generally.

While primarily conversing about the past, we also discussed some contemporary events that shed light on their attitudes toward the Sandinista government. In the first few months after the Chamorro government's inauguration, the municipality of La Concepción became the site of a series of invasions of farms that had been redistributed through the agrarian reform. Almost uniformly, those who attempted to take over the land were associated with the former owners of the property.[12] The follow-up interviews provided an opportunity to address the issue of property ownership rights with my informants. Although several of them sympathized with the cooperatives that had their land invaded, more than half of them took the side of those who were trying to take back the land from the cooperatives. This second group of informants revealed an implicit, and in some cases explicit, assumption that the legitimate owners of the affected farms were those who had lost their land through the agrarian reform. In essence, they did not conceive of the redistribution of land that was carried out by the Sandinista government as a lawful process.

The views of several informants exemplified this position. One of these, a former CCS member, was married to a farmer who had organized a different CCS with a number of others and had received land through the agrarian reform. As a consequence, the immediate family of my informant, Doña Rafaela, had access to almost 10 manzanas of land, which placed them at the very top end of the small-farmer category. Although the informant's husband had not participated in Los Patios, he and a few other family members sat in on several interviews that I conducted with Doña Rafaela between mid-1990 and mid-1992. In the first of these interviews I asked her husband, Don Juan, if his cooperative had received any communication from the former owner of its land, to which he replied in the negative. But the previous foreman of the farm had recently come onto the cooperative and an argument about its ownership had ensued. Doña Rafaela's husband did not feel that the foreman had any right to the land. But, he clarified, "if Solorzano [the former owner] came, that would be different. We would turn back the land to him. We would, however, ask to be able to collect the harvest of the crops we have been growing there now" (interview no. 22, June 16, 1990).

In our next interview—approximately six months later—we returned to the topic of the land takeovers, referring especially to those that had occurred close to them. When I asked them to recount the events to me they began by saying that "the UNO people entered [went onto the land of] the cooperatives and those who they encountered there mistreated them" (interview no. 46, January 6, 1991). When I asked why the former had gone onto the cooperative's land, Doña Rafaela and her husband said, "They wanted to get the Sandinistas [the cooperative members] out. They had a right to take back the land, because the UNO won [the elections]."

Even before the land invasions of July 1990, however, there was much talk of UNO activists threatening to take cooperatives' lands away from them to give to UNO sympathizers. I raised this topic with Don Roberto, a former CCS member whose family engaged in a variety of activities, (e.g. basket making and selling sweets out of the house) to supplement their earnings from the one-half manzana he had planted with pitahaya.[13] My goal was to explore his feelings about the cooperatives that had been formed in the 1980s. He responded, "It's right that others who don't have land move into the cooperatives, because there were [cooperatives] in which each person had perhaps up to ten manzanas and they couldn't work it all, while there are others who have no land" (interview no. 54, June 21, 1990]. Don Roberto, in contrast to some of my other informants, still sympathized with those peasants who had less than he did. But the fact that he expressed no concern about the manner in which these new "beneficiaries" were to be "given" land and about the illegality of the procedure suggests that he viewed the region's existing cooperatives as not entirely legitimate.

Another informant, Don Rogelio, was actually married into a family that had lost its land in the agrarian reform. Over the course of the few years following the installation of the Chamorro government, his wife's family engaged in an ongoing battle (which ranged from juridical to military in nature) to recover the three farms that he said they had "lost to the Sandinistas." In fact, on several occasions our interview appointments had to be canceled as pitched battles took place on one of the farms. For Don Rogelio and his family, it was taken for granted that it was their right to have the land back. The issues of concern to them were how to actually take control of the land and how to get the farms functioning again: "We retook the farm in Santa Teresa four months ago without an incident. But the following night the people [the cooperative members] came back armed, and there were gunshots fired. Nonetheless, we negotiated a solution there. The farm in San Jorge we [also] retook about four months ago. Since it was abandoned, there was no problem in retaking it. [Finally,] the farm in Las Esquinas we retook three days ago. There were thirty of us and we only encountered one boy there—another forty people came later to spend the first two nights with us there" (interview no. 52, January 12, 1991).

Once most of Don Rogelio's friends had left, however, the cooperative members came back and retook the farm from them. Besides being anxious to get the third farm back, Don Rogelio complained, "They left the farms in shambles. Those people don't know how to work. A farm needs a lot of care. Each of the farms had a little house on it, which they also destroyed. But that doesn't really worry us, we can rebuild them just as we can put the farms back together again."

The attitude held by many Los Patios beneficiaries toward the Sandinistas' agrarian reform program was evidenced in another area as well. In comparing La Concepción's voters in the areas of influence of Los Patios with those in neighboring municipalities where electoral support for the Sandinistas was significantly greater (see the discussion and data in chapter 7), the question arises as to what distinguishes these populations so much that the latter's identification with the FSLN would be noticeably greater. At least one of the key differences, if not *the* key difference, is the fact that significantly more land was redistributed through the agrarian reform in these municipalities (specifically in San Marcos, Masatepe, and Nandasmo) than in La Concepción.[14] Moreover, the land redistribution occurred much earlier in the former areas than that which took place in La Concepción.

Even more important, in the municipalities neighboring La Concepción, the redistribution of land was carried out in response to demands made for it by the rural population. In contrast, La Concepción's land redistribution followed an effort by the FSLN to organize the population to ask the government for it. Hence the initiative came from above, not below. When asked why these processes had been so varied, an informant with extensive knowledge of the area stated that it stemmed from the nature of the people of La Concepción.[15] That is, the fact that this community's population is predominantly composed of independent small farmers affected the posture it adopted concerning the redistributive policies of the Sandinista government. This explanation of La Concepción's population fits with the opinions expressed by those residents who participated in my follow-up interviews when asked about the land confiscations that occurred there in the post-Sandinista era.[16]

In sum, despite the positive socioeconomic impact that the Los Patios agrarian reform project had on its beneficiaries' lives, the beneficiaries withheld support from the Sandinistas when the latter's tenure in power was being disputed. Many of these producers strongly opposed the Sandinista government's attempts to modify crucial aspects of Nicaragua's prerevolutionary economic and social structure. Instead, Los Patios participants overwhelmingly favored a return to unfettered capitalism.

In order to comprehend the conservative reaction of Los Patios beneficiaries, we need to look at them, as well as at the project itself, more carefully. Los Patios, as an agrarian reform project, was largely successful in attaining the economic goals that had motivated its implementation. Numerous individuals who participated in it clearly did find their living standards raised, as seen in the shift in family labor patterns and in material improvements on their farms. Yet, while the project redistributed various resources to its beneficiaries, changes in landholding patterns were not integrated into its design. Thus Los Patios reinforced the socioeconomic differentiation already existing among its participants, and between them and the rest of the region's minifundio population.

It is also important to take into account the fact that even though Los Patios beneficiaries were predominantly minifundistas, many of them were at the upper reaches of this category relative to the vast population of poor peasants in this area. Undeniably, as seen in chapter 3, most of the project's participants were not rich peasants and would not even have qualified as medium-scale peasants if a strict definition were applied to describe them. What is key to note here and will be developed at greater length in chapter 7 is that, *comparatively* speaking, this population was not among the region's poorest peasantry.

Interestingly, one of the hamlets that formed part of the Los Patios area of influence within the municipality of La Concepción—San Caralampio—is the subject of a six-community study that was carried out by Leslie Anderson. Anderson's (1994) socioeconomic characterization of San Caralampio—to which she refers by its post-1979 name, Pikin Guerrero[17]—conforms quite closely to the situation described by the informants who participated in the survey I coordinated in 1988 of Los Patios beneficiaries. She found (1994, 147, 151) that while a problem of landlessness and insufficient land certainly existed in this area—as clearly evidenced in an average deficit of 1.1 manzanas per household in terms of what a family needed to support itself—"many villagers were essentially middle-peasants." Moreover, "they knew that relatively speaking, they were more fortunate than many" (Anderson 1994, 154). Yet Anderson's informants reported a significant level of differentiation in terms of land ownership, with the village including several medium- and large-scale landholders (using the criteria established for this region earlier).

Still, Anderson found that even those who did not have sufficient access to land (based on ownership) were usually able to rent land at reasonable prices. She concluded that although many of San Caralampio's dwellers had a rough time in economic terms, poverty levels were not overwhelming and most people were able to get by. Anderson considered these socioeconomic factors to have contributed to the community's relative quiescence during the war against Somoza, leading its residents to have become involved in the struggle against his regime only very late in the war (i.e., during approximately the last nine months).[18] That is, until the regime began to engage in repressive activities in this community (in about 1978), San Caralampio's residents preferred to "retreat as much as possible and mind their own business" (Anderson 1994, 154).[19]

The *relative* economic security that Anderson speaks of, which was also evident among the Los Patios beneficiaries who formed part of my survey sample, was only strengthened for those who became beneficiaries of the project. This positive economic outcome was, in fact, sought by the Los Patios planners. However, when the socioeconomic improvements that the project's beneficiaries experienced through the project were combined with their social origins, even more distance was created between them and the area's poorest peasants. In the process, many of the beneficiaries were pushed in the direction of, if not into, the category of middle peasant.

In an effort to counterbalance the tendency toward increased differentiation, the project's planners encouraged the formation of CCS among its beneficiaries. But, even though the CCS did bring their members together to receive certain resources, those who composed them continued to farm on an individual basis. Hence, their individual orientation and class differences were never completely eliminated[20] and, therefore, neither was their potential for adopting a conservative political stance.[21]

Many analysts of peasant politics have argued that with the transition from poor peasant to small commercial farmer status, a conservatizing process takes place (Huntington 1968, Paige 1975, and de Janvry 1981). With the achievement of greater economic security, however slight, these peasants shift their concern from that of demanding a redistribution of agricultural resources to that of ensuring the permanence of their recently acquired positions. One informant, Don Gregorio, in explaining the problems that existed in the CCS to which he belonged, complained of all the new members (who were agrarian reform beneficiaries) that "the government" had pushed into the cooperative. This particular CCS had been founded during the Somoza era by a group of relatively well-off peasants and larger producers—including Don Gregorio, who had 5 manzanas of land. From his point of view, the agrarian reform beneficiaries were "a lot of vagrants and drunks who didn't pay their entry dues . . . and wasted a lot of [the cooperative's] money" (interview no. 89, June 1, 1990). He went on to propose that "it would be good to kick out all of the new members that the government let in [the cooperative], so that only the founding members would be left," as a solution to its troubles.

A neighbor of Don Gregorio and fellow Los Patios participant held a similar view of the area's agrarian reform beneficiaries. This informant—Don Edgar—owned approximately 12 manzanas, which he farmed on an entirely individual basis. In recounting the ambiance in the pre-electoral period, Don Edgar said that "those from the nearby cooperatives told me that if they [the FSLN] won, they would take away my farm" (interview no. 70, June 18, 1990). When I asked him why this was, he responded "because I'm working it well. They [always] took away things that were working well to grab [the profits] themselves—or they ran them into the ground."

Clearly, neither Don Gregorio nor Don Edgar sympathized with those who formerly had nothing and had only become farmers through the agrarian reform. Instead, they identified with the rich peasants and larger landowners. For both of these farmers and others in their position, their aspirations were turned toward upward mobility, and their sights were set on joining the rural bourgeoisie. Rather than continue to empathize with the needs of their poorer counterparts, they begin to share the fears of the agrarian upper class concerning threats to property rights and other benefits derived from their relatively privileged position within the peasantry.

Certainly the sympathy expressed by Los Patios producers for former landowners in La Concepción demonstrates this perception of having interests in common with the landed classes. Their resentment of government interference in produce commercialization further underlines their identification with the capitalist sector. Complaining of the Sandinistas in this regard, as well as in others, one Los Patios beneficiary said, "Your yucca, your corn, you had to sell as if you were a thief, in secret. I don't understand how some campesinos can continue to support the FSLN given its commercialization policies. They even took away [produce] baskets from one's wife" (interview no. 50, July 25, 1990).

This particular informant was an individual producer who had entered the project when it was extended to MIDINRA's development pole in Diriomo. He owned more than 100 manzanas, of which slightly less than 40 were cultivatable. Thus his social origins distinguished him from the average minifundista in the area. Yet his participation was a reflection of the Sandinistas' efforts at this time—especially in the Diriomo area—to reach out to individual producers and try to bring them into the fold of agrarian reform beneficiaries and regime supporters.

Another informant, when asked why he felt bad under the Sandinistas (in response to an earlier comment of his) stated, "The people are still upset about the government's efforts to control their production . . . what they want is a free market" (interview no. 28, June 22, 1990). Interestingly, the CCS of this informant had been more responsible, over time, than any state agency for controlling his produce marketing. Yet, it was the state's unwelcome marketing schemes that stood out most in his mind.

In essence, instead of supporting the government's efforts to buffer the poor peasantry from the negative effects of the free market—effects that have a stronger impact on this sector than on larger producers because of the former's minimal margin for error and misfortune—the Los Patios producers' ascension in status predisposed them to resist any control over their own profit-making possibilities. For them the Sandinistas' efforts to control their flow of produce to the market symbolized all of the government's interference in their affairs. As Don Rogelio went on to say, "Those communists wanted to control everything . . . even my own home, which I built with my own sweat. They would say 'another four people could live here'" (interview no. 28, June 22, 1990).

In addition, the extent to which internal stratification leads to divisiveness within the peasantry has also been highlighted by those who study peasant politics (Paige 1975 and de Janvry 1981). According to Paige, this occurs because of the high degree of competitiveness that characterizes peasant communities. Hence, "as long as such differences in wealth exist, it is always possible to imagine gaining wealth or status by outmaneuvering or outstealing one's neighbors."

One informant, Doña Socorro, had a new tale to tell each time I visited her about her problems with her neighbors. At first the problem was with the neighbor across the road from her house, who had killed one of the pigs she was raising as a source of income. According to Doña Socorro, the problem stemmed from the fact that her neighbor "was very jealous because her [the neighbor's] son had been drafted, and my own remained working on the cooperative's land" (interview no. 58, January 7, 1991). Two years later, she spoke with concern of another neighbor whose land adjoined the small farm that she owned, which was located at some distance from her house. This neighbor "has let his animals graze on our land on various occasions, in the process damaging the beans we had planted there. The last time, which was the sixth time, we caught his horse grazing there and took it to the police.... Now he's putting up a new fence around his property and he has grabbed some of our land in the process" (interview no. 128, April 3, 1993).

In discussing these problems, she told me that this neighbor and his family were supporters of the UNO and that he was always trying to trick her into revealing her politics. Doña Socorro and her family continued to support the FSLN, and it was clear that political differences had come to exacerbate other differences between her and her neighbors. Thereby, tensions were created between peasants who, objectively speaking, shared many problems in common.

The exacerbation of social differentiation in rural communities, through the creation of a pampered minority of the peasantry, has often been an implicit aim of agrarian reform projects in capitalist settings, given its potential for reducing the cohesion of peasant movements (de Janvry 1981). Hence, the fact that Los Patios strengthened already existing social differentiation in its areas of influence may well have reduced the solidarity between the project's beneficiary population and the surrounding community of poor peasants.

Finally, the process of repeasantization itself that Los Patios facilitated would have reinforced one of the key tendencies that Paige (1975) identified: that growing dependence on the land for one's income was directly related to a weakening in the incentives for revolutionary political organizations. The reasons for this were several. First, the small margin between survival and starvation that typifies the lives of the peasantry leads to risk-averse behavior among those who compose this sector. That is to say, the dramatically negative outcomes that most peasants associate with the possibility of being landless usually limit their willingness to engage in political or technical change. Second, their structural isolation and dependency on people who are not peasants reduces their identification with other peasant producers. As independent farmers, they have traditionally had to rely upon non-peasants for assistance in a variety of areas, including with the provision of social services, agricultural credit, and other economic resources. Because peasants have not historically been able to help resolve the needs of other peasants in these areas, their allegiance lies with those from outside of this sector who have proven their ability to do so. Their "patrons" are often larger landowners who live in the area, thus strengthening the tendency for small farmers' identification with the landed classes. And finally, the above-mentioned competitiveness that commonly exists among the peasantry also inhibits solidarity within this sector.

In a situation of collective land ownership, this inclination toward individualism would be ameliorated. Instead of looking to wealthy benefactors, cooperative members would rely on each other to find the means of meeting their production-related and other needs. The identification with others from the peasant sector would grow, while that with the landed classes would decrease. Yet in the case of the Los Patios project, its beneficiaries became more tied to the land precisely as individual farmers. Therefore their openness to seeking collective solutions, especially those arising from within the peasantry, for the problems that characterized their lives dropped off accordingly.

The dramatic deterioration that occurred in the national economy after 1987 probably contributed to this phenomenon. Along with the rest of the country's population, Los Patios beneficiaries were strongly affected by Nicaragua's profound economic crisis. The crisis reduced domestic demand for a number of the crops promoted by the project and undermined the government's ability to prioritize redistribution of resources over economic efficiency. As the country's entire population was increasingly forced to seek survival strategies, individual pursuit of survival became very common. Consequently, the campesinos' willingness to participate in further collective experiments in social reform diminished.[22]

The political results of the Los Patios project underscore the indispensable nature of efforts to stimulate the active participation of the peasantry in the process of development and transformation. Its beneficiaries were passively incorporated into these overall processes through their relationship with the project, and in some cases their membership in CCS. But their general orientation continued to be that of independent peasants. As argued in chapter 1, in the context of the transition to socialism the mobilization or organization of the population in a variety of forms is crucial, both for fostering development in a situation of scarce resources as well as for maintaining the political legitimacy of the regime that is pushing forth such change. As the difficulties that almost inevitably accompany the transition to socialism become accentuated, the role of mobilization only increases in importance as a means of maintaining the popular classes firmly behind the socialist regime and making them fully aware of the causes of the difficulties. In essence, in contrast to the thesis Huntington (1965) had set forth in which the mobilized population overburdens the regime with excessive demand—demand which existed within this particular population even though it was left unmobilized—thereby creating political instability, the failure of Los Patios to mobilize its participants contributed to their growing alienation from the Sandinista government and its socialist project. The end result was their strong support for the UNO, which promised a more traditional, capitalist orientation in government policymaking.

Conclusion

Nicaragua's agrarian reform program represented the most important piece of a comprehensive process of social transformation. The reform was designed to move the country away from its extreme agroexport dependence while simultaneously ameliorating the socioeconomic conditions of the rural poor. At the same time, agrarian reform planners assumed that the redistribution of resources brought about by the reform would generate an increase in support for the Sandinista government and its overall goal of initiating the transition to socialism.

The Los Patios project was part of this effort, although it also reflected the shift that was under way by the mid-1980s in the Sandinistas' agricultural development model. Los Patios targeted the minifundio sector, with the aim of improving its economic potential and living standard. The project responded to shortcomings in previous reform policies, especially the attempt to proletarianize and/or collectivize the region's peasants.

Even though Sandinista policymakers had originally considered these two approaches to dealing with the "peasant question" to be the most appropriate ones, by the time Los Patios was implemented they had begun to modify their position somewhat. Proponents of the new campesinista strategy assumed that more intermediate steps could be taken that would appeal to the peasantry while also stimulating development in this sector of the economy. That is to say, through redistributive policies that were flexible enough in nature to allow for their receipt by individuals, it would be possible to reach a broader spectrum of the peasantry than had heretofore been the case. At the same time, the incorporation of this population into the agrarian reform would facilitate an increase in the level of the productive forces employed by the peasantry and therefore growth in its production. These two phenomena, taken together with the improvements that were anticipated in its members' standard of living, would represent an advance in the overall process of rural and agricultural development.

The results of the Los Patios project, as evidenced through my survey findings, were generally positive in the economic sphere. Indeed, the improved technologies utilized by project participants led to production increases (particularly for marketed goods) and symbolized a raising of the forces of production that were employed by its peasant beneficiaries. Likewise, the progression upward in their standard of living that was revealed in the absorption of their labor on the farm, home construction and repairs, and related purchases also signaled the economic success the project had. Despite the partial economic reversal that had affected its beneficiaries as a result of the country's economic crisis generally and the economic reform specifically, in relation to their social conditions and agricultural production, the salutary economic impact Los Patios had had for its participants remained tangible.

Yet to the degree that Los Patios was successful in the social and economic spheres, it raised questions about how best to implement a strong pro-peasant policy and what the consequences of such a policy would be. The strengthening of peasant production that resulted from the project reinforced already existing differences within the peasantry in its areas of influence, and a new process of differentiation was begun in this sector of the population. In addition, it fortified the peasants' production in a manner that bolstered its individual nature. Furthermore, the growth of the region's CCS that was fostered by the project, while collectivizing some aspects of the production and commercialization processes, did not fundamentally alter the beneficiaries' individual production patterns.

In implementing the Los Patios project, Sandinista agrarian planners had assumed that the larger context in which this agrarian reform project was being carried out would counter any conservatizing tendencies that might have been stimulated by the recampesinización resulting from it. The project was only one of a number of endeavors undertaken, which together had the goal of bringing about that change in the countryside. Whereas other projects had been especially focused on redistributing resources such as land, Los Patios was designed to complement them by responding to the needs of those minifundistas outside of their reach.

Nonetheless, the political impact of the Los Patios agrarian reform project suggests the difficulties inherent in implementing policies that will benefit the peasantry economically *and* produce political results for a socialist regime. Agrarian reform planners in capitalist regimes are at a great advantage in this sense, because their policies simply have to facilitate a slight increase in the economic security of the peasantry in order to achieve their objective of maintaining the status quo. In contrast, given the explicit objective of promoting social transformation held by socialist planners, it becomes essential for their policies to ameliorate the conservative potential inherent in agrarian reform.

At the same time, the efforts of socialist planners are often constrained by the existence of a mixed economy and a large peasant sector. Dilemmas such as that described above are likely to arise wherever the possibility is limited of implementing strategies that serve to counteract this tendency. In other words, without a comprehensive redistribution of productive resources, agrarian reform will tend to produce the same conservative results regardless of the more general sociopolitical context in which it is carried out. And redistribution must be combined with a reorganization of production relations that incorporates the peasantry into the process of societal change that composes the transition to a socialist model of development. As discussed in chapter 1, the mobilization of the population is a crucial ingredient in development efforts during the transition to socialism. The fact that insufficient mobilization, or organization, had accompanied the implementation of Los Patios was highlighted in the independent production patterns of its small farmers. When combined with the conservative potential produced by this type of agrarian reform program and the economic decline that characterized the country in the late 1980s, the organizational weakness of Los Patios was almost bound to result in a withdrawal of support for the Sandinistas' socialist project.

Other region-specific economic development strategies were implemented as part of Nicaragua's agrarian reform program that put in evidence the political benefits of alternative strategies, such as collectivization of production. One agrarian reform project that embodied these alternative strategies was Plan Masaya. As will be shown in chapters 5 and 6, this project succeeded in bringing about a fundamental redistribution of resources and in moving its beneficiary population away from individual production. Consequently it achieved its political objectives as well as its economic ones to a much greater extent than Los Patios. The Plan Masaya agrarian reform project suggests some of the conditions under which the promotion of socioeconomic development can generate political identification with the regime that is responsible for its realization, which in this case was a regime oriented toward furthering the transition to socialism.

The Los Patios project was only one of the many agrarian reform projects that were implemented by the Sandinista government. Although the project did not completely transform the nature of agricultural production in the Carazo plateau region, it clearly advanced that process of change. Los Patios opened up new horizons to those small-scale producers who were slowly being pushed off the land by the development of agricultural capitalism. Ironically, that achievement would eventually contribute to the termination of the agrarian reform.

5

Plan Masaya
Its Roots

Between June and July 1985, Nicaragua's agrarian reform ministry turned over 4,509 manzanas of prime agricultural land to 1,011 peasant families in the area of Masaya and Diriomo (MIDINRA n.d.[a]). This *entrega de tierra* (redistribution of land) was known as Plan Masaya. Its beneficiaries were organized in a variety of forms, including in several types of cooperatives and as individual farmers. They subsequently began to grow corn, beans, and other traditional "campesino crops" in this former agroexport region.

In addition to bringing about a dramatic change in cultivation patterns, Plan Masaya simultaneously set in motion a major modification in the social relations of agricultural production in the two regions where it was implemented. The most publicized expression of this process of modification was the case of Agro-Industrial Systems of Masaya, Inc. (SAIMSA). SAIMSA was a streamlined agroindustrial enterprise par excellence that was directed by Enrique Bolaños, then president of the Superior Council of Private Enterprise (COSEP).[1] This company specialized in cotton production, with operations ranging from crop cultivation to processing. Due to its owners' lack of willingness to negotiate a settlement with the government, all of SAIMSA's property was confiscated. On some of the company's farms, the workers organized and forcibly took over the land. On others, the government stepped in to orchestrate its confiscation. Although SAIMSA was the only company (or set of individuals) to have its land confiscated by the implementation of Plan Masaya, the shift in production relations that occurred on the affected property was characteristic of the change that had taken place on all of the land affected by the project.

The transformation of agricultural production and class relations that Plan Masaya brought about underlined the wholesale adoption of the new orientation in agrarian policymaking that was consummated during this period. In contrast to the Los Patios agrarian reform project, in which only the first indications of the shift in strategy that was being contemplated were evident, Plan Masaya entailed its comprehensive implementation. Whereas Los Patios initiated the new policy of extending the benefits of agrarian reform to farmers organized in various forms, through means other than land distribution, Plan Masaya went a step beyond that and included land among the benefits. That is, it expressed the increased flexibility that described land redistribution policy, in that individual farmers and those organized in CCS were accepted as legitimate candidates for receipt of land through the agrarian reform. This flexibility was designed, in part, to further the goal of recampesinización of the peasant population. Further, Plan Masaya brought about the replacement of medium- and large-scale capitalist producers with peasant farmers in one of Region IV's key agricultural areas.

Moreover, while Los Patios promoted the cultivation of domestically oriented crops by its small-scale farmer beneficiaries, it did not alter the general export emphasis of production in its areas of influence. Rather, it only affected those areas which had already been categorized as marginal for coffee production when CONARCA's coffee renovation program was carried out. Plan Masaya, however, completely supplanted the export-oriented production in its areas of influence. In the process, the latter project ruptured the dominance of cotton and beef production that had continued to exist in the development strategy that Sandinista policymakers had elaborated for this region at the beginning of the 1980s. Food crop production was brought back to the areas it had occupied before the various waves of agroexport expansion had marginalized it earlier in the century.

The Plan Masaya agrarian reform project was implemented for many of the same general reasons that had led to the Los Patios project's being undertaken. Through it, agrarian reform planners sought to raise the standard of living of its beneficiaries by providing them with the resources necessary for their full employment in agricultural production. At the same time, they aimed to increase food crop production in this region by expanding the area under cultivation with crops destined for the domestic market and by improving the level of technology utilized in their production processes. Hence, food crops and their producers were to be given access to all of the resources from which they had formerly been excluded, especially fertile land, agricultural credit, and technical assistance. And, for many Plan Masaya participants, agricultural machinery was an additional benefit they obtained through the project.

Like Los Patios, Plan Masaya was seen to be a means to promote socioeconomic development in the regions in which it was implemented. By bringing about an increase in the area's agricultural diversification and in its production, raising the level of the forces of production, and facilitating an improvement in the standard of living of its beneficiaries, the project would stimulate an advance in the overall process of rural and agricultural development. It was also taken for granted that the land redistribution that formed the core of Plan Masaya and the socioeconomic progress that it would bring to its beneficiaries would serve to convince this population that the Sandinista government did indeed represent its interests. This in turn would lead to a growth in support for the government and its project of social transformation.

Plan Masaya was quite successful in meeting the socioeconomic objectives that had been set out for it within several years of its implementation. Through an evaluation of the project's impact (see the Brief Discussion of Methodology), it became evident that participation in Plan Masaya had led to a betterment in its beneficiaries' socioeconomic well-being. It also was clear that the project had accomplished its goal of integrating more advanced technologies into basic grain production, which resulted in a dramatic increase in the region's food crop output.

Yet it was not until Nicaragua's 1990 elections that it became possible to assess the political results of Plan Masaya. A first glance at the electoral data from 1990 would seem to suggest that the project had had a similarly negative impact in the political sphere as that produced by Los Patios. In the precincts that were included in the areas of influence of Plan Masaya, the vote in favor of the incumbent party was only slightly greater than that in the Los Patios areas of influence and of the country's rural population as a whole (see table 2.1). But as will be described below, upon closer inspection, several indicators in these data imply a higher level of identification with and support for the FSLN than is revealed by a brief look. These indicators coincide with my findings from follow-up interviews conducted with the project's beneficiaries after the elections. Through the interviews it became apparent that a significant level of support for the FSLN and its social project continued to exist among those who had received land through this agrarian reform project.

The political impact of the Plan Masaya agrarian reform project conformed to what many social theorists (e.g. Paige 1975, Alavi 1965, and Lenin 1980) would hypothesize to be the outcome of such an endeavor, and to what Nicaragua's agrarian planners had hoped to achieve through its implementation. Given the differences in the level of support for the Sandinista government in the population as a whole, the rural population, and Los Patios beneficiaries on the one hand, and that of Plan Masaya beneficiaries on the other, it behooves us to examine at greater length the dynamics that led to this outcome. Such an examination should also help to shed light on the larger question which underlies our study—that of the nature of the relationship between socioeconomic development brought about through agrarian reform and politics during the transition to socialism.

This exploration of the dynamics that underlay the political impact of Plan Masaya will begin with a review of the socioeconomic context in which the project was carried out and the circumstances that led to its implementation. In addition, it is necessary to become familiar with the social origins of those who participated in the project. These three phenomena will be the foci of this chapter. With this background in hand, we will then move on, in chapter 6, to look more closely at exactly how Plan Masaya affected the lives of its beneficiaries. This should facilitate an understanding of what distinguished them from other agrarian reform beneficiaries and the rural population more generally with regard to their levels of commitment to the Sandinistas' project of social transformation.

Plan Masaya

The Political and Economic Situation That Gave Rise to the Project

The comprehensive adoption of a new strategy of agricultural development and agrarian reform was the result of a number of issues that came to the fore in the mid-1980s. Nonetheless, in the case of Plan Masaya, these issues (which will be described below) had only compounded the need to address preexisting socioeconomic problems that had their roots in the area's developmental history. Like Los Patios beneficiaries, Plan Masaya participants also had been casualties of the region's agroexport booms. There were differences, however, in the degree to which each of these populations was affected. Through a closer look at both the process of development that had occurred in this region and the manner in which it had marginalized the area's peasantry, we will gain a better sense of the precise nature of the project's participants. This will provide a foundation for understanding the extent of the change that Plan Masaya brought to their lives.

The two areas in which Plan Masaya was implemented, the plains of Masaya and Diriomo, had been prime agricultural zones prior to 1985 (see map 3). Agroexport production had spread into these areas in the preceding decades. In the process, it pushed aside the basic grains that had been grown there previously. This process, though, differed somewhat between Masaya and Diriomo, affecting the areas' peasants to varying extents.

In Masaya (see note 2 in the introduction for a listing of the municipalities included in this area) the crop which had brought about the most significant alterations in the social and productive structures was cotton. The widespread adoption of cotton production dated from the 1950s, when a number of Region IV's major coffee-growing families joined the rush to cultivate this new boom crop. Although cotton had been cultivated in Nicaragua since colonial times, it was not until the advent of chemical pest control in the mid-twentieth century that its production for export was expanded in a long-lasting way (Williams 1986). Granada and particularly Masaya were the primary areas of cotton cultivation in the region.

The expansion of cotton growing in Region IV was as dramatic as that in the nation as a whole. Whereas in 1950–51, 2,058 manzanas were cultivated with cotton in Region IV, by the next year this figure had leaped to 15,234 (calculated from CONAL 1973, table II-9). The average number of manzanas dedicated to cotton production in the 1950s and 1960s was 12,739. Region IV was not, however, the country's most important cotton-producing area.[2] What later became known as Region II, León and Chinandega, has always been Nicaragua's foremost cotton-growing area. Yet Region IV's contribution to national production was not insignificant, and cotton was one of its key crops. Moreover, for Masaya, cotton was its principal crop.[3]

As had occurred elsewhere in the nation, the expansion of cotton cultivation gave new impetus to the process of land concentration that had advanced with each agroexport boom. Another characteristic of Nicaraguan cotton production made this situation of land concentration even more extreme: given that cotton is an annual crop, and it has been common for Nicaraguan cotton growers to move in and out of its production according to variations in the international price for it. Cotton producers particularly relied on land rentals to facilitate this movement. When the world market price for cotton was low, they restricted its cultivation to their own land, at times even planting their land with other crops. When the price rose, growers not only planted their own land with cotton, but also rented large tracts of additional land for its cultivation. According to MIDINRA (1983, 16), cotton planted on rented land fluctuated between 55 and 85 percent of the total cotton acreage in Masaya. This study further concludes that producers who rented land represented more than half of all cotton growers. One of the consequences of this phenomenon was an upsurge in the rental prices for agricultural land whenever the international price made cotton production profitable. Thus, landless and land-poor campesinos in this area were effectively excluded from access to rental land by competition from larger cotton producers.[4]

The Nicaraguan state facilitated the expansion of cotton cultivation by showering it with productive resources and developing the infrastructural base required to sustain large-scale production. At the national level, state banks dramatically increased their credit allocations for cotton after 1950, and cotton producers were disproportionately favored over other farmers with regard to credit distribution (cf. CONAL 1973 and Enríquez and Spalding 1987). Yet the banks' generous provision of credit was not designed to stimulate cotton production among all sectors of the rural population. Beginning in the 1959–60 cotton cycle, a number of stipulations were placed on the receipt of credit that effectively restricted its use to those producers who employed more advanced technology in the production process—typically the larger growers (see Ordóñez Centeno 1976). In addition, the government showed a clear interest in cotton production in its expenditures for infrastructural development (cf. Belli 1975). This infrastructural development included the construction of roads, storage facilities, and so forth.

In sum, the expansion of cotton production in Region IV represented an extension of the bourgeoisie's historical pattern of looking outward to the world market for stimuli to trigger its movement into new areas of production. It also served to reinforce Region IV's reliance on export crop production as the essence of its economy. Furthermore, it greatly accentuated the concentration of agricultural resources that already existed, particularly that of land. Nonetheless, cotton was only the first product, albeit the most important, in this wave of agroexport expansion.

In contrast to Masaya, Diriomo was affected by the growth that took place in beef production in the 1960s. The beef industry's resurgence in Region IV at that time was part of a dramatic increase in beef exports that was occurring at the national level. The country had not experienced a major boom in beef production since the 1500s. The tremendous growth that Nicaragua's beef industry underwent during the 1960s was, in large part, a response to the nascent fast-food industry in the United States. Once again the state—with international financing—played a major role in this growth. Breeding cattle were imported from the United States, an artificial insemination center was established, and more infrastructural development occurred. The Somoza family assumed a prominent position in the new industry, although some non-Somoza capital from Granada and Rivas was also invested in this sector of the agricultural economy.

As was the case elsewhere in the country, cattle ranching consumed an increasing proportion of the region's agricultural land. Rivas was the department (province) most affected by this expansion in Region IV. Nonetheless, Granada's municipalities of Diriomo and Diriá also saw their proportions of pastureland grow and come to occupy the most fertile areas in these two municipalities. Following the pattern that had characterized the nation as a whole, this new wave of agroexport production also pushed food crop production out of the areas it had occupied. Along with the marginalization of food crop production went the marginalization of those who were responsible for it—the peasantry. As we saw in chapter 3 (especially table 3.1), peasants were not typically central to export production. Rather, it was medium- and large-scale capitalist farmers who specialized in its production. This general pattern held true for cattle raising, as it had for coffee, sugarcane, and cotton cultivation before it, thereby contributing to the already striking levels of land concentration that characterized Region IV. But in contrast to the cotton production that monopolized agriculture in Masaya, cattle ranching did not usually entail the use of rented land. Thus, to the extent that rented land existed in Diriomo, at least the campesinos living there did not have to compete for it with larger producers who could afford to pay more for its use, in the process driving up its price.

As a consequence of the expansion of both cotton production and cattle ranching, insufficient land and landlessness had become serious problems in Masaya and Diriomo by the 1970s. In fact, the entire department of Masaya and the municipalities of Diriomo and Diriá in Granada were among the areas with the highest levels of landlessness (and insufficient land) in Region IV. This phenomenon was a result of the fact that the population density was higher in these areas than it was in the rest of the region: in 1978, while the population density for Region IV as a whole was 106.3 inhabitants per square kilometer, in these municipalities the same figure was 197.4 (calculated from CIERA 1980a, 12; 1980b, 7; 1980c, 7; and 1980d, 9). The phenomenon also stemmed from the fact that these areas were characterized by their particularly heavy reliance on agroexport production, with all of its attendant effects in terms of land concentration.

The Early Years of Agrarian Reform in Masaya and Diriomo
Development plans for Masaya and Diriomo formed part of the larger strategy that was designed for Region IV in the early 1980s. In Masaya and Diriomo, the more general strategies of nationalization and proletarianization and, later, land distribution with cooperative formation also held sway. Moreover, agrarian reform policies in these two areas were subject to similar constraints to those that characterized the Carazo plateau region. That is to say, given the areas' agroexport orientation and the country's continuing need to generate foreign exchange earnings, MIDINRA set limits in terms of the degree to which the reform could restructure agricultural production.

One of the "development poles" that had been planned for Region IV was slated to be located in the project's area of influence. The selected site was Tisma-Los Malacos, on the eastern border of the plains of Masaya. Cotton cultivation had previously been predominant in this area and of necessity would remain a priority. However, the introduction of basic grain production was also supposed to take place. Combined crop production was to be made possible by the installation of irrigation systems that would facilitate year-round production. Thus, the cultivation of cotton and basic grains would be alternated on the same land. The strategy's rationale was to produce basic grains on the region's most fertile land so as to respond to the growing demand for them. The primary actors in this development effort were to be the new cooperatives, which were composed of small- and medium-scale campesino producers who had benefited from the redistribution of agricultural land.

This was the plan. What was eventually implemented in order to respond to the urgent problem of minifundismo was the Special Project Camilo Ortega Saavedra (PECOS), which was carried out in the Tisma-Masaya area. PECOS' implementation in 1983 entailed the distribution of 1,853 manzanas to 259 campesinos who had been organized into 17 cooperatives.[5] Although the project had envisioned these cooperatives producing basic grains, the high price of cotton induced them to continue its cultivation on the newly distributed land. Thus the project initially reinforced the region's traditional emphasis on agroexport production. It was not until 1984 that it succeeded in fulfilling the goal set forth in the regional development plan of growing grains in the off-season.

More problematic than this delay in working toward the goal of balancing export and domestically oriented production was the fact that following the first harvest, approximately 30 percent of the cooperatives' members deserted them (MIDINRA 1984, 3). This alarming precedent pointed, among other things, to the resistance to cooperative production that existed even within the population of campesinos who had initially been willing to experiment with this type of social organization.[6] Moreover, PECOS had only benefited a very small proportion of the region's landless and land-poor, leaving unresolved the tremendous demand for land in this sector of the population.

It would be another two years before a major effort would be undertaken to address this dilemma. This new effort was embodied in the Plan Masaya agrarian reform project. The policy shift that Plan Masaya represented was triggered by several specific factors. The expansion of the Contra war into more and more of the central mountain region called attention to the need to bolster support for the regime among the area's peasantry. Extending agrarian reform benefits to an ever-greater number of campesinos there became a crucial part of the defense effort. Land redistribution in this region accelerated, and land titling to those who had been squatters on agricultural land (some for several generations) was rapidly increased (cf. CIERA 1989a). Individual families also became eligible for receipt of redistributed land there. In addition to serving as a rear guard—in the sense of being a civilian barrier to the advance of the Contras—it was hoped that the campesinado's production could fill the gap left by the withdrawal of a significant portion of the rural bourgeoisie from participation in the agricultural sector. In sum, political, economic, and military concerns underlay the impulse toward a shift in strategy in this part of the country.

In other regions, especially in the Pacific Coast region, political and economic concerns also led to an increasing willingness to consider such a shift.

One contributing factor of a political nature was the 1984 elections. This was particularly evident in the case of Plan Masaya. The outcome of the general election of 1984 lit the fuse that ignited the implementation of Plan Masaya six months later.

Prior to the 1984 election, expression of a loss of support for the FSLN and the government had already manifested itself in the areas that would eventually be incorporated into Plan Masaya. Nevertheless, the election results highlighted the campesinos' perception that their need for land had still not been satisfied by the agrarian reform. In fact, they were apparently quite justified in holding this perception. By the end of 1984, when the elections were held, only 16 percent of the peasant population in this area had received land through the agrarian reform (cf. IHCA 1985b, 12c). This was even less than the national figure of 22 percent.

Even though the FSLN did not lose the elections in any of the municipalities included in the Masaya-Diriomo area, these were among the municipalities in which support for the incumbent party was weaker than in the rest of the country. For example, in the municipality of Tisma, the FSLN won 45 percent of the total votes cast, followed by the PCD, which won 38 percent (IHCA 1985a, 20b). These figures contrast strikingly with those for the nation as a whole, in which the FSLN won 63 percent of the total votes cast and the PCD, 13 percent.

The newly elected government reacted to these results by conducting a census of Masaya's and Diriomo's minifundio populations in early 1985. It revealed that 7,491 families (85 percent of the campesino population) owned fewer than 5 manzanas of land and urgently needed access to more (cf. CIERA 1985, 2).

Another issue that Plan Masaya addressed was that of the accelerated process of rural-urban migration, which had likewise contributed to the implementation of Los Patios. It was hoped that Plan Masaya would be able to provide its beneficiary population with a viable alternative to urban-bound migration, thereby helping to slow the flow of people out of this area.

Despite the multiplicity of arguments in favor of the Plan Masaya implementation, with the most important being the need to shore up support for the government, not all of the actors representing the various institutions involved in carrying it out were in agreement about the project. The principal differences of opinion centered around the pace of its implementation and the extent to which it would affect private producers in the area. The distinct positions that the various actors adopted vis-à-vis these issues reflected the more general debate that existed (which was described in chapter 2) about the form agrarian reform should take in Nicaragua. The technocrats were slowly brought around to the position that a significant need for land redistribution prevailed in the areas eventually affected by Plan Masaya. What convinced them were the general election results and a precinct-level study of those results that demonstrated a close correspondence between the areas that had lacked land redistribution and those with low levels of support for the FSLN (interview no. 151, former MIDINRA official, national level, July 13, 1995).[7] Yet they argued for a very gradual process of redistribution, which would take place over several years. They also were concerned about maintaining "national unity" and were therefore opposed to the idea that Plan Masaya might affect the land of large private producers in the area, especially that of Enrique Bolaños.

On the other side of this ongoing debate were the propeasant forces. Their position was that too much time had lapsed without a response by the government to the peasantry's need for land. In addition, they felt that the moment had come to give priority to the demands of the peasantry over continuing efforts to reassure the agrarian bourgeoisie that its interests would be protected (interview no. 151, former MIDINRA official, national level, July 13, 1995; and interview no. 150, former MIDINRA official, Region IV, July 12, 1995).

The propeasant forces won out in this important test of wills, through the organizational work of local FSLN, UNAG, and Agricultural Workers' Association (ATC) activists. Though the technocrats were beginning to accept the need for land redistribution in Masaya and Diriomo, the occurrence of a series of land invasions—which were heavily supported by activists from these organizations—succeeded in eliminating any remaining resistance to the idea within the government. Invasions took place on state farms and on SAIMSA's land. When faced with this fait accompli, on June 14, 1985, MIDINRA officials complied with a recommendation made earlier by the campesinistas and declared the area an "Agricultural Development and Agrarian Reform Zone."

The designation of these areas as such facilitated a change in land tenure under a legal clause that allowed for all of the land in a given area to be affected, even if it was being used productively, should it be deemed necessary to do so in order to promote development projects of strategic importance.[8] The development zones specified by MIDINRA in this region were composed of eighteen farms, most of which were either purchased by the government, or their owners negotiated their exchange for land located elsewhere (MIDINRA, n.d.[a]). Lists of potential beneficiaries (including those who had participated in the invasions) were put together by community-based organizers, and the land was turned over to them almost immediately.

Thus as an agrarian reform project, Plan Masaya was not a neatly implemented program. Rather, it was the end result of a struggle between opposing factions within the agrarian reform process. As such, the fact that it did take place symbolized a hard-fought victory for the pro-peasant forces over the previously dominant technocratic approach to land redistribution.

Redistribution of the eighteen farms affected by Plan Masaya took various forms. Most of the land was turned over to newly organized cooperatives, both CCS and CAS. Sixty-two cooperatives were formed with the project's implementation: ten were CAS, thirty-five CCS, and seventeen CT, (which have fewer than ten members and are seen as being precursors to CAS) (MIDINRA, n.d.[a]). Sixty-two individual farmers also received land to work independently. Although cooperatives were still clearly the preferred form of social organization for MIDINRA, the inclusion of individuals in this entrega de tierra was noteworthy.

During the first agricultural cycle following the Plan Masaya implementation, its beneficiaries employed primarily what in Nicaragua is considered to be a medium level of technology in basic grain production: they combined the use of oxen with manual labor to carry out the tasks that compose these crops' production processes. The crop yields that year were more than those characterizing production in the central mountain region. However, MIDINRA's planners did not consider production levels to be high enough to guarantee the self-sufficiency of these producers and to make a significant contribution to the national supply of basic grains. Thus the ministry implemented a second project, the PATD, which was designed in part to complement Plan Masaya.

The PATD, in essence, consisted of ongoing provision of technical assistance to combat the incidence of pests. It was reasoned that constant supervision would make the utilization of pesticides both more efficient and more effective. The program also had a training component, which was designed so that each cooperative participating in it would have at least one *plaguero*, or member with extensive knowledge of pest management techniques. PATD had an additional purpose, which was to raise the level of technology employed in its area of influence. Tractors were supposed to replace the oxen that were previously relied upon in some, if not all, stages of the production process.

Overlap in participation between the two projects was extensive but not complete. After two years of implementation, the PATD was servicing 3,816 manzanas of corn and 1,216 manzanas of sorghum.[9] Of this area, 63 percent of the land planted with corn consisted of farms included in the Plan Masaya project.

The Social Origins of Plan Masaya Participants

Who were those benefited by Plan Masaya? What were their social origins? Did participation in this agrarian reform project mark a shift in their labor histories? What benefits did Plan Masaya bring them? In order to answer these questions I coordinated a survey of the project's participants. The following

Table 5.1. Economic activity of two generations of Plan Masaya campesinos (AP = agricultural producer; AW = agricultural worker; FP = family plot; SE = self-employed; UW = urban worker)

	Parents	Informants
One economic activity	45.8	16.7
AP	25.0	—
SE	4.2	—
UW	—	—
AW	16.7	16.7
FP	—	—
Two economic activities	52.1	31.3
AW/AP	41.7	8.3
FP/AP	—	8.3
SE/AP	2.1	2.1
UW/AP	—	—
FP/AW	—	—
SE/AW	8.3	4.2
FP/SE	—	2.1
UW/AW	—	4.2
FP/UW	—	2.1
Three economic activities	2.1	45.8
FP/UW/AP	—	4.2
FP/AW/AP	—	16.7
SE/AW/AP	2.1	2.1
AW/UW/AP	—	12.5
SE/UW/AW	—	4.2
FP/AP/SE	—	2.1
FP/AW/UW	—	2.1
FP/AW/SE	—	2.1
Four economic activities	—	4.2
FP/AW/UW/AP	—	4.2
Five economic activities	—	2.1
FP/AW/UW/AP/SE	—	2.1

Source: Author's survey data, 1989 (N = 48).

discussion summarizes the survey's findings, while highlighting the subtle but important variations in the extent to which separate fractions of the peasantry had been affected by the socioeconomic changes of the preceding decades.

Through the survey it became apparent that Plan Masaya had succeeded in incorporating the sector of the peasantry it had been designed to reach, the region's minifundistas. The life histories of the Plan Masaya beneficiary population present a microcosm of the marginalization process experienced by the campesinado as a consequence of the recent boom in export crop production in Masaya-Diriomo. The peasantry was increasingly excluded from access to land, credit, and other resources that make agricultural production possible. More and more of its members were forced to sell their labor in the wage labor market as their capacity for self-sufficiency on the farm diminished.

The ties of Plan Masaya beneficiaries to this area were long-lived. In fact, almost all of the informants were natives of the small rural communities surrounding the region's former export estates. However, the peasantry's relationship with the area's agricultural land had already begun to change by their parents' generation. Although the majority of the informants' parents had been farmers (71 percent), only 25 percent of them were able to maintain themselves and their families on their farm-generated income (see table 5.1).[10] This situation was much more extreme in Masaya than in Diriomo: in Masaya a mere 15 percent of the informants' parents had been able to support themselves with agricultural production, while in Diriomo the figure was 75 percent. As a consequence of their difficulty in this regard, most of the informants' parents complemented their agricultural production with income earned through wage labor. A few also engaged in various kinds of self-employment.

The primary cause of this older generation's inability to be self-sufficient farmers was their limited access to land. Fewer than half (41 percent) of those who had been farmers had owned their own land.[11] And even those who were lucky enough to own land were not endowed with much: most owned 5 manzanas of land or less. The remaining producers either rented land or sharecropped. Nevertheless, the land situation was more problematic in Masaya than in Diriomo, as seen in the discrepancy between the situations of the informants' parents in these two areas: only approximately 28 percent of those living in Masaya had owned land, while 38 percent of those from Diriomo had.

This phenomenon can be explained by the fact that cotton cultivation had led to a much higher level of land concentration in the former region than had cattle raising in the latter (cf. CIERA 1980b and 1980c). For those with little or no land of their own, land rentals made it possible to continue farming. But because of the pervasive use of rented land in cotton cultivation, its availability for small-scale basic grain farmers was severely restricted in Masaya. This dramatic state of land tenancy was exacerbated when the next generation, that of the informants, came of age to support itself, as inheritance customs led to plots being subdivided among the children within each family.

Given these circumstances, the economic possibilities of the informants were more limited than those of their parents. Even their childhoods ended early, with the majority of them having begun to work before the age of twelve.

These youths found employment in a variety of situations, from rural and urban salaried labor to working on their families' parcels of land. Although many of the informants later became agricultural producers in their own right, their access to land was extremely precarious. Of this generation of campesinos, only 6 percent owned their own land (through inheritance or purchase), and all of their parcels were less than 5 manzanas in size (see table 6.2). Once again, the situation for the project's Masaya-based beneficiaries was more stark than that for those from Diriomo: in the former area a mere 5 percent of Plan Masaya participants had land of their own (through the above-mentioned means) prior to the implementation of this project, in contrast to 13 percent in the latter area. Clearly, the impact of cotton production on the peasantry had been more severe in Masaya than had that of cattle raising in Diriomo. Still, the beneficiaries from Diriomo evidenced a notable lack of resources that were essential for maintaining a farm-based livelihood.

The beneficiaries' tenuous relationship with the land led them, inevitably, to search for other means of support away from the farm. Although 63 percent of the informants had worked at some point as farmers before their inclusion in Plan Masaya, *none* of them had been able to support themselves from farm-generated income alone. Most had turned to agricultural wage labor, with a smaller number participating in the urban labor force or in self-employment activities. Here again, differences existed between the beneficiaries in the project's two areas of influence: the vast majority (83 percent) of the Masaya-based participants had resorted to rural wage labor at some point prior to their entry into the project, whereas fewer (63 percent) of Diriomo's beneficiaries had. These data complement those described above in demonstrating the greater degree of marginalization that had been experienced by the peasantry of Masaya as opposed to those of Diriomo. One of the principal results of this marginalization was the comparatively higher level of proletarianization among Masaya's peasants in relation to those from Diriomo.

The labor histories of Plan Masaya beneficiaries illustrate the dramatic manner in which export agriculture affected the lives of the peasants who resided in areas suitable for this type of production. Yet the degree of its impact varied depending on the specific export product. Cotton had a more thoroughgoing effect than any other export crop, leading to a qualitatively different level of marginalization for the peasantry wherever it was cultivated (cf. Enríquez 1991 and Williams 1986). But cattle raising also clearly disrupted traditional production patterns and structures.

In sum, by the mid-1980s the peasants of Masaya and Diriomo were well on their way to being pushed completely out of subsistence production and into the wage labor force. Despite this overarching historical trend, which seemed to march inexorably ahead, the areas' peasants continued to aspire to a life of full-time farming. Through the elections of 1984, they put into evidence their disappointment that the Sandinistas had failed, to that point, to make this possible.

CONCLUSION

Plan Masaya was designed to reverse the process of marginalization that had been set into motion with the widespread adoption of cotton production in Masaya and cattle raising in Diriomo. In this it shared with the Los Patios project the goal of recampesinización. And, like Los Patios, it was also aimed at increasing the levels of production destined for the domestic market. In working toward these goals, both projects were seen as means to promote regional rural and agricultural development.

However, Plan Masaya went beyond Los Patios with respect to the resources it made available to its beneficiaries. It embodied the nationwide shift that was under way in terms of accelerating the redistribution of land and in permitting the receipt of that land by peasants organized in a variety of forms. The project also represented the step that had been taken away from the original development strategy designed for this region. Whereas Los Patios worked within the crevices that existed in that strategy, Plan Masaya symbolized a break with the strategy, in both the type of production it introduced to the former agroexport areas where it was carried out and the differing organizational forms adopted by its participants.

Further, as will be discussed at length in chapter 7, Plan Masaya drew on a fraction of the peasantry that was significantly more marginalized than that of Los Patios. This can be seen in the former's more limited access to agricultural resources when compared with the latter's. It can also be seen in the consequences of that reduced access for the Plan Masaya beneficiaries: that is, their higher level of dependence on sources of income other than what was generated on the farm, and especially on that of wage labor.

Despite being able to identify these several major differences between Los Patios and Plan Masaya, we must now look more closely at exactly how Plan Masaya affected its beneficiary population before we can go any further in comparing the two projects. That is, if we are to begin to understand why two projects which had similar objectives produced such varying political results, it is necessary to assess to what extent Plan Masaya achieved its goals and changed its beneficiaries' lives. Thus, in chapter 6, we will focus on the project's socioeconomic and political impact.

6

Plan Masaya
The Social and Political Impact of the Project

The Plan Masaya agrarian reform project both reflected the change that was under way in Sandinista policymaking in the mid-1980s and embodied an important divergence from larger sociopolitical trends that characterized Nicaraguan society at that time. It was part and parcel, in fact a forerunner, of the shift in agrarian reform policy that was legislated in the aftermath of the project's implementation. Yet, the organizational effects of Plan Masaya, in terms of incorporating a new sector of the rural population into the revolutionary project, symbolized a break with the general process of demobilization that was taking place throughout the society. By closely examining the project and its impact we will be provided with a window onto the nature of these two phenomena and can thereby gain an appreciation for their significance in the overall societal transformation that the Sandinistas sought to bring about.

The implementation of Plan Masaya represented the new era of agrarian reform, which was formalized in legislation early the following year (cf. *La Gaceta* 1986). In addition to the project's noteworthiness with respect to the variety of organizational forms through which it permitted its beneficiaries to receive redistributed land, its implementation also made a statement about the government's prioritization of the campesino sector in its agrarian policymaking. Giving high priority to the peasantry culminated at the national level in 1986. That year, the amount of land redistributed to the peasantry, 315,032 manzanas, reached its peak for all of the 1980s (see table 6.1). The portion of this land that was turned over to individual peasants—which represented the most radical aspect of the mid-1980s shift in strategy—also set the record for the decade at approximately 35 percent. This latter pattern was even more striking in Region IV, where the land redistributed to individuals rose from 2 percent of the total in 1984 to 53 percent in 1985 and 49 percent in 1986 (com-

Table 6.1. Land redistributed and families benefited, nationwide and Region IV, October 1981–December 1988

	1981–82				1983			
Form	Area	(%)	Families	(%)	Area	(%)	Families	(%)
CAS								
Nationwide	106,398	(80)	6,739	(85)	240,119	(82)	10,734	(79)
Region IV	7,991	(83)	918	(76)	42,411	(78)	2,431	(73)
CCS								
Nationwide	3,342	(3)	771	(10)	36,179	(12)	2,533	(19)
Region IV	990	(10)	263	(22)	11,509	(21)	882	(26)
CT								
Nationwide	—		—		245	(0)	32	(0)
Region IV	—		—		63	(0)	8	(0)
Individuals								
Nationwide	22,827	(17)	383	(5)	17,398	(6)	298	(2)
Region IV	647	(7)	34	(3)	584	(1)	19	(1)
CSM								
Nationwide	—		—		—		—	
Region IV	—		—		—		—	
Totals								
Nationwide	132,567	(100)	7,893	(100)	293,941	(100)	13,597	(100)
Region IV	9,628	(100)	1,215	(100)	54,567	(100)	3,340	(100)

	1984				1985			
	Area	(%)	Families	(%)	Area	(%)	Families	(%)
CAS								
Nationwide	195,558	(81)	8,604	(76)	61,235	(57)	5,119	(44)
Region IV	41,295	(77)	1,854	(66)	505	(15)	584	(35)
CCS								
Nationwide	28,146	(12)	2,347	(21)	15,388	(14)	4,344	(37)
Region IV	11,090	(21)	920	(33)	1,106	(32)	922	(55)
CT								
Nationwide	2,993	(1)	139	(1)	3,033	(3)	313	(3)
Region IV	—		—		16	(1)	22	(1)
Individuals								
Nationwide	14,141	(6)	264	(2)	20,790	(19)	264	(2)
Region IV	1,281	(2)	41	(2)	123	(4)	16	(1)
CSM								
Nationwide	—		—		7,443	(7)	1,574	(14)
Region IV	—		—		1,682	(49)	140	(8)
Totals								
Nationwide	240,838	(100)	11,354	(100)	107,889	(100)	11,614	(100)
Region IV	53,666	(100)	2,815	(100)	3,432	(100)	1,684	(100)

112   Chapter Six

	1986				1987			
	Area	(%)	Families	(%)	Area	(%)	Families	(%)
CAS								
Nationwide	149,759	(48)	6,310	(41)	129,569	(73)	4,457	(50)
Region IV	6,635	(23)	1,298	(34)	n.a.		n.a.	
CCS								
Nationwide	26,147	(8)	2,146	(14)	18,788	(10)	1,446	(16)
Region IV	6,887	(24)	1,057	(28)	n.a.		n.a.	
CT								
Nationwide	12,107	(4)	707	(5)	3,949	(2)	177	(2)
Region IV	1,684	(6)	176	(5)	n.a.		n.a.	
Individuals								
Nationwide	110,652	(35)	4,531	(30)	15,512	(9)	1,880	(21)
Region IV	8,960	(31)	712	(19)	n.a.		n.a.	
CSM								
Nationwide	16,367	(5)	1,523	(10)	10,191	(6)	918	(11)
Region IV	5,177	(18)	548	(15)	n.a.		n.a.	
Totals								
Nationwide	315,032	(100)	15,217	(100)	178,009	(100)	8,878	(100)
Region IV	29,343	(100)	3,791	(100)	n.a.		n.a	

	1988				Total			
	Area	(%)	Families	(%)	Area	(%)	Families	(%)
CAS								
Nationwide	38,853	(68)	5,102	(57)	921,491	(69)	47,065	(61)
Region IV	n.a.		n.a.		n.a.		n.a.	
CCS								
Nationwide	5,630	(10)	1,656	(19)	133,620	(10)	15,243	(20)
Region IV	n.a.		n.a.		n.a.		n.a.	
CT								
Nationwide	1,182	(2)	202	(2)	23,509	(2)	1,570	(2)
Region IV	n.a.		n.a.		n.a.		n.a.	
Individuals								
Nationwide	8,654	(15)	866	(10)	209,974	(16)	8,486	(11)
Region IV	n.a.		n.a.		n.a.		n.a.	
CSM								
Nationwide	3,059	(5)	1,051	(12)	37,060	(3)	5,066	(6)
Region IV	n.a.		n.a.		n.a.		n.a.	
Totals								
Nationwide	57,378	(100)	8,877	(100)	1,325,654	(100)	77,430	(100)
Region IV	n.a.		n.a.		n.a.		n.a.	

Source: CIERA (1989a).

bining the figures for Individuals and Dead Furrow Cooperatives, or CSMs, in which adjacent plots are worked individually but there are no physical barriers except an empty furrow between them and which are seen as an intermediary stage between individual and cooperative farming). Meanwhile, the land turned over to CAS dropped from 77 percent of the total in 1984 to 15 percent in 1985 and 23 percent in 1986 (see table 6.1).

The accelerated redistribution of land to the peasantry rested, in part, upon a reversal in the government's earlier policy of leaving untouched the farms of medium- and large-scale producers who were working their land if the redistribution of those farms was deemed necessary to satisfy the needs of the landless and land-poor. In the process, it highlighted the major reorientation that was under way in Sandinista thinking about the role of the peasantry in the country's development. That is to say, it shifted from seeing the peasantry as a sector that had to be "modernized" through its proletarianization, to one that could play an important role in the economy and should, therefore, be strengthened through recampesinización.

The repeasantization that would be brought about by the project would be of quite a different kind than that which Los Patios had stimulated. Plan Masaya was implemented in response to the "demand" for land that was voiced through the 1984 elections. That demand had come from a sector of the rural population that was poorer, in terms of ownership of agricultural resources, than its Los Patios counterparts. Moreover, the project promoted collective production relations, whether expressed in CAS or CCS. Hence, it was aimed at mobilizing its participants into organizational efforts that were social and political in nature. To the extent that the project approximated this goal, it stood in contrast to the tendency characterizing other sectors of Nicaraguan society toward demobilization from sociopolitical organizing. Consequently, the project contained within it the potential of bringing its beneficiaries into the larger process of social transformation.

In the interest of assessing the extent to which Plan Masaya realized this as well as its other objectives, it is essential to look at the project's impact on its beneficiaries. A review of the findings from my survey of its participants, as well as the follow-up interviews conducted after the 1990 elections (see the Brief Discussion of Methodology), will permit such an assessment.

PLAN MASAYA

The Project's Socioeconomic Impact

As was the case with the Los Patios agrarian reform project, the designers of Plan Masaya believed that its implementation would facilitate the achieve-

Table 6.2. Access of Plan Masaya beneficiaries to productive resources (percentages)

	Before 1985	After 1985
Owned land		
Through purchase/inheritance	6	—
Through agrarian reform	6	100
Received credit	33	100
Received technical assistance regularly	8	73

Source: Author's survey data, 1989 (N = 48).

ment of its socioeconomic and political goals. While Los Patios reached many of its socioeconomic goals, it failed abysmally with regard to its political objectives. Through interviews with Plan Masaya beneficiaries I found that this project had realized, to a significant degree, the various objectives that had stimulated its being carried out.

In recounting the survey's findings, I will begin by focusing on exactly how the informants' prospects changed with the implementation of Plan Masaya. As mentioned above, some land redistribution had occurred in the region prior to 1985. However, for the vast majority of those interviewed (95 percent in Masaya and 88 percent in Diriomo), it was their participation in Plan Masaya that afforded them their initial opportunity to receive land through the agrarian reform. With access to this new resource, the project's beneficiaries were able to return to their familial tradition of being agricultural producers.

In addition, those benefited by Plan Masaya adopted the cultivation patterns that had been passed down through generations of campesino families. That is, their production emphasis was placed on basic grains. One hundred percent of those of the informants' parents who had been agricultural producers had grown corn, beans, and yucca, or some combination of these crops. The figure was the same among their offspring who participated in Plan Masaya.

This next generation was also provided with access to other resources that facilitated its agricultural production. One such resource was agricultural credit. All of the informants relied on credit to furnish the working capital required throughout the agricultural production process (see table 6.2). For most (67 percent), the first time they received credit through the banking system was after they were incorporated into Plan Masaya. A much smaller group within the sample (27 percent) had begun to receive credit prior to its entry into the project, as a result of the expansion in credit distribution that formed part of the Sandinistas' agrarian policy. Only 6 percent of the sample of Plan Masaya participants had access to this important resource prior to 1979. Although the better part of the credit that the beneficiaries received after their entry into

Table 6.3. Access to technical assistance among Plan Masaya beneficiaries versus nonbeneficiaries (percentages)

	Before 1985	After 1985
Masaya		
Plan Masaya/PATD (N = 26)	8	85
Plan Masaya (N = 14)	14	36
PATD (N = 4)	75	100
Control (N = 6)	33	66
Diriomo		
Plan Masaya (N = 8)	—	100
Control (N = 1)	—	100

Source: Author's survey data, 1989.

the project was utilized to finance basic grain production, a growing number of them used it in the cultivation of summer crops (e.g. watermelon) as well.

Another resource that was made more available to the project's beneficiary population was technical assistance. The designers of Plan Masaya designers had envisioned it as an integral part of the project. Yet, the survey revealed that technical assistance was received most regularly by those who also participated in PATD (see table 6.3). A comparison of those in Plan Masaya but not in PATD, and the control group, which was not associated with either project, showed that the latter had even more access to technical assistance than the former. That is to say, participation in Plan Masaya, in and of itself, did not guarantee special treatment with respect to this resource. However, only a small percentage of those participating in either project had received this service prior to 1985 (see table 6.3).

A final change in agricultural production practices that should be mentioned here is that of the level of technology the project's beneficiaries employed. Prior to the implementation of Plan Masaya in 1985, most of those informants who had been farmers (70 percent of these) had either relied on oxen or had manually carried out the various tasks that composed the production process.[1] In contrast, 71 percent of the informants utilized tractors in one or several stages of this process after their entry into the project; in the case of those beneficiaries who participated in both Plan Masaya and PATD, the figure was 85 percent. In other words, Plan Masaya succeeded in raising the level of technology of its beneficiaries' agricultural production.

Aside from the modifications that participation in Plan Masaya and PATD brought about in their beneficiaries' relationship with agricultural production, the projects stimulated a number of other alterations in the lives of these campesinos. First among these was the fact that the majority of the project beneficiaries became fully employed as farmers. Only a small group of the informants still participated in additional economic activities off the farm at the time of the survey. Of this minority who did have other sources of income, the better part simply continued to engage in the self-employment activities that had been initiated prior to 1985.

Most of the informants also had traditionally participated in the cotton and/or coffee harvest as a means of supplementing their farm-generated income. Nevertheless, production on the land they received through Plan Masaya had begun to keep the majority of them occupied the entire year. During the dry season—when corn cannot be cultivated without irrigation—many beneficiaries began to grow watermelon and vegetables, and others engaged in maintenance activities on the farm.

Just as important, work on the newly established farms required the incorporation of other family members and hired laborers in production-related tasks. In the case of the informants, most (73 percent) employed family labor at peak moments in the production process. Hired labor was about as common on these farms. Thus the greater part of the informants had been transformed from employees into employers through their participation in Plan Masaya.

In sum, contrary to its circumstances prior to 1985, the Plan Masaya beneficiary population was able to support itself from income earned through its own agricultural production after entering the project. Its farm-generated income had increased significantly as a result of the access provided by the project to a variety of agricultural resources. Many Plan Masaya participants were also able to purchase farm animals and work implements with the income earned on their farms. Others made home improvements or built new homes with their profits from the corn and bean harvests.

These kinds of indications of socioeconomic improvement stemming from participation in Plan Masaya were particularly associated with the 1986–87 and 1987–88 crop cycles. In contrast, inclement weather conditions and the credit and pricing policies that were established as part of the government's economic reform in early 1988 made the 1988–89 crop cycle a difficult one for the project's producers. Taken together, however, these first few crop cycles left Plan Masaya participants with a considerably improved standard of living.

The standard-of-living improvements experienced by the project's beneficiaries differed markedly from the situation of several other sectors of the "popular classes" during this period. Severe inflation combined with partial wage controls led to a drastic drop in income for most salaried workers between 1986 and 1989.[2] Agricultural producers, who were in a position to grow an important part of what they and their families consumed, had an advantage over those who depended on their ever-shrinking salaries for sustenance. The fact that the income of Plan Masaya beneficiaries had risen was extraordinary. In effect, in the midst of the country's deepening economic crisis, the economic situation of the minifundista population benefited by Plan Masaya actually became more secure.

Yet the impact of the Plan Masaya implementation extended beyond its beneficiary population. The project stimulated a replacement of export production by domestic crops in its areas of influence.[3] This represented a divergence from the regional development strategy that had been designed several years earlier and that had called for a consolidation of the area planted with cotton on the region's most productive land. The installation of irrigation systems in certain of these areas was to permit year-round production, so that basic grains could be grown there a few months each year. But the displacement of cotton by corn embodied a dramatic shift in policy.

This policy shift had been evolving for some time, however. Cotton production was dependent on many imported inputs. As a consequence, its cultivation was increasingly problematic to sustain because of the country's extreme shortage of foreign exchange earnings. Further, maintenance of the smooth flow of the cotton production process was becoming more and more difficult due to numerous factors, including import shortages. This resulted in growing production and profit losses for the crops' farmers. At the same time, the price of cotton in the international market had begun to experience a downturn by 1984.[4] A decision was made to concentrate Nicaragua's cotton production in the northwestern departments of León and Chinandega, where ecological conditions were the most appropriate for its cultivation and much of its related infrastructure was located. Although this new policy orientation was not fully articulated until the 1986–87 period, the Plan Masaya implementation signaled the initiation of the process (see table 6.4 for production figures that illustrate this change.)[5]

The shift in policy orientation also expressed the recently adopted goal of bringing food crop production back to the Pacific coastal region. Although the Sandinistas' development strategy for Region IV had called for an increase in basic grain cultivation in Masaya, it had not envisioned such a significant expansion in area. In addition to the need to ensure Nicaragua's food supply, which was being threatened by the war, the accelerated rural-urban migration that had affected the country's Pacific Coast cities expanded the demand for food in this area. Hence, Plan Masaya sought to augment the country's food crop production and bring it closer to the areas of greatest demand. Moreover, given the Masaya-Diriomo region's superior ecological conditions for basic grain production (in comparison with the central mountain region), the policy shift emphasized the government's efforts to achieve a better balance in resource allocation between food and export crop production.

The Plan Masaya project brought about an expansion in the area cultivated

Table 6.4. Evolution of cotton, corn, and bean production, nationwide and Region IV

	1979–80[a]	1980–81	1981–82	1982–83
Cotton[b]				
Nationwide	1,244,700	4,878,590	4,080,999	5,070,136
Region IV	301,094	374,247	400,894	392,006
Corn[c]				
Nationwide	3,168,300	3,995,306	4,199,695	3,602,600
Region IV	424,783	732,915	513,013	183,339
Beans[c]				
Nationwide	635,200	624,681	904,918	1,030,081
Region IV	74,440	65,591	130,615	92,229

	1983–84	1984–85	1985–86	1986–87	1987–88
Cotton[b]					
Nationwide	5,690,739	4,608,645	3,349,900	3,289,037	2,200,000
Region IV	523,016	389,800	143,814	94,624	49,600
Corn[c]					
Nationwide	4,516,600	4,581,200	4,241,600	4,703,600	6,160,859
Region IV	552,691	480,000	725,200	877,900	894,000
Beans[c]					
Nationwide	1,226,100	1,259,800	1,007,800	1,290,000	740,067
Region IV	186,784	138,900	175,000	223,300	103,700

Source: CIERA 1989b.
[a]Region IV data from MIDINRA, unpublished data 1989.
[b]In hundredweight of unginned cotton.
[c]In hundredweight.

with—and production levels of—basic grains, as well as an improvement in their yields. The acreage planted in corn in Region IV increased by 86 percent between 1984–85 and 1986–87 (calculated from MIDINRA 1989 unpublished data), while production during the same period increased by 83 percent (see table 6.4). An even more striking expansion occurred in bean acreage (98 percent), and bean production grew by 61 percent. Furthermore, with the implementation of PATD in 1986, corn yields in Masaya rose from an average of 27 hundredweight per manzana in the pre-1979 period to 50–60 hundredweight per manzana.[6]

This dramatic expansion in production suggested that if production in the country's other regions remained constant, the gap between supply and demand for basic grains at the national level would be reduced. However, while Masaya's corn and Diriomo's bean output pushed up Region IV's production levels, production in the central mountain region dropped off notably. Not surprisingly, the drop was greatest in Region V, the area that was most affected by the war at this time. Corn output in Region V in 1985–86 was only 39 percent of what it had been the previous year (calculated from CIERA 1989a, 138–44 and 150–51). Likewise, bean production in this region in 1985–86 was only 47 percent of that of the year before. But with the military advances that were made by the Sandinista army in 1986 and 1987, corn and bean production began to recover in Region V, and national output of both crops was greater that year (1986–87) than any other since 1978–79 (see table 6.4). In sum, the expansion in corn cultivation brought about by Plan Masaya contributed to the increase in Pacific coast grain production, thereby helping to counterbalance losses experienced in the regions affected by the war. Later, as the effects of the war on production diminished, the areas that were newly opened up to basic grains along the Pacific coast complemented the increase in their cultivation that occurred on the national level.

While Plan Masaya had transformed the Masaya-Diriomo region's productive profile, it had also brought about a change in the social relations of production. As stated above, most of the project's beneficiaries organized themselves into cooperatives in order to receive the land. Thus, the project provided an impetus for the cooperative sector's development. In quantitative terms, the implementation of Plan Masaya led to the formation of sixty-two cooperatives. As a consequence, in the course of a few months, the number of cooperatives functioning in the project's areas of influence doubled. In the process, a significant number of previously unorganized campesinos were brought into the reformed sector of agriculture. Moreover, Plan Masaya, and particularly its complementary program, PATD, had a qualitative impact on the cooperative sector. By providing participating cooperatives with greater access to agricultural resources, their economic base was fortified. That is, these resources gave new life to already existing cooperatives and helped establish those that had recently been formed.

Nonetheless, the adoption of a higher level of technology was not without its drawbacks, either for the project's beneficiaries or for the country as a whole. The mechanization introduced by the PATD stimulated a dramatic rise in the farmers' production costs. Most of the inputs required in mechanized production had to be imported. These inputs ranged from chemical fertilizers and pesticides to tractors, their accessories, and fuel. The economic reform enacted in early 1988 made mechanized production even more costly than it had been before, because it cut existing subsidies for imported inputs. Simultaneously, credit policies became more restrictive. While yields had improved, unless the agrarian reform beneficiaries had already assimilated comprehensive administrative skills and an entrepreneurial vision of their production—qualities that were not widespread within this population—profitable production became increasingly problematic.

In addition, importation of the requisite inputs necessitated an expenditure of Nicaragua's extremely scarce foreign exchange earnings. Yet, corn—as compared to some other heavy users of imported inputs (e.g. cotton)—was not employed to generate foreign exchange earnings.

Several other factors must be taken into account in assessing this issue, however. First, increased domestic production of these crucial food products was bound to lessen the need to import them. Although expanded basic grain production may have reduced the country's foreign exchange earnings to a limited extent, it also lowered expenditures of these earnings for food imports. Second, it is essential to bear in mind that certain temporary losses were bound to occur as a result of the changes that were taking place in Nicaraguan agriculture. In order to advance toward the goals of diversifying the country's agricultural production and raising the level of the productive forces characterizing this sector, some sacrifices were inevitable. If the project of socioeconomic transformation and development was to move ahead, traditional production systems—with all their pros and cons—would have to give way to new ones. If short-term losses in foreign exchange earnings were to lay the groundwork for socioeconomic development in the medium to long term, they would have to be considered as one of the costs of this overall social project.

The Political Impact of Plan Masaya

The implementation of Plan Masaya had costs in another sphere beside the economy: that of the polity. The initiation of Plan Masaya had required the confiscation of some of the land in its area of influence. Even though ultimately only one enterprise was affected in this way and negotiations for the government's purchase of its property had been proposed by the Sandinistas and rejected by SAIMSA, its director's response was publicized around the world by the international press.[7] The fact that its director, Enrique Bolaños, was the president of COSEP was what had lent weight to his angry denunciation of the Sandinista regime. International interest in the Bolaños case stemmed from the fact that he was seen as an exemplar of the beleaguered private farmer who had kept his production going only to have it confiscated by the Sandinistas. What underlay this perception was the idea that COSEP represented all private producers. At least in numerical terms, this was a serious misconception, as UNAG had a larger membership of private farmers: UNAG's membership in 1984–85 was 84,693 (Luciak 1995, 95), in contrast to the 6,397 members of UPANIC, the agrarian association within COSEP (Spalding 1984,

226). Yet, COSEP did represent a prominent part of the large-scale growers and industrialists, and for the international players who took up Bolaños's cause, the term *private sector* was synonymous with large growers.[8]

The confiscation of the property of one very visible member of the private sector was heralded as definitive evidence that, with the 1984 elections behind them, the Sandinistas were about to embark on a new wave of confiscations. For international observers—especially those with ties to Washington—the Sandinistas had thereby revealed their true intentions of eliminating the private sector in their quest to establish communism in Nicaragua.

In addition to its international impact, Bolaños's overtly hostile response was also heard within that part of the private sector that COSEP represented. COSEP had consistently questioned the Sandinistas' intentions with regard to the private sector—routinely suggesting that its own continued existence was a mere tactical and temporary policy of the Sandinistas, which would be altered the moment the Sandinistas were politically able to do so. Coming a mere six months into the Sandinistas' new term in office, the measure undoubtedly raised concerns among those large growers who had been openly opposed to the Sandinistas. It revealed that merely keeping production going on one's farm would no longer be enough to safeguard it from confiscation, given the government's new emphasis on the peasantry.

What was not publicized in either the international press or domestic opposition circles was the fact that the Sandinistas had successfully negotiated with all the other landowners in the area, providing them with either a cash settlement, an equivalently valued piece of land elsewhere, farm equipment, vehicles, or some combination of these. Nor did these various critics consider the number of peasant families who were benefited by this action. Because of COSEP's openly political agenda—it being the foremost opposition organization at that time—neither of these latter aspects of the Plan Masaya project gained attention. Consequently, the implementation of Plan Masaya undoubtedly had a political cost in terms of the government's relationship with this organization's membership.

But the Sandinistas' main concern in carrying out Plan Masaya was not that of continuing to protect the interests of a producer group whose support it perceived as lost in any case. Rather, priority was placed on addressing the minifundista sector's needs, because its allegiance was thought to hold considerable potential for the Sandinista government. In essence, the government decided that meeting the demands of the landless and the land-poor in this region was more crucial than attempting to sustain a modus vivendi with the agroexport elite. In numerical terms alone, the novel forms of organization in agricultural production that were introduced by Plan Masaya clearly benefited a greater number of people than production there had previously.[9] Moreover, gaining the peasantry's political support and strengthening its economic contribution to national production had taken on new importance for government policymakers, as they acknowledged the increasing difficulty of maintaining the bourgeoisie as an active and constructive force in the country's mixed economy.

Yet, the extent to which the project's beneficiaries considered their needs to have been met was not apparent until early 1990. The general election of February 25, 1990, provided an opportunity to explore the level of political support that had been gained by the project's implementation. The first evidence we will turn to in this exploration is that of the electoral data produced by those elections. This will provide an idea of the degree of support that existed for the incumbent government within the general area that was affected by Plan Masaya. As described in chapter 5, at the level of the precincts encompassing Plan Masaya beneficiaries, the vote was only 39.8 percent in favor of the FSLN, compared with 34.5 percent for the areas that the Los Patios project had reached (see table 2.1).

But it is important to look more closely at several specific precincts where Plan Masaya beneficiaries resided to find a clearer suggestion of the project's political impact than it is possible to obtain through a general analysis of electoral data. Diriomito, Cofradia, and Pilas Occidentales were three rural communities in the area of Masaya in which an appreciable number of Plan Masaya participants lived.[10] The FSLN won the election in each one of these communities (with 44.1 percent, 58.9 percent, and 50.1 percent of the total votes cast, respectively).[11] Similar examples can also be drawn from the Diriomo area: several of the rural hamlets most heavily benefited by Plan Masaya in this area were Los Jirones, General Sandino, and La Curva.[12] The incumbent party won the elections in each of these communities, with 50.9 percent, 58.4 percent, and 46.0 percent of the vote, respectively. These figures differ widely from national figures, both for the voting population as a whole and for that from rural areas.

In spite of the fact that these data might seem to indicate that Plan Masaya had a noticeably positive impact on the level of identification that its beneficiary population had with the Sandinista government, we should bear in mind the problem with assuming a direct correspondence between the project's impact and the way these communities voted, as mentioned in chapter 4. That is, ultimately, the absolute number of project beneficiaries was quite small within the overall population of each community. For example, in Cofradia approximately 160 people were incorporated into the project, while the total number of people casting votes there was 1,328.[13] Thus, even if we assume that all of the project beneficiaries voted, they still only represented approximately 12 percent of the total vote.[14]

Yet, these specific, precinct-level data coincide closely with the findings generated by my follow-up interviews with project beneficiaries several months after the elections. Those interviews, which were conducted in both Diriomo and Masaya, revealed a conspicuous level of support for the FSLN within this population (see table 6.5). In fact, a full 60 percent of my informants expressed a preference for the Sandinista government at that time. This suggests that support for and identification with the incumbent party was even greater among Plan Masaya beneficiaries than among the voters in general in the rural hamlets where they resided.

In sum, Plan Masaya and its complementary project, the PATD, appeared to have been relatively successful in working toward their goal of gaining political support for the government and its socialist program within the populations they reached. This is especially noteworthy if one takes into account the larger context in which these projects were implemented—of war, of economic crisis, and so forth. There were many other phenomena that affected the lives of Plan Masaya beneficiaries that could have undercut the project's potential for generating positive political results. But even if they did reduce support for the Sandinistas to some extent within the beneficiary population, it was not enough to negate the positive political impact that the project had on its beneficiaries.

Given this political outcome, it would seem necessary to explore further what had distinguished this population, and the project itself, so as to produce these results. In doing so, the first factor that must be taken into consideration is that the essence of Plan Masaya was the redistribution of land. Of secondary importance, but without which the land would not have yielded significant fruit, the project also provided its beneficiaries with agricultural credit, technical assistance, and improved technologies. Hence its implementation entailed a comprehensive redistribution of agricultural resources. In the process, the project fundamentally altered the social relations of production in its areas of influence. It brought about a wholesale replacement of large-scale capitalist producers, by peasant farmers—most of whom were organized in cooperatives.

Plan Masaya differed, then, from the types of agrarian reform projects typically carried out in Latin America.[15] Rather than simply tinkering with the relations and structure of production in Masaya and Diriomo, it transformed them. Most of the agrarian reform projects that Latin American governments have implemented have sought to create a select group of beneficiaries that they convert into peasant capitalists (cf. Grindle 1986 and de Janvry 1981).

Without calling into question the overall structure of land tenure, given the tremendous inequality in land ownership patterns that is common to capitalist regimes throughout the region, these programs have provided a small number of beneficiaries with enough resources to instill in them an interest in maintaining the status quo. As a consequence, these individual campesinos have shifted their demands to those of securing their new advantage over other peasant producers. Their concern with more fundamental reform is thereby forgotten.

In contrast, it was readily apparent to Plan Masaya beneficiaries that it had only been through a rupturing of the status quo that they had received the land that was turned over to them. That is to say, far from shifting their identification from the peasantry to the landlord class, as is the norm in the former type of land reform, the participants of this project could see the basic conflict between their own interests and those of the larger landowners. In the words of Don Jorge, one of Plan Masaya's beneficiaries, "the rich say that this land [i.e., that of the cooperatives] is 'stolen land.' But it belongs to us—it belonged to us [peasants] before, but they took advantage of our great-grandparents," and grabbed the land from them (interview no. 65, July 24, 1990). When asked about the threat to their land ownership implied by the change in government, Don Jorge went on to say, "we are here legally—we won't let go of this land. Without the agrarian reform we are nothing."

The CAS that Don Jorge belonged to—and had helped to direct in the capacity of being a member of its Junta Directiva—had received 96 manzanas of agricultural land (62 of which were cultivable) on the plains of Masaya. Its situation was particularly poignant, as the land that formed the cooperative had belonged to a colonel in Somoza's National Guard prior to 1979. The colonel had died defending the Somoza regime in 1979. Thus the members of this CAS felt no threat from him as far as an attempt to take the land away from them. Yet it was possible that his relatives in Miami might place a demand before the government to have the land returned to them. As Don Jorge's statements indicate, he was not about to let that happen.

A very different legal situation prevailed in relation to the land of which Don Eugenio's CAS formed a part. Its 55 manzanas belonged to SAIMSA until June 1985, and its return was very strongly sought by the Bolaños family.[16] Nonetheless, Don Eugenio, who was the CAS's plaguero, did not seem the least bit inclined to cede to SAIMSA's demands. Even while lamenting the cooperative's bad harvests of the previous few years and the consequent economic difficulties its members had encountered, Don Eugenio concluded by saying: "But we'll always hold our spirits high; we have to hold on to this land to the [bitter] end; this land was given to us by the revolution" (interview no. 112, February 5, 1991). And finally, Don Carlos, a CAS president from Masaya, summed up quite simply his thoughts about the elections and the position of the Sandinista government regarding the peasantry: "For us a vote for the FSLN was a guarantee that we would be able to keep our land" (interview no. 36, July 24, 1990). Thus, it was apparent to these peasants that only through the government's consideration of the beneficiaries' needs over those of the previous owners had it been possible to provide them with land.

Despite the fact that Plan Masaya provided its beneficiaries with access to land, a number of factors that were built into the project inhibited the formation of a new group of peasant capitalists. First, there was the fact that the agrarian reform gave them usufruct rights, but it did not give them the right to sell the land or use it in a number of other ways characteristic of traditional land ownership. The logic behind this was to avoid a reconcentration of land should agrarian reform beneficiaries decide to sell it for whatever reason. Likewise, avoiding the parceling of land—ultimately leading to *minifundización* (the process of minifundio formation)—inevitably resulting from the customary passing on of land to offspring, was another objective underlying this policy. The upshot was the creation of a different kind of relationship with the land. This relationship allowed the campesinos to reap all the benefits of its productive use and for their offspring to join the cooperative—as space permitted. Beneficiaries received a title for the land, which guaranteed them the right to its use in perpetuity. Hence, they could make long-term plans for its development and so forth, but they did not have precisely the same kind of link with it as would an individual peasant capitalist.

A major influence on the nature of this link, the second factor that needs to be highlighted in explaining the political anomaly presented by Plan Masaya, was that the vast majority of its beneficiaries were organized in cooperatives. Although some individual farmers did receive land through Plan Masaya, they represented only a small part of the beneficiary population. The beneficiaries were organized into three distinct types of cooperatives, the largest number of which were CCS.

The CCS formed through the Plan Masaya implementation, however, were characterized by a much higher degree of cooperation among their members than is typically the case in this kind of cooperative. Most of the country's CCS were formed on land already owned by their members, which was clearly not the case for this project's participants. Even more important, whereas normally CCS members complete virtually the entire production process in an individual fashion, this was not true for the Plan Masaya CCS. Given the fact that much of the production process was mechanized on the farms that were included in the project, a number of stages in this process were collectivized. This included preparation of the land, planting, pest control, and harvesting. The only points at which CCS members acted as individuals were in everyday maintenance activities and in the sale of their crops. In essence, the Plan Masaya beneficiary population consisted by and large of peasant farmers engaged in collective production.

Engaging in collective production inhibits the development of an individual outlook among agrarian reform beneficiaries. For some of precisely the same reasons that resistance against participation in cooperatives had emerged within the peasantry, cooperatives served this critical function. When, as we saw in chapter 2, peasants complained about having to comply with the will of the majority, they were expressing a desire to be able to act as individual peasant farmers. In contrast, through a process of collective decisionmaking, cooperative members are required to abide by preferences that may not be their own as individual members. The cooperatives, therefore, force their members to look beyond their own individual interests to take into account what is best for the whole group. Their orientation is much more social than individual.

As a consequence of this process of socialization, the tendency among small-scale farmers who receive agrarian reform land to become more conservative is undercut. Instead of concentrating on how to secure their newly won advantage over other peasant producers, the focus of cooperative members becomes one of looking for ways to improve production and, as a result, the standard of living of the entire group. That is, their search for means of resolving problems that the cooperative members share becomes collective. This willingness to focus on the collectivity was expressed in Don Jorge's response to my inquiry as to whether he would prefer that the new government change the title of the cooperative's land so that each of its members would have a title of his/her own: "We prefer to stay united—that would be better for the social and economic development of the cooperative" (interview no. 65, July 24, 1990).

Once the initial individual orientation has been broken, this more collective orientation has the potential of fostering a greater sense of cooperation with the society as a whole. Like wage labor—especially where there are more than just a few workers—collective production creates interdependence among those who engage in it. This is simply a result of the fact that the division of labor that exists in most production processes relying on more than one or two laborers requires that each must depend on the others in order to continue working. Interdependence plays a key role in generating solidarity among workers (or cooperative members), in that it becomes much easier for them to identify their common position and interests in relation to other groups in a society (Paige 1975). The words of one cooperative member (who was the president of his cooperative at the time of this interview, but not our earlier one), spoken slightly more than a month after the inauguration of the Chamorro government, confirm this hypothesis. In the face of overt threats to the land held by his cooperative, Don Luis stressed the importance of maintaining collective title to the group's land, as opposed to requesting multiple, individual titles, by arguing that "each one of us would be weaker—it would be [that much] easier to win out over each one of us, while if we're united it will be more difficult for our land to be taken away from us" (interview no. 18, member of a CAS that had been a CCS until 1989, June 4, 1990). He concluded that only by staying together and struggling collectively would it be possible for the cooperative to survive.

The impact of interdependence is particularly strong in terms of cultivating workers' or cooperative members' ability to distinguish between themselves and other classes. The interests each cooperative's members share with those who compose other cooperatives should likewise be stimulated by collective production. Don Sergio, who formed part of his CAS's Junta Directiva, articulated this new identification with great clarity when he said to me in a conversation in mid-1990, "We are going to stand firm—the cooperatives have to stand firm—because if one goes down, we all go down" (interview no. 57, May 31, 1990). A sense that their interests are distinct from, and perhaps incompatible with, those of larger landowners should also emerge in this process of developing class consciousness. The words of two informants suggest the extent to which the development of a class consciousness had progressed. In speaking of the change in government that had occurred several months earlier, Don Eugenio said: "The life of the campesino is pretty difficult, they feel it [the difficulties] more strongly . . . this government is only thinking in terms of saving the big ones [the rich]" (interview no. 72, June 8, 1990). Likewise, when asked how he felt about the Chamorro government, Don Jorge stated that "it would not work to the benefit of the campesinos, rather [its interest] is to reactivate capitalism" (interview no. 65, July 24, 1990).

Don Antonio (a CCS president who will be described at greater length below) voiced the same concern and awareness of differing class interests when speaking of the UNO government several years into its administration. In response to my question about how he saw the country's economic situation, he had replied that it was very difficult and that he didn't see any future for it (interview no. 15, March 19, 1992). I followed this up by asking him what he thought the government considered to be the way out of the current situation. To this, Don Antonio said that "the big ones will eat up the small ones—that the big ones will assume the production once again and that the small ones will get left behind." The class consciousness expressed in the comments made by these informants should serve to counter any tendency that might exist toward growing conservatism within this population of agrarian reform beneficiaries.

Finally, in addition to facilitating increased class consciousness, collective production should lead to greater social consciousness more generally. According to Burawoy (1985), production relations are the most critical influence on an individual's consciousness. It follows from this that collective agricultural production relations, as opposed to individual farming, are much more likely to produce a socially oriented perspective among those who engage in them. Like participation in a mass organization, membership in a cooperative moves the individual's sights beyond his/her own needs and demand, to those of the group. The next step, toward an understanding of the needs and demands of other social groups and to those of the society as a whole, is a comparatively easy one.

Furthermore, as with the mass organizations, participation in collective production organizes the respective population. This organization not only helps it to more loudly articulate its demands but also encourages its involvement in satisfying those demands. In his study of cooperatives in Nicaragua, Serra (1991, 201) noted the close relationship between the degree of cooperation that existed in production and the level of participation of the members in the organizational aspects of their CAS or CCS. He summarized this relationship by pointing out that "there is no doubt that collective ownership and collective work in the CASs facilitated the process of collective decision-making. . . . On the other hand, the general assemblies [the organizational form for participation that incorporated the entire membership] were weak in the CCS that lacked investments or collective land ownership, because the common interests of the members were limited to the obtention of credit and agricultural inputs." In addition to the positive impact that the collective nature of the work process had on increasing the involvement of members in the internal affairs of their cooperatives, Serra (1991, 237) also mentions three key changes brought about by the cooperatives that have laid the foundations for their members' active participation in politics more generally: (1) in most cases they have raised the standard of living of their members; (2) they have broken the relations of subordination between those who compose the cooperative and the local landed class; and (3) a sense of solidarity between members has been developed, where before it only existed between family members.

The goal of increasing the political participation of the peasantry is certainly a valuable aspiration in and of itself. But the deepening involvement of this sector of the population in matters that reach into their cooperatives and their communities also has the potential of contributing to larger development efforts. That is to say, in a situation of underdevelopment, the organized participation of the population is crucial for advancement toward fulfilling the population's needs. Where an extreme scarcity of resources prevails, such popular participation can make socioeconomic development possible.

In the case of cooperatives, this organization made the redistribution of agricultural resources—especially land—to the minifundista sector much more feasible. Undoubtedly their redistribution would have proved to be a much more prolonged and complicated process if all of its beneficiaries had been organized as individual farmers. Additionally, the introduction of higher levels of technology would have been virtually impossible to realize among the multitude of minuscule, scattered parcels that land reform to individual campesinos would have resulted in. Finally, to the extent that UNAG was able to influence Sandinista policymaking toward the rural sector, it was a consequence of the strong base of support the organization had within the cooperative sector. Thus in a variety of ways, cooperative production relations enabled their members to progress in their efforts to have their needs met.

At the same time, the organization of cooperatives brought those who participated in them into the larger process of societal change that was taking place. In the case of Plan Masaya beneficiaries, it integrated them into the new productive structure being established in agriculture and put them at the forefront of the attempt to replace agroexport production with new, more balanced production priorities. Furthermore, even as much of the rest of the population experienced growing hardship because of the war and the economic crisis in the mid-1980s, the resources that were showered upon the cooperatives in the Plan Masaya areas of influence only highlighted the fact that Sandinista policymakers were indeed concerned with responding to their members' needs. The cooperatives' privileged position made evident the priority the government had come to place in representing the interests of the rural poor.

All of this is to say that the organization of the Plan Masaya beneficiaries into collective production relations produced results that were quite different from those that might have been expected from a careful reading of Huntington's 1965 theses on popular mobilization and political stability. Far from generating demands that the government would be unable to meet, the cooperatives made it possible for the Sandinistas to address many of the project beneficiaries' demands. In addition, they also facilitated the development of a deeper understanding within the peasantry of the importance the Sandinista government placed on it as an economic actor in the country's development and transformation. When this sector also began to experience the severe effects of the economic crisis—especially after the economic reform of 1988—its members' awareness of the reasons for the crisis would certainly have been much stronger than that of the individual producer sector. Its identification with the Sandinistas' social project would also have been more firmly established than its unorganized counterparts.

This dynamic, which I am arguing operated at the level of the project as a whole, also appears to have existed within the population of those benefited

Table 6.5. Voting pattern of Plan Masaya beneficiaries

Organizational form	FSLN	UNO	No answer
CAS	5	—	—
CCS	—	2	1
Individual	1	1	—
Totals	6	3	1

Source: Author's interview data, 1990 (N = 10).

by the project. As seen in table 6.5, among those I talked with in my follow-up interviews in 1990, the beneficiaries who were still organized in CAS at that time were solidly behind the FSLN and its project for social change. In contrast, those interviewees who were organized in CCS or farmed individually were less supportive of the Sandinista regime. Although the number of those interviewed from each organizational form was small, the outstanding pattern with regard to the CAS members' support for the FSLN would appear to echo the general tendency I believe to be true for Plan Masaya as a whole: that is, where levels of organization and participation were higher, support for social transformation (as represented by the FSLN party) was greater.

In an extensive study of the role played by the various organizations representing Nicaragua's rural poor in the construction of democracy during the Sandinista regime, Luciak (1995) provides an example that would seem to contradict my assertions about the positive impact of participation. He describes at length the formation and functioning of the *Tiendas Campesinas* (also referred to as ECODEPA), which were the basis for the rural supply network set up by the UNAG in the mid-1980s. Interestingly, Luciak (1995) found that in the two regions that were the focus of his study (Regions V and VI), it was in those communities where the stores were most successful—in economic, managerial, and participatory terms—that the membership appeared to be most favorably inclined toward the UNO in the months leading up to the 1990 elections. According to Luciak (1995, 147), "Many producers indicated that they supported the goals of the revolutionary project while being critical of the Sandinista government. Moreover, a vote for UNO was not necessarily an endorsement of the opposition but was foremost intended to end the massive killing and economic deprivation resulting from a decade of U.S.-sponsored aggression."

The concerns expressed in these statements were echoed in the voices of Los Patios and Plan Masaya beneficiaries, as was mentioned in chapter 2. Yet it was evident that these concerns—which were held by many in Nicaragua's countryside—could not completely explain the varying levels of support for the continued implementation of the Sandinistas' social project that were evidenced in these two projects' populations.

In looking more closely at the case Luciak presents, however, it becomes apparent that several other factors were at play—which would seem to have counteracted or confounded the effects of participating in a project that formed an important piece of the process of change in the countryside. The first was that the region where this pattern was clearest, Region V, was also that most seriously affected by the Contra war in the latter part of the 1980s.[17] Unlike Region IV, where the Los Patios and Plan Masaya projects were carried out, Region V was the scene of ongoing battles, ambushes, kidnappings, curfews, and so forth. Relief from such dramatic and traumatic circumstances was undoubtedly sought by many of the region's residents.

Still, a few of the characteristics that Luciak points to in describing the differences between the membership makeup of Regions V and VI would seem to shed further light on what appears to be a lack of support for the FSLN in Region V, at the same time as they coincide with the findings from the present study. Among these is the fact that while the membership of Region VI's Tiendas was predominantly composed of peasants belonging to CAS, those from Chontales—one of the two departments that Luciak studied in Region V and the only one for which he provides a description in this sense—were composed primarily of individual producers (Luciak 1995, 144). Despite the fact that the farmers from Chontales had opted to participate in a project that was promoted by the UNAG—and was, therefore, consistent with the larger goals of the Sandinista government—they had yet to concretely express an interest in moving away from their individual orientation to agricultural production. Participation in the Tiendas did not in any way contradict their individual approach to farming. If anything, it facilitated the production arrangement they preferred by responding to a number of their needs as farmers—just as it did for those who had opted to join cooperatives.

At the same time, Luciak (1995, 145) also mentions that in the departments of Boaco and Chontales (both of which are in Region V), medium-scale producers controlled the Tiendas by the late 1980s.[18] And, "following the change in government [in 1990], it became clear that the ECODEPA project was increasingly controlled by rich producers." Given the control that medium (if not large) producers had over this project in Region V, it seems reasonable to suggest that it was their perspective that had the strongest representation in the Tiendas. The logical outcome of this dynamic was that the Tiendas were transformed from a project of the poorer sectors of the peasantry to one of medium- and large-scale producers. In sum, differences of class origins and class interests had come into play in this project.

In the case of the Plan Masaya agrarian reform project, class origins and class interests also appeared to have influenced the political position of its participants. The influence of class origins was closely related, but not identical, to the impact that collective production had on this project's beneficiaries. The Plan Masaya beneficiary population had been even more marginalized by the expansion of agroexport production—especially that of cotton in Masaya—than was the case of the remainder of the minifundista population in the regions where it was implemented. This was already evident by the time that its parents' generation was in its prime productive years. The heightened marginalization of the beneficiaries' lives is revealed in their *comparatively* high level of participation in the wage labor force, which resulted from their almost complete lack of access to agricultural land.

The hamlet of Quebrada Honda, which fell within the area of influence of the Plan Masaya project and is located in the municipality of Masaya, was another of the communities that Leslie Anderson (1994) included in her study of peasant political behavior in Costa Rica and Nicaragua. She, too, found an extreme problem of landlessness and insufficient land in this area. In fact, Anderson (1994, 123) calculated an average deficit of 6.1 manzanas per household, in terms of the land area needed to support a family. She comments that virtually no one owned enough land to live on, and land rentals were very difficult to come by. Anderson's informants also spoke of the difficulty of finding steady employment off the farm. Hence, she points to the community's extreme poverty—resulting from landlessness and chronic unemployment—as playing a key role in its members' early, extensive commitment to, and cohesive involvement in, the revolutionary struggle against Somoza.[19]

The problem of landlessness still existed in 1985, when Plan Masaya was implemented. Even though its beneficiary population resided in rural communities—including Quebrada Honda—and perhaps grew small amounts of produce on the tiny plots where its homes were located, it was heavily proletarianized prior to entering the Plan Masaya project (particularly that group which resided in Masaya, as opposed to Diriomo). A full 83 percent of the beneficiaries from Masaya had been employed in the rural wage labor force at some point before 1985, which underscores the degree to which the expansion of cotton had pushed this population out of the category of peasant farmer and into the category of agricultural proletariat.

Participation in wage labor, as suggested above, creates an interdependence among those thus engaged. This interdependence, in turn, creates solidarity among those who work together and an increase in their class consciousness. One beneficiary of Plan Masaya, Don Antonio, when comparing the Sandinista and Chamorro governments, expressed this sense of solidarity with other poor peasants. He commented that "the former government robbed, but [at least] it remembered the poor. It shared [its earnings] with the poor . . . [whereas] this government doesn't share [with the poor], only with the bourgeoisie" (interview no. 130, CCS member, April 24, 1993). Although this peasant farmer (and CCS president) admitted to have voted for UNO in the 1990 elections, three years later he said he felt betrayed by the Chamorro government because it had done nothing to help the poor.

Speaking of quite different matters, Don Jorge (interview no. 124, CAS member, March 19, 1992) expressed this same kind of identification with other poor peasants, and lack of sympathy for those who have (or aspire to have) more than they do. I had asked him if he was not worried about people stealing the cooperative's harvest of yucca (a serious problem at the time). Don Jorge responded: "It's not theft if a campesino takes a plant once and awhile—he does it for necessity. . . . But, yes, if they enter with a cart and take various sacks of yucca, that is theft." Thus, Don Jorge clearly distinguished between the neighboring peasant who might not have any food to put on the table—and, therefore, was forced to take it from others like him/herself—and those who sought to profit off the labor of the cooperative members by stealing their crop and selling it to others. His comments reflected a genuine sense of solidarity with the former (a poor peasant like himself) and a disdain for the latter (an exploitative middleman).

In addition to increasing political solidarity, wage labor has a number of other effects on the consciousness of those employed in this manner. Paige (1975, 30) hypothesizes that "the greater the importance of wages as a source of income, the less the economic competition and the greater the incentive for political organization." These effects of wage labor flow logically from the increased solidarity and class consciousness that result from this kind of economic activity. Once a sense of identification with others in one's same position emerges, the disadvantages experienced by this sector vis-à-vis the land-owning class should become evident. It should also become apparent that competing with others from the same class is less likely to yield tangible benefits in terms of the level of marginalization characterizing one's life, than cooperating with others to call for a change in their relationship with the landed classes. This sector of the rural population is not noted for having a one-to-one patronage relationship with larger producers as that which frequently characterizes the peasant-capitalist sector. Hence, uniting to demand redis-tributive justice from the landowning class is much more feasible for wage laborers.

Moreover, Paige (1975) argues that those engaged in wage labor are more accepting of risk and are more receptive to revolutionary appeals than are peasant farmers who have not experienced a significant degree of proletarianization. Once the rural proletariat has lost its access to the principal resources employed in agricultural production, it also sheds the fear of their loss, which is so distinctive among small-scale peasants. Then the potential exists for that fear to be replaced by a willingness to participate in activities that are seen to contain the possibility of bettering its circumstances as a class. This process is not automatic, however. It requires, first and foremost, the consciousness and organizational strength this population has attained as a class.

In sum, Plan Masaya benefited a sector of the rural population, the smallest of the minifundistas, that had largely lost its ties to the land. Its participation in the wage labor force prior to 1985 had led to an increase in its class consciousness and an openness to seeking alternatives to the status quo. Once the Sandinistas had achieved power and initiated an agrarian reform, a new factor came into play that fortified the predispositions of this project's beneficiaries, that of collective production. Their membership in cooperatives provided them with organizational strength and deepened their class consciousness, thus buttressing their receptivity to revolutionary appeals. Finally, the collective work in which they engaged incorporated them into more socially oriented production relations, thereby laying the basis for the adoption of socialist production relations. Likewise, their integration into the Sandinistas' larger project of social transformation, through their cooperative membership, solidified their identification with the government. In essence, all of these factors reinforced the social consciousness of Plan Masaya beneficiaries, leading to a notably higher degree of support for the Sandinista government and its efforts to promote the transition to socialism than was the case elsewhere in the Nicaraguan countryside.

Conclusion

The implementation of Plan Masaya in 1985 and 1986 represented a major departure from the model of development that Sandinista policymakers had envisioned for this area, within the general plan they had elaborated for Region IV in the early 1980s. That model had taken for granted the continued predominance of agroexport production in the region, due to the country's ongoing need for the foreign exchange earnings that agroexports generated. A corollary of this strategy was that agroexport production was to remain concentrated on medium- and large-sized estates, whether part of the state or private capitalist sectors, because of the presumed appropriateness of this size of producer for the streamlined, high-technology enterprises that it involved. Efforts were to be made to expand permanent employment in the export sector so as to absorb labor from within the peasantry. Proletarianization of the campesinado was assumed to be the most suitable means to raise its members' standard of living and incorporate them into the modernization process that was to be brought about in the countryside.

A minor modification of this general strategy occurred a few years before the implementation of Plan Masaya when a relatively small area in Tisma-Masaya was turned over to cooperatives that had been established in order to receive it. The formation of these cooperatives symbolized the other suitable alternative that government policymakers had set forth for peasants not interested in proletarianization. Nonetheless, cotton cultivation was to remain the primary agricultural activity on the farms in this area. To the extent that it was feasible to introduce irrigation systems there, food crops would be grown during cotton's off-season.

Plan Masaya, however, broke with the predominant development model in several important respects. It completely replaced export production with that of basic grains, leading to a dramatic increase in their production levels in Region IV. It shifted the focus of agricultural modernization away from products destined for the export market and toward the formerly marginalized basic grain sector. In the space of two years, corn and bean cultivation evolved from being carried out manually, at one extreme, to having virtually their entire production processes mechanized, at the other extreme. Finally, Plan Masaya put into practice the more flexible attitude that prevailed in the mid-1980s among agrarian policymakers regarding the means through which to incorporate the peasantry into the overall process of agricultural transformation. By redistributing land and other agricultural resources to campesinos organized in a variety of forms, Plan Masaya succeeded in raising their standard of living appreciably. Thus the project largely achieved the socioeconomic goals on which it was based.

At the same time, the results of the 1990 elections revealed the relative accomplishment of the project on the political front. In a context in which support for the FSLN had dropped off dramatically all over the country—and especially in rural areas—the fact that the FSLN actually won in a number of the precincts where a large percentage of Plan Masaya beneficiaries voted was noteworthy. More importantly, however, it reinforced the conclusion that I had already drawn from interviews with the project's participants: that the project had had a positive political impact.

Additionally, these results, especially as expressed in my interview data, demonstrate that means do exist to ameliorate the tendency toward conservatism that may be stimulated by agrarian reform. Those who study the implementation of agrarian reform programs undertaken by capitalist regimes have consistently observed the beneficiaries' new concern with maintaining the status quo following such reform. But Plan Masaya highlighted the potential inherent within some fractions of the peasantry to become more radicalized as a result of such programs.

The effects of this project suggest that the fraction of the peasantry that is most likely to respond favorably to a socialist regime that carries out agrarian reform is that which had been most marginalized under capitalism. That is, it will be those campesinos who had been increasingly proletarianized as a consequence of the expansion of export agriculture. As numerous analysts of peasant politics have argued (cf. Paige 1975, Wickham-Crowley 1989, and Lenin 1966), it is among the poorest of the peasantry that the greatest promise of support for revolutionary change is to be found. In addition, my study shows that even after the transition to socialism is begun, this fraction remains the most likely source of sustenance within the rural population for this endeavor.

But another factor that was part and parcel of Plan Masaya was also crucial in facilitating the achievement of the project's political goals. It was the fundamental restructuring of agricultural production and its accompanying social relations. Both the effective overthrow of medium- and large-scale capitalist production brought about by the project, and organization of the beneficiaries into forms of production that varied but were in their essence largely collective in nature, led to increased class and social consciousness. As well, their collective production relations incorporated them into the overall process of social change that was under way throughout the society. As a result of this mobilization, the level of identification with the Sandinista government—which had given priority to this sector over the bourgeoisie through the Plan Masaya implementation—and with its socialist project increased. Thus, in strong contrast to Huntington's 1965 assertions, this phenomenon highlights the critical role that popular mobilization can play in development and social transformation.

To the extent that Plan Masaya was only relatively successful in political terms, and not overwhelmingly so, its impact had been undermined by the multitude of factors that were mentioned in chapter 2, particularly the war and the country's profound economic crisis. It was almost inevitable that they would produce a drop in confidence in the Sandinistas' capacity to govern within at least a small part of this project's—or any other's—beneficiary population. What is remarkable is that the level of identification with the FSLN remained as high as it did in the project's areas of influence.

In sum, the political and economic results of Plan Masaya suggest that a much more optimistic view of the *potential* role of the peasantry in socioeconomic development efforts is in order. They point to the possible means by which to undercut conservative tendencies that may exist within this population, so that it can be incorporated into a socialist project of societal change. This finding is of great relevance for those Third World countries that are still characterized by the existence of a large peasant population, and which seek to carry out a profound social transformation.

7

The Lessons to be Drawn from Los Patios and Plan Masaya

On April 25, 1990, with the inauguration of Violeta Chamorro as president of Nicaragua, the agrarian reform process that had been brought about by the Sandinista government came to an end. In a period of slightly more than a decade the reform had initiated major changes in a number of key aspects of the country's agrarian sector. Given the extreme importance of this sector within the national economy, these changes were crucial for the overall process of social transformation that was under way in the society at large. Fundamental alteration of the productive and social structures in Nicaragua's countryside was essential if progress was to be made toward firmly establishing a new model of development. The new model of development took into account more than economic factors, however. It also presupposed that democratization of the means of production would lay the groundwork for democratization in other spheres of society, such as the polity. That is, the redistribution of productive resources, such as that implied in the agrarian reform, was a central component of the more general effort to initiate a democratic transition to socialism.

The decade-long revolutionary transformation that was set into motion by the Sandinistas experienced some significant modifications before it was overthrown in 1990. Although many of those modifications served to undercut the socialist-oriented aspects of the Sandinista economic program and institutionalize the new political reality, agrarian policy instead underwent a radicalization over the course of time. Ironically, while the former two modifications had the effect of demobilizing much of civil society and channeling its political activities more and more toward outlets characteristic of traditional representative democracy, it was precisely the continued mobilization of the rural poor that led to the deepening of the agrarian reform. Furthermore, as the reach of the reform widened, it incorporated a growing number of rural dwellers into the socialist project.

The two case studies analyzed above, however, highlight the fact that the reform did not succeed in integrating all of its beneficiaries into the overarching effort to promote social change. Rather it produced contradictory outcomes, fully mobilizing some campesinos and pushing others into the conservative opposition. How is it possible that such distinct positions were adopted by its beneficiaries?

The answer to that question points to some of the social dynamics which underlay Nicaragua's agrarian reform. It also sheds light on several larger questions and issues. The first of these is that of which aspects of Sandinista policymaking were important in determining the degree of commitment held by the population to thoroughgoing societal transformation.

Looking beyond Nicaragua, a second issue that this study addresses is that of the role of the peasantry in socioeconomic development, particularly that of a socialist orientation. It would seem to behoove us to examine, however briefly, the Nicaraguan agrarian reform in a comparative fashion in order to be able to assess the potential it offers for suggesting alternative responses to "the peasant question" for those engaged in the transition to socialism.

Finally, the varying political outcomes arising from Nicaragua's agrarian reform also provide abundant material for reflection with regard to a number of debates in the theoretical literatures addressing development and peasant politics. This study presents several new elements that should be taken into account if one is to understand the relationship between socioeconomic development and politics, especially in terms of the participation of the peasantry in that equation. It is to a discussion of all of these questions and issues that we now turn.

The Contradictory Political Results of Plan Masaya and Los Patios

This exploration of the broader implications that can be drawn from studying the nature and outcomes of Los Patios and Plan Masaya must of necessity begin with a closer examination of the factors that distinguished these two projects and their beneficiary populations. Although some of these differences have been suggested in earlier chapters, they need to be underlined at this point and others need to be added to the picture. These differences include the varying class origins of the beneficiaries, the alternative organizational forms they adopted for their production after entering the projects, and the differing approaches to dealing with the problem of minifundismo implied in each project (see table 7.1).

The principal difference that requires further elaboration here is that of the

Table 7.1. Profiles of project participants (percentages)

	Los Patios	Plan Masaya	
		Masaya	Diriomo
Profiles			
Land ownership (prior to the project)	52	10	25
Inherited	36	0	13
Purchased	27	5	0
Agrarian reform	5	5	13
Employment history			
Only farmer	0	0	0
Rural laborer	46	83	63
Urban laborer	30	38	25
Informal sector	34	23	13
Benefits received (through the project)			
Land	—	95	88
Organization of production			
CAS	11	63	50
CCS	52	33	50
Individuals	36	5	—
Voted for the FSLN (N = 21)	36	63	50

Source: Author's survey data, 1988 and 1989; author's interview data, 1990. Los Patios: N = 44; Plan Masaya: N = 40 in Masaya, N = 8 in Diriomo.

Note: Employment history should not be expected to add up to 100 percent because most of the beneficiaries participated in more than one economic activity.

class origins of the Los Patios and Plan Masaya beneficiary populations. Despite the facts that the projects both targeted the minifundista populations in their respective areas of influence and that it was effectively from this sector that most of their beneficiaries came, there were some important distinctions between the two groups. Although Los Patios beneficiaries were not predominantly middle or rich peasants, their access to agricultural resources and ability to maintain themselves as independent farmers was significantly greater than that of Plan Masaya beneficiaries prior to each group's entry into their respective projects. Several key indicators reveal this reality.

Given that access to land is the most crucial resource sought by agricultural producers, our comparison of these two beneficiary populations must begin there. The major differences existing between them were already evident in their parents' generation. While more than half the parents (55 percent) of Los Patios participants owned land, only approximately a quarter (28 percent) of those of Plan Masaya beneficiaries who lived in Masaya did.[1] Although the parents of the Plan Masaya beneficiaries who resided in Diriomo had greater access to land (38 percent) than their Masaya-based counterparts, it was still significantly less than the Los Patios participants. This factor alone was enough to determine which fraction of the peasantry their offspring would join.

A clear reflection of the impact that this would have on the next generation can be seen in a comparison of the economic activities in which these two groups engaged. While approximately 42 percent of the parents of Los Patios beneficiaries were able to sustain themselves and their families from their own agricultural production, a mere 15 percent of the parents of Plan Masaya beneficiaries who were based in Masaya were able to do so.[2] Obviously, the prospects for the next generation to work as independent farmers were limited for both groups, but much more so for the Plan Masaya project's beneficiaries.

Moving on to the generation of the beneficiaries, we find that while more than a third (36 percent) of Los Patios participants inherited land, *none* of Plan Masaya beneficiaries from the Masaya area did.[3] Although a small number from both groups were able to obtain land through other means—purchasing it or receiving it through the agrarian reform prior to entering the project—once again, Los Patios beneficiaries were more fortunate than those of Plan Masaya from Masaya.[4]

Indeed, none of the beneficiaries from either project were able to depend exclusively on their farm-generated income as a means of sustenance. Yet the types of economic activities upon which they relied in order to support themselves also differed between beneficiary groups. The vast majority (83 percent) of Plan Masaya Masaya-based participants had to resort to rural wage labor to supplement their farm earnings.[5] In contrast, less than half (46 percent) of Los Patios participants had ever entered this work force prior to being incorporated into the project. Both groups participated to a lesser extent in urban wage labor and informal sector activities, falling roughly into the same range on both counts.

Despite the fact that the contrast between these two populations is not black and white, all of the above indicators provide us with enough evidence to conclude that even within the minifundista sector there were important gradations in the degree of marginalization that characterized its fractions. Los Patios beneficiaries clearly had more access to agricultural land than those of Plan Masaya, and this phenomenon had existed for at least two generations. Their access to land played a determining role in the extent to which they had been pushed into the wage labor force in order to supplement the earnings they derived from farming. Los Patios beneficiaries had depended on a variety of other economic activities in addition to farming, among which was agricultural wage labor. However, fewer than half of them resorted to wage labor. In contrast, an overwhelming number of Plan Masaya beneficiaries had been proletarianized as a consequence of their extreme margin-alization from the agricultural means of production.

These differing social origins predisposed the projects' beneficiaries to respond in distinct forms to the possibilities opened up through the agrarian reform. With the new resources provided to them through the project, Los Patios beneficiaries saw their standard of living rise. The increase in farm-generated earnings permitted them to retreat to their land and maintain themselves through their agricultural production alone. In the process, they moved significantly closer to, if not into, the middle peasantry. Without anything to mediate the influence of this change on their lives and their thinking, the project's participants experienced the classic move to the political right that campesinos who form part of a pampered minority of agrarian reform beneficiaries within a sea of minifundistas have repeatedly undergone. Their reinforced ties to the land increased the level of socioeconomic differentiation within their rural communities, and they came to identify with other, larger-scale landowners in their desire to maintain the new status quo.

Plan Masaya beneficiaries also achieved greater economic security through their participation in the project. The resources it provided them, especially land, served to liberate them from their constant search for means of survival. They regained what had been lost during their parents' generation—the ability to support themselves and their families from earnings generated by their own agricultural production.

Nonetheless, a major mediating factor existed which kept these campesinos from turning their sights toward the landed classes as a new source of identification. That factor was the organizational form that their production took. These minifundistas were organized largely into cooperatives in which their farming was undertaken in a collective fashion. Therefore they did not have the opportunity to develop a conception of themselves as individual farmers. And although it is logical to assume that they would have been anxious to ensure their continued rights to the land that was turned over to them, they would not have felt the same kind of threat from a further deepening of the agrarian reform as Los Patios beneficiaries, because it was that same reform which had provided Plan Masaya beneficiaries with their own land.

It is also crucial, however, to see the beneficiaries' cooperativization as something more than a prophylactic measure against their moving to the political right. Membership in a cooperative was to play an important role in ensuring the full participation of the reform's beneficiaries in making decisions about the production that was to provide them with a livelihood. This participation was important for a number of reasons, including that it was an essential component of the larger process of democratization that was going on in the entire society (cf. Serra 1991).

Carmen Diana Deere (1986) has argued that without the existence of participatory mechanisms at the point of production, it is highly questionable whether a society can achieve socialist democracy.[6] She asserts that cooperatives present much greater potential in this regard than state farms, which have always been seen as being the superior form of production within socialism. Deere draws this conclusion from an analysis of the agrarian reforms which were carried out in thirteen Third World countries that experienced a socialist transition. Although admitting that collective ownership of the means of production does not guarantee democracy in the work place, Deere (1986, 139) contends that "what production cooperatives offer is worker control over the labor process and over the appropriation and allocation of the surplus produced." Both of these phenomena are critical for the development of socialist democracy.

Nicaragua's agrarian reform established state farms as well as agricultural cooperatives. While the former organization of production was given priority in the first few years of the reform, by the mid-1980s cooperatives had been accepted as an important means of incorporating campesino producers into the socialist project. Although it is also necessary to acknowledge that the Plan Masaya beneficiaries had not achieved complete control over the production process, they were certainly closer to it than they had been as agricultural wage laborers on capitalist estates. That is, as we saw in chapter 2, a number of limitations affected the degree of democracy that characterized decisionmaking regarding their production and accumulation processes. Yet if one takes into account that the cooperative sector in Nicaragua was still young—and the one resulting from Plan Masaya especially so—its weaknesses can be understood as arising from the fact that fully democratic decisionmaking was still very much in the process of evolving. The political and social consciousness of the members, as well as that of the agricultural technicians, ministry officials, and UNAG organizers, would require time to reach the level that was necessary for the cooperatives to function in an entirely democratic fashion.

On the road to reaching this goal, however, the cooperatives also served to secure the participation of their members in a new, more socially oriented form of production. Their participation represented an active engagement in the overall project of changing the agricultural relations of production. Despite the fact that, as we saw in chapter 2, resistance to cooperative production relations still existed in the countryside, and that the development of these relations was only one piece of the societal transformation that was occurring, it nonetheless constituted participation in that transformation.

The participation of Plan Masaya beneficiaries in collective production was therefore a second factor distinguishing this population from that of Los Patios's beneficiaries.⁷ Moving to the level of the projects themselves, we come to a third major distinction which played a role in the emergence of the differing political outcomes that they produced. This distinction consists of the fact that Plan Masaya brought about much more far-reaching changes in the agrarian social structure than did Los Patios. The massive redistribution of land underlay these changes. It was this that facilitated the conversion of its beneficiaries from a largely proletarianized population into agricultural producers, an aspiration their participation in the project implied. For many of the beneficiaries, the FSLN was seen as the party that had made this aspiration a reality.

The conversion process had been contingent upon the de facto removal of an important number of medium- and large-scale capitalist producers from this key agricultural region. Collective peasant production effectively replaced capitalist production in a significant part of Masaya's and Diriomo's rural areas. Not surprisingly, many Plan Masaya beneficiaries saw the UNO alliance as being closely linked to the landed classes, including the large capitalist producers who had lost their land with the implementation of Plan Masaya. Hence their support for the FSLN, and opposition to the UNO becomes more understandable. In contrast, most of the Los Patios beneficiary population had owned some agricultural land prior to its inclusion in the project. Given this situation, and the still only incipient stage of transition that characterized the agrarian reform when the project was first implemented, a complete transformation of the area's social structure was not envisioned or realized. Thus while Los Patios beneficiaries did experience some change in their living standard and agricultural production, it was not as great as that of Plan Masaya beneficiaries.

A striking exception to this pattern can be seen in several of the rural areas that Los Patios had reached into—such as San Marcos and Masatepe—where a considerable amount of land *was* redistributed. The population residing in these communities, in contrast to that which lived in the area at the heart of the project, La Concepción, had in fact witnessed a dramatic change in their access to productive resources and in their employment situation. And they—like the Plan Masaya land reform beneficiaries—demonstrated a much higher level of identification with the government that had brought about this change. Notably, the FSLN actually won in each one of these municipalities (focusing only on the precincts where there were Los Patios beneficiaries).⁸

Nonetheless, for most Los Patios beneficiaries, the change was much more partial in nature and had not noticeably come at the cost of the landed sectors of the rural population. The potential threat implied by the UNO's strong links with the country's agricultural bourgeoisie was not as worrisome to Los Patios participants precisely because so few of them had received land through the agrarian reform. That is to say, the nature of the projects themselves also contributed, to a significant extent, to determining the responses of their respective beneficiary populations to the distinct political and economic programs offered to them in the 1990 elections.

BROADER IMPLICATIONS OF PLAN MASAYA AND LOS PATIOS

Lessons for the Sandinistas' Project of Popular Hegemony

The political results of Los Patios and Plan Masaya have implications that reach beyond the areas of influence of each project and the populations that participated in them. Their implications extend in several directions; the first of those we will address is that of suggesting at least a few of the aspects of Sandinista policymaking that facilitated the development of the population's commitment to the FSLN's project of social transformation.

As argued above, the very nature of each one of these projects contributed to the political results they produced. This dynamic can be restated so that its broader relevance becomes clearer, as: where a fundamental restructuring of agricultural production relations occurred, a deeper identification with the overall process of social change was more likely to emerge. There were a number of subprocesses at work to generate this overall process, among which was the fact that with such thoroughgoing restructuring, the government demonstrated in a tangible way its prioritization of the popular classes over the former propertied classes. With each entrega de tierra to the peasantry, for example, a statement was made that the privileged position of the former rural bourgeoisie no longer held sway. Instead, it was the poorer sectors of the rural population that had become the focus of government policymaking.

Given the level of development characterizing Nicaragua's economy and society when the Sandinistas came to power in 1979 and the broad class alliance that brought them to power, their political strategy did not consist of the establishment of a dictatorship of the proletariat (cf. Stahler-Sholk 1990b, Vilas 1988, and Núñez Soto 1980). Rather, they saw themselves as "the articulator of a pluralist project, continually redefined by the broad masses that had constituted themselves as the social subject of the revolution" (Stahler-Sholk 1990b, 11).[9] In essence, the political project of the Sandinistas was to consolidate the hegemony of the popular classes.

Yet that political project was to evolve in the context of a mixed economy, in which the capitalist sector continued to play a major role. With time, Sandinista policymakers became well aware of the capacity of this sector to voice its concerns at both the national and international levels in an effort to have its interests represented. Thus a constant tension pervaded politics and policymaking in Nicaragua throughout the 1980s between advancement toward the goal of consolidating popular hegemony and the maintenance of national unity (the participation of the capitalist sector in the mixed economy). Policymaking in all areas was affected by this tension, including in the agrarian sector.

Some analysts have argued that increasingly, over the course of the decade of Sandinista rule, the interests of the popular sectors lost out to the perceived need to cater to the concerns of the bourgeoisie (see especially Vilas 1991). Others suggest that different periods were characterized by distinct emphases, but that ultimately, in the midst of such a strong interplay of pressures on the regime and the society, balancing popular hegemony with national unity proved to be an untenable strategy (e.g. Stahler-Sholk 1990b). I would add to this latter position a recognition of the fact that those who were responsible for somehow maintaining this balance were burdened by the war and shortages of all kinds of resources—including basic information about the country, experience in policymaking, and obvious models from which they could derive a clear picture of how to pull off this feat. Hence, they engaged in a tremendous amount of experimentation in a relatively short period of time, in an attempt to move ahead toward their larger goals. Nonetheless, the point that is most relevant to the present discussion is that given this type of complex political context, programs and projects that demonstrated the government's commitment to the popular classes were particularly important.

The deepening of the agrarian reform in the mid-1980s was one such demonstration. Despite the fact that it represented a piece of the larger effort to fight the Contra war, the shift in the reform embodied the "popular" side of the Sandinista political project. Such a strong expression of this emphasis was significant at that time because of the impact that the economic crisis had had on other parts of the popular classes, and because of the effects of a number of contradictory policies that had been imposed on the peasants in the preceding few years.[10]

At the same time, the serious restructuring of agricultural production relations brought about during this stage of the reform reduced the possibility of a new, privileged sector of the peasantry emerging whose interests would tend toward maintaining its recently improved socioeconomic position to the detriment of the vast majority of poor peasants. Since implementation of the broadened reform affected whole areas at a time, far from pampering a small group of peasants and leaving the remainder untouched, it incorporated large numbers of poor peasants from each community. And it severely weakened the position of the rural bourgeoisie, thereby lessening its importance as a source of identification for the newly enfranchised peasantry. One of the consequences of these dynamics was to undermine any conservatizing tendencies that might have arisen within the beneficiary population as a result of the reform.

The second aspect of Sandinista policymaking that our case studies revealed to be key to fostering "popular hegemony" was that of efforts to promote the active participation of these sectors in the process of change. As Stahler-Sholk (1990b, 21) succinctly states, "the possibility of establishing a hegemonic popular project depends not simply on wise leaders or objectively correct goals, but on the ability to mobilize and sustain broad popular support during the transition." Through this means the popular sectors could come to identify with the process of change that was under way and see it as something that they could shape so as to best address their concerns and needs.

That participation could take a variety of forms, including the collective organization of production. What was crucial, however, was that it incorporate these sectors in an ongoing fashion and link the societal transformation to their own lives. Their formal membership alone in an organization—through which they might occasionally be mobilized to carry out some specific task or attend a political rally—was not enough to either foster a strong identification with the government that was promoting that transformation or ensure that their concerns would be responded to consistently over time. This is not to say that the periodic mobilization of the mass, and other, organizations by the government for community development efforts and so forth was, in and of itself, detrimental to their participatory well-being. But their existence had to consist of much more than these mobilizations. What was necessary to guarantee both the development of a well-founded identification with the project represented by the government and a relationship characterized by continuous dialogue between policymakers and the popular sectors was the establishment of organizational forms that provided a genuinely participatory experience—internally, as well as vis-à-vis the government.

Yet, as described in chapter 1, a number of factors led to a serious weakening in the organizations of the popular sectors and their gradual demobilization, especially after the mid-1980s. These included the war, the growing economic crisis, and the perceived need to maintain national unity.[11] Ironically, as resources became increasingly scarce and decisions had to be made with regard to which sectors would receive those that remained, the sectors that continued to be organized and that strongly voiced their demands became the principal recipients of government attention. This process can be seen quite clearly in the case of the beneficiaries of the Plan Masaya project. Through UNAG's mobilizational efforts, which were commensurably strengthened as the agrarian reform expanded, the organized peasantry was able to bring about a deepening of the process of agrarian restructuring. That is, through mobilization it was able to become a key focus of government interest. And within the population of agrarian reform beneficiaries, those who were organized collectively had the closest relationship with UNAG.

The growing organization of the peasantry, through UNAG, contrasted strongly with that characterizing other parts of the popular classes. The organizations representing women, workers, and urban neighborhoods were especially hard hit by the demobilization that occurred within the popular classes in the mid-1980s. Yet from the point of view of achieving popular hegemony and the consolidation of the popular project, the active participation of all of these sectors—not just the peasants organized by UNAG—was crucial. In sum, the demobilization of most of the population in and of itself greatly reduced the prospects for attaining the sought-after popular hegemony. And the organized sectors of the peasantry were among the few sectors in which identification with the Sandinistas and their social project remained strong by the end of the 1980s.

Nonetheless, those sectors of the peasantry who remained unorganized throughout the 1980s failed to develop an identification with the Sandinistas' social project. The Los Patios beneficiary population was characterized by this phenomenon. Despite its lack of organization, this group was designated to receive certain benefits by government policymakers. But the latter's efforts to organize this population, first through "Producers' Associations" and later through CCS, never produced the kind of collective orientation that was hoped for.

The question of how that orientation might have been achieved brings up the issue of how the class origins of Los Patios beneficiaries interacted with this process. Given that its beneficiaries were drawn from a sector of the peasantry that was still strongly tied to the land—in the form of independent farming—it would have been virtually impossible for the Sandinistas to "impose" collective production relations upon them without using coercion. That is, because most of them did not receive land through the reform—but instead were able to improve their economic security simply through the receipt of other productive resources—short of using force there was little more that the Sandinistas could do than promote the less collectivized forms of organization among them. But the latter forms of organization were insufficient in terms of eliminating the strong sense of individualism that characterized these producers. Rather than supporting the government that had provided them with additional productive resources, Los Patios participants resented the intervention of the state in their affairs and felt threatened by the potential of further land reform. In the end, they did not identify with the "popular classes" that the Sandinistas' project sought to represent.

Parallels with Agrarian Reform Elsewhere in the Third World

One of the major questions that the political results of these two projects raises is the potential role that the peasantry can play within the processes of social transformation and development. By comparing the findings from my two case studies with the achievements and limitations encountered in the incorporation of the peasantry in other socialist-oriented agrarian reforms in the Third World, we can begin to see some patterns. It is to such a comparison that we now turn.

The overarching pattern that becomes apparent from even a brief perusal of the various agrarian reforms that have been implemented by socialist-oriented governments in the Third World is that the shape of the reform is largely contingent upon the previously existing class and productive structures. This means that, for example, the continuing existence of a large peasantry makes a policy of gradual collectivization more feasible than one of massive nationalization followed by the formation of state farms. Several especially clear examples of the way in which formerly existing class and productive structures influenced a government's broad strategy of agrarian reform can be seen in the cases of Mozambique, Cuba, and Nicaragua.[12] The first two countries had been characterized by having a large foreign presence in their agricultural economies: in the former, it had taken the shape of a settler population that fled with the overthrow of the colonial regime; in the latter, it was the major holdings of multinational (particularly U.S.) sugar companies, which were expropriated by the revolutionary government shortly after it came to power. This presence was concentrated in relatively high-technology agroexport production, which led the respective regimes to conclude that the subdivision and redistribution of its property to the peasantry made little economic sense. Moreover, in the case of Cuba, the rural population had been quite heavily proletarianized by 1959, so it was even less practical to consider a strategy of recampesinización (cf. Pollitt 1979). In Nicaragua, as described in previous chapters, the significant holdings of Somoza and his close allies provided the state with a large, modernized productive base upon the dictator's flight into exile and the expropriation of these holdings that followed shortly thereafter. Thus what appeared to be the most logical strategy to pursue in all three cases was to nationalize these estates and to convert them into state farms. The goal then became to improve the lot of the workers through more benevolent and participatory employer-employee (i.e., state-employee) relations.

Yet, two problematic issues related to this strategy emerged, even in the cases in which there appeared to be no question as to its appropriateness. The first was the fact that despite having placed worker participation high on the list of goals for the new state farms, little success was achieved in this regard (see especially Deere 1986 and Ortega 1985). The stable employment and improvements in other areas that were brought about with the formation of the state farms undoubtedly benefited the workers they hired and represented a change from formerly prevailing conditions. However, resistance by administrators, the overall government policy of central planning, and worker inexperience presented huge obstacles to the achievement of genuine participation by the workers in the management of these "enterprises of the people."

In the cases of Mozambique and Nicaragua, the formation of and early policymaking emphasis on state farms as the centerpiece of agrarian reform also meant that a major restructuring of the social relations of production in agriculture was forestalled until a later time. Given that state administrators replaced the former administrative staff and did not incorporate workers into the management process in a thorough manner, *and* that the priority given to the state sector left the peasantry largely untouched, the better part of the rural population remained outside of the process of social transformation. The economic and political issues raised by this oversight, as well as the state sector's continuing lack of economic success, eventually led to a shift in policy in both cases.[13] In Mozambique, the need for this shift was clearly articulated by 1983, along with a call for a new emphasis on cooperative production and smaller-scale, more locally oriented projects. As we already have seen, in Nicaragua the shift toward promoting the development of cooperatives as a means of incorporating the peasantry into the agrarian reform was initiated in 1981 and more fully implemented as of 1983.

Even in the case of Cuba, whose rural population was significantly more proletarianized than those of either Mozambique or Nicaragua, a change occurred with regard to the government's strong preference for state farms to form the backbone of agricultural production. There, throughout the 1960s and early 1970s, the incorporation of small farmers' land (i.e., land that had not been subject to expropriation by the agrarian reform) into state farms had been the government's goal with respect to this sector. Completing the process of proletarianization of the rural population and organizing the vast majority of agricultural land into state farms had been perceived as the most rational and correct way of pursuing agricultural development. However, by the mid-1970s, a recognition had emerged within policymaking circles that those farmers who remained outside the state sector could be organized into cooperatives, which would facilitate an expansion in the provision of services to them and bring them within the orbit of state planning.[14] Since that time, the cooperative sector has grown and become increasingly consolidated.

In addition, the crisis in Cuban agriculture (and in the economy as a whole) that arose following the breakdown of the Council of Mutual Economic Assistance (COMECON) has triggered a whole new move toward cooperative relations of production. Prior to the tearing down of the Berlin Wall, the COMECON had been Cuba's principal trading partner, being the source of or market for more than 80 percent of the country's imports and exports (CEE 1989, tables 9.3 and 9.4). The massive drop in imported inputs that was produced by the changes under way in the COMECON hit agricultural production especially hard. Because of the resultant need to shift to alternative, if not lower, levels of technology, the organization of smaller units of production than those typical of Cuba's state farms became more and more critical. Likewise, the urgency of encouraging production increases on what had been until then state farms, called for a modification of the predominant social relations of production. Consequently, in the fall of 1993 the government introduced a novel strategy that entailed the organization of cooperatives on what were formerly state farms (cf. *Granma* 1993a, 1993b, 1993c, and Enríquez 1994). Thus, an appreciation for the benefits inherent in cooperative production relations emerged, even where the prerevolutionary social structure had earlier pointed to state farms as the logical successor to the massive sugar estates of the pre-1959 period.

A realization of the important role that the peasantry plays in agricultural production, and of its significant presence within the rural class structure, has led to the promotion of cooperative formation in some other agrarian reforms as well. But the organization of cooperatives, in and of itself, will not necessarily resolve either the economic or political concerns that lead to the adoption of this strategy. Where it is not voluntary, does not receive sufficient government attention, and/or does not follow from a complete restructuring of agrarian class relations, its results will be mixed at best, in terms of facilitating socialist transformation in the countryside. The agrarian reform experiences of several countries have a special bearing in this sense and find a resonance in—as well as suggest the potential implications of—the dynamics revealed by my case studies from Nicaragua.

The agrarian transformation initiated in 1967 in Tanzania provides us with a clear example of how crucial it is that collectivization of agriculture proceed in a voluntary fashion.[15] The transformation gave rise to two related, but not identical, strategies that were used to promote rural development there: the organization of communal production and the resettlement of the rural population in consolidated villages, which was supposed to foster the former. Nyerere's government began to encourage communal production with the provision of extensive social services, agricultural inputs, and so forth immediately following the Arusha Declaration in 1967. Yet its voluntary adoption by the population remained an unrealized goal despite its high priority in terms of receipt of government resources: as late as a decade after it became the key to government policymaking for agricultural production, communal production still only incorporated 5 to 8 percent of the agricultural land.[16]

Given the slow pace with which communal production was being assimilated and the perception held by policymakers that the provision of services would be made more feasible by concentrating the rural population in larger settlements, the "villagization" program was initiated in 1973. As a result of this program, up to 55 percent of the rural population was resettled (Barker 1985, 68). Yet neither the resettlement effort nor the spread of communal agriculture was left to proceed in a voluntary fashion. Inevitably, the government's coercive actions provoked resistance on the part of the "beneficiaries." Barker (1985, 67) argues that where communal production emerged from within the rural population it was usually quite successful. In contrast, where an attempt was made to force it on the population, various types of passive, and in some cases active, resistance resulted. Nonetheless, it was not until 1983 that the Tanzanian government announced a shift in agricultural policy. In so doing, it implicitly recognized the problems that had been produced by forcing the rural population to adopt communal forms of production and to be relocated to large settlements, neither of which had readily appealed to them.

The experience of Tanzania provides us with abundant evidence of the potential negative outcomes—both in terms of politics, as well as production (or economics)—of imposing collectivization on a population. The lessons to be derived from this case suggest that the Sandinistas could not have pushed harder than they already had done in promoting the formation of CCS among Los Patios's participants. That is to say, forcing them to collectivize their production (especially by organizing CAS) through coercive means—in order to avoid the possibility of their becoming conservative as a result of the agrarian reform—would have only reinforced this process and increased the beneficiaries' resistance to government-sponsored social change.

Another pattern that emerges from a brief perusal of other agrarian reforms is that cooperative production will not thrive unless it receives adequate government attention and resources. Here the case of Mozambique is once again enlightening. Although the Mozambican government called for the establishment of collective production at the same time as it set up the state farm system on the ex-settlers' land, the bulk of its resources were devoted to the latter type of production. The cooperatives that formed were left to languish, while the government focused all of its attention on creating a viable state sector.

Yet that goal had still not been achieved after eight years, when policymakers called for a change in strategy. Moreover, drops in peasant production had occurred and a process of demobilization of the peasantry had begun as a result of the government's neglect of this sector. Because of its limited access to resources, as well as several other factors,[17] a severe economic crisis had enveloped the peasant sector in general and the newly formed cooperatives in particular. This gave rise to a political and ideological crisis within the cooperative sector, as "enthusiasm and goodwill began to be replaced by apathy and cynicism . . . [with the resultant demobilization of the sector] . . . effectively . . . block[ing] the processes of social, political and ideological transformation that the creation of the communal villages had set in motion" (Roesch 1984, 309). A concern for the potentially negative political consequences of this dynamic, combined with the lackluster performance of the state farms, eventually led to the shift in the government's strategy of rural development.

Finally, an additional pattern is readily apparent, which represented a source of problems for the continuing process of social transformation in many of the agrarian reforms I reviewed—the lack of a thoroughgoing restructuring of social relations in the countryside. As a number of social analysts have hypothesized concerning agrarian reforms carried out in capitalist settings, unless a fundamental redistribution of resources—and especially land—is brought about by such reform, the end result will be increased differentiation within the peasantry and the emergence of a new sector of middle and rich peasants that seeks to block further reform. This pattern can be seen in a variety of settings, from Vietnam, to Chile under Allende, to Kerala under the rule of the Communist Party of India (CPI-M).

In the case of Vietnam, the pattern actually had a name, "the middle peasant problem."[18] Due to the fact that the agrarian reform implemented by the government of North Vietnam had left the middle peasantry untouched, the latter was able to strongly influence policymaking toward, and within, the recently formed collectives. Consequently, the middle peasants were able to protect their privileged position relative to the poor peasants. Werner (1984) suggests that this problem was bound to worsen with the revisions of the agrarian reform that were initiated in 1979. That is, the decollectivization process that was embodied in the newly adopted emphases on subcontracting production and relying on the family as the appropriate unit of production would in all likelihood lead to increased differentiation within the peasantry and weaken the bonds between the peasantry and the state. The need to increase production, which had stagnated, and strengthen rural incomes led to this policy shift. But the political ramifications were profound in the sense of their potential for undermining the continuing transformation of Vietnam's countryside.

The cases of Chile and Kerala represent slightly different contexts than those discussed thus far in that the social transformations that were carried out in each were the result of the electoral victory of leftist governments rather than products of revolutionary governments that had gained power through military victories over the center and right. Hence certain limits were set on policymaking in these two cases, due to the continuing presence and legitimacy of some institutions, parties, and/or forces of the opposition (a situation which bears some relation to that arising from the Sandinistas' efforts to maintain a mixed economy and national unity, despite their military victory over the Somoza regime). Yet, a number of the problems that arose in their processes of agrarian reform bear a strong resemblance to the other cases. One particularly salient example of these is the issue of the tensions resulting from the lack of a fundamental restructuring of agrarian social relations.

In Chile, an agrarian reform that had been carried out by the Christian Democratic government of Eduardo Frei during the 1960s set the stage for that undertaken by the socialist government of Salvador Allende. The first of these reforms followed the classic strategy of converting latifundios into somewhat smaller, modernized estates, and providing some land to the peasantry through the formation of *asentamientos,* or rural cooperatives. Those among the peasantry who were benefited were far and away the minority: approximately 6 percent of all rural workers had received land in an asentamiento by the end of the Christian Democratic regime (Kay 1978, 124). Thus within the pool of rural workers and peasants, a privileged minority was formed that would come to act as a block against further reform.

The Allende government attempted to use the previous government's legislation to implement its own agrarian reform, pushing that legislation to its limits in the process. Moreover, it based its strategy of reform on the same groups who had benefited from the Christian Democratic reform, the *asentados,* leaving unincorporated the more proletarianized sectors of the peasantry. Often when these latter sectors engaged in *tomas* (land takeovers) on the larger estates, they were opposed by the Allende government on grounds of their illegality and the delicacy of the political balance of forces. What eventually occurred was a demobilization of the more radicalized sectors of the rural workers and peasantry and a blossoming of conservativism among the few who did receive land. In the face of an increasingly hostile rural bourgeoisie, the Allende government failed to take advantage of that part of the peasantry that might have been capable of pushing the reform far enough so that those opposed to it would have been prevented from having a firm base from which to participate in the counterrevolution.

In the case of Kerala, the agrarian reform promoted by the CPI-M proved to be only partial in nature.[19] The reform succeeded in largely eliminating the productive base of the landlord class by turning over its vast holdings to those who had previously been its tenants. In the process, it improved the standard of living of this new middle peasantry. But the rural workers who had formerly assisted these same tenants in tilling their rented fields did not receive any part of the benefits derived from the reform. Instead, they remained landless workers. An antagonistic relationship developed between these two sectors, as the former tenants opposed having to pay the cost of better conditions for the workers, despite the fortification of their own economic position.

What the CPI-M's agrarian reform did was to create a middle peasantry that sought to resist further reform, in the interest of maintaining its recently acquired privilege. At the same time, the CPI-M ceased its mobilizational activities in the countryside following the ouster of the landlord class, thereby undermining the chances for rural workers to push for a widening of the reform. The end result was the continued existence of social tension in rural areas, which was clearly manifested in reduced productivity and ongoing labor conflicts.

This brief review of several agrarian reform processes that have been carried out in the Third World illustrates the problem-laden nature of such efforts. Each one of these reforms attempted, in varying degrees, to transform the relations of production in agriculture, to improve the standard of living of the rural poor, and to introduce a more balanced model of development in the agrarian sector of the economy. As we have seen, that process was partially conditioned by the previously existing productive structure. But even beyond that, a few dilemmas seemed to arise, almost inevitably, for the regimes responsible for implementing agrarian reform. These dilemmas included the problem of how to secure sufficient participation on the part of those whom the reform was supposed to benefit, as state farms appeared incapable of doing this as well as involuntary formation of cooperatives proved to be counterproductive, and the fact that anything less than fundamental restructuring of rural social relations eventually worked to undermine further progress toward socialist-oriented social transformation. These problems certainly find a resonance in my two case studies from Nicaragua. At the same time, the Nicaraguan cases add nuances to these general patterns because of their having been carried out simultaneously within the same overall context of social change. Thus the findings they generated confirm and extend the principal lessons we can draw from comparative analysis of agrarian reform in the Third World.

The Relevance of the Nicaraguan Agrarian Reform for Theoretical Debates on Development and Peasant Politics

Analysis of the political impact of the Nicaraguan agrarian reform, as seen through the lenses of the Los Patios and Plan Masaya projects, offers a number of important insights for theorizing about development and peasant politics. More specifically, the fact that the reform produced contrasting results through the two projects provides an ideal opportunity for reflection on existing theories in these fields and assessment of the need for their "reconstruction" or simple extension. The following discussion will suggest some of the contributions that these two case studies can make to our theoretical understanding of development and the role of the peasantry within it.

As described in chapter 1, one of the leading theorists on the topic of the relationship between politics and development, Samuel Huntington (1965) had argued that democracy represented an obstacle for economic development in the Third World. This dynamic was articulated through the popular mobilization that inevitably emerged within democracy. Popular mobilizing would give voice to a degree of demand that the government would not be able to contain. As Third World countries progressed in their level of economic development, demands and political mobilization expanded commensurably, eventually leading to an excess of both. The government's very stability would be challenged, as would be ongoing economic development.

It is my contention that our review of "transformation and development" in Nicaragua reveals this thesis to be severely flawed. In fact, my case studies point in precisely the opposite direction with regard to the relationship between mobilization and development in the context of the transition to socialism. That is to say, they highlight the importance of popular participation in implementing a socialist model of development. This is particularly the case where an effort is made for the process of change and for the newly established regime to be democratic in nature. In so doing, my case studies complement findings from elsewhere in the Third World where agrarian reform has been part of a larger process of social transformation.

Before going on to argue the logic of my assertions, perhaps it would be useful to very briefly examine exactly what is meant by the concept of "a democratic transition to socialism." According to Lowy (1986, 264, emphasis in original), democracy and socialism are integrally related: "Democracy is not a problem of 'political form' or institutional 'superstructure': it is the *very content* of socialism as a social formation in which . . . the people, effectively exercise power and democratically determine the purpose of production, the distribution of the means of production, and the allocation of the product." In order for socialism to be achieved, democracy must be created simultaneously. In essence, whereas Huntington (1965) considered democracy to be a problem for development, Lowy posits that without it, there can be no truly socialist model of development.

But what exactly does democracy consist of within socialism? In the Nicaraguan context it was supposed to consist of a number of things. For the Sandinistas, democracy was defined as "participation by the people in political, economic, social, and cultural affairs. The more the people take part in all of these areas, the more democracy there will be. It is important to say something once and for all, democracy neither begins nor ends with elections. It is a myth to try and reduce it to this" (*Barricada* 1980, 6). Thus democracy would include representative forms of governing, which would be facilitated by the holding of elections, but it was also to extend much further than that in terms of its economic and participatory aspects.[20] In fact, "democracy begins in the economic order, when social inequalities begin to diminish, when the workers and the peasants improve their standard of living . . . in a more advanced stage, democracy means the participation of the workers in the running of factories, farms, cooperatives and cultural centers. In synthesis, democracy implies the involvement of the masses in all aspects of social life."

On the one hand, the economic aspect within this conception called for a redistribution of productive resources, such as that which occurred through the agrarian reform. On the other hand, the participatory aspect was principally promoted through the activities of the mass organizations. That is, the mass organizations were supposed to represent all sectors of the population on an ongoing basis—even in the several-year periods between the holding of elections—and to ensure their participation in the making of decisions that affected their daily lives. Both the perennial nature of these organizations and the fact that they were especially geared to incorporate the popular sectors of Nicaraguan society were what distinguished them from traditional political parties and made their existence so crucial for social transformation there.

At a more concrete level, the mass organizations, as well as the various other organizational forms utilized by the population to participate in the process of social change, were essential for several additional reasons. First, they facilitated the achievement of development-oriented objectives that would have otherwise been very difficult to realize. For example, in the case of rural and agricultural development, the formation of cooperatives made it possible to raise the level of the productive forces through, among other means, the mechanization of several stages of the production process. Given the prevailing scarcity of resources, it would not have been practical to mechanize the production of the multitude of individual farms that would have been created by a redistribution of land to an unorganized beneficiary population. The redistribution of land itself would have proved to be a much more time-consuming and costly process if all of the recipients had been individuals, thereby making it much less feasible. In sum, the population's organization opened the way to development, in spite of tremendous resource scarcity.

It is also my contention that the organization of the population is not only possible but actually necessary during the transition to socialism—for political reasons. Instead of generating instability for the new regime, the population's participatory mobilization is crucial for its continuing existence. The Nicaraguan case illustrates this point quite clearly. In the face of a worsening economic situation and growing class polarization (as expressed by the Contra war and various types of civic opposition), only the incorporation of the popular sectors in the process of change would have made it possible for the Sandinista regime to remain in power. Yet by 1990, most of those in the popular sectors had already been demobilized for five to six years and their participation in decisionmaking had increasingly become restricted to periodic elections, thereby dramatically reducing their identification with the regime. Moreover, their lives had become totally overshadowed by the multiple problems confronting the society. This combination of factors resulted in their support for the Sandinistas being undermined. Ultimately, it was solely in those "pockets" of the population that remained organized—such as in the cooperatives formed by Plan Masaya beneficiaries, as well as in their participation in UNAG—that the social project the FSLN represented still found a resonance.

In sum, over time it will become increasingly difficult for a socialist-oriented regime to maintain its legitimacy without the active engagement of the greater part of the population in the process of social transformation.[21] This dynamic diverges sharply from Huntington's (1965) hypothesis, betraying the fundamental weakness within it. To give Huntington some credit, his thesis would appear to be quite reasonable in the context of a regime that does not claim nor intend to represent the interests of the majority. In this type of situation—one which characterizes most of the capitalist states of the Third World—popular mobilization for redistributive justice would indeed constitute a serious threat. But where the regime is concerned with and gives priority to meeting the needs of the majority and attempts to function in a democratic fashion, its continuing existence is contingent upon the genuine, ongoing participation of the popular sectors in determining the course of change the society is to undergo.

In addition to speaking to the literature on the politics of development, my findings from the Nicaraguan agrarian reform also suggest some important insights for theoretical discussion about peasant politics and about agrarian reform and agricultural development. At the core of these discussions lies the major question of what role the peasantry is capable of playing in agricultural transformation and development.

The first issue on which my findings shed light is that of which sector of the peasantry is more likely to engage in revolutionary organizing activities. Historically, a debate has raged as to whether the middle or poor peasantry has greater potential in this regard. According to the "middle peasantry" theorists (cf. Wolf 1969, Migdal 1974, and Alavi 1965), this fraction has more revolutionary potential than its poorer counterparts because of its relative economic independence, which makes it less subject to pressures from the rich peasantry and rural bourgeoisie. Additionally, it is capable of offering more to the struggle in the way of tactical resources and experiences more of a genuine threat of loss in the face of the spread of agricultural capitalism than those who have nothing to lose. In contrast, many theorists argue that the middle peasantry will be less inclined to engage in revolutionary activities than poor peasants precisely because it does have something to lose. That is to say, it has a stake in the status quo. Rather it is the poor peasantry, who already has experience in working with and relying on others and has virtually nothing to lose, to whom revolutionary organizers should turn (e.g. Lenin 1966, Paige 1975, Saul 1974, and Wickham-Crowley 1989).

A comparison of the social origins of Los Patios's and Plan Masaya's beneficiary populations and of their political positions leads me to concur with the school of thought that sees the poor peasantry as potentially the more revolutionary subject. But it also suggests that the scope of this thesis should be extended beyond the stage of the struggle to overthrow the old regime to posit the relatively greater importance of this fraction of the peasantry in terms of assisting in the formation and consolidation of the new regime. In addition to the arguments set forth by the "poor peasant" thesis, I would assert that it is the poorest of the peasantry, who have become partially or largely proletarianized, who have the most to gain from a thorough restructuring of the agrarian productive structure. Furthermore, it is the poor peasants who least identify with, and will feel the least threatened by the elimination of, the large landholding class through a serious process of agrarian reform.

Another area of theorizing about the peasantry speaks of the conservatizing tendency that often affects those who are benefited by agrarian reform within a capitalist setting (cf. de Janvry 1981, Grindle 1986, and Feder 1970). That is, where only a minority of the peasantry is benefited by reform, and their inclusion within it does not entail major modifications in the prevailing land tenure system, it has been common to find that this population shifts its concerns from demanding—and, perhaps, organizing for—agrarian reform, to being anxious to maintain the new status quo.[22]

In the areas in which the Los Patios agrarian reform project was implemented, and especially in La Concepción where it was initiated, land redistribution was relatively limited and the project itself did not rely fundamentally on this policy mechanism. Thus, although these areas were subject to other kinds of redistribution—such as that of social services—the project inadvertently replicated the strategy of targeting a limited population to receive benefits without introducing any mediating factors that might have ameliorated the common tendency for it to become more conservative and eventually even oppose further change. Ultimately, then, this project came to embody the very dynamic that capitalist regimes have sought as a way of quelling rural unrest.

My findings from Nicaragua also suggest, however, that there is a means by which this dynamic can be ameliorated. That means is through the organization of collective relations of production. Prior to explicating the mechanisms that make this possible, a qualifier for this assertion seems to be in order. Lessons from agrarian reform elsewhere suggest that unless this process of collectivization is voluntary in nature, it has little potential for incorporating the beneficiaries into the larger project of social change.

Interestingly, my two case studies also point to the poorer peasantry as that which will be the most amenable to engaging in collective production relations. As the case of Los Patios demonstrated, its members—who were not among the poorest peasants in the area—were largely unwilling to move beyond participation in credit and service cooperatives to work together in fully collectivized production. As long as they were able to sustain themselves on their own—which the project had made possible—they were not inclined to join a cooperative. Thus they effectively remained individual farmers with the consciousness of small-scale capitalist producers.

In contrast, Plan Masaya beneficiaries showed a greater disposition to experiment with collectivized farming. The vast majority of these campesinos were notably poorer than Los Patios participants and represented a much more proletarianized sector of the rural population. Hence this case further confirms the hypothesis that the poor peasantry have the greatest potential within the peasantry to become active participants in social transformation.

But exactly how does the collectivization of production relations ameliorate the potential for conservatization within an agrarian reform beneficiary population? Several mechanisms work together to make this possible. First, the fact that beneficiaries come together to work as a group makes economic advancement feasible where it otherwise would not be. As argued above, it would be much more costly, if not totally untenable, to provide land, credit, and technical improvements to an unorganized beneficiary population. Such economic advancement would demonstrate, in a tangible way, the government's prioritization of this population over those who previously had privileged access to productive resources. Theoretically speaking, the likely economic gains from having access to these resources would be the same for cooperative members and individual reform beneficiaries. But their collective receipt would inhibit the emergence of an individual farmer consciousness within the cooperative membership.

At the same time, receiving the redistributed resources as a group and utilizing them as a group would serve to reinforce their members' consciousness as to the interests they shared in common. In addition, the fact that in order for redistribution to occur, these resources—especially land—would have had to be taken out of the hands of large-scale capitalist producers would make clear the distinction that exists between the cooperative members' interests and those of the rural bourgeoisie. Just as engaging in wage labor can foster a sense of interdependence among workers and of sharing a similar status vis-à-vis the owners of the means of production (cf. Paige 1975), collective production following agrarian reform can do the same, with the exception that the point of opposition would now be with the former owners of the means of production (and other large growers). Thus in contrast to such individual agrarian reform beneficiaries as those who participated in Los Patios, whose identification with the larger landholders would tend to increase with their improved economic security (especially in relation to the poorer peasants), it was significantly more probable that collectivized agrarian reform beneficiaries would experience a growing identification with others in their own position and more generally with their own class.

Finally, collective production relations would serve to actively incorporate those who participated in them into the overall process of social transformation. The case of Plan Masaya illustrates this point in that by turning over a massive area of land to its beneficiaries—most of whom were organized in cooperatives—they took part in rupturing the previously existing structure of production relations. This was a major step in the process of social transformation. Furthermore, given that their new relations of production were more socially oriented—in terms of working as a group and in terms of producing for the larger society, not just their own subsistence—this too brought them into the process of social change. Lastly, the cooperatives' close relationship with UNAG meant that through this organization they had an open channel to those making policies that affected their daily lives.

Conclusion

Several conclusions can be drawn from all of the foregoing. The most significant of these is that, in a society characterized by the continuing existence of a large peasant sector, the peasantry can indeed be brought into the process of social transformation and development. This conclusion is of considerable importance for those attempting to promote such far-reaching change, as well as for analysts of social change.

There are, however, at least a few conditions under which the peasantry's incorporation must take place, if its potential for contributing to that process is to be realized. The first of these conditions is that of its becoming the beneficiary of a comprehensive redistribution of agricultural resources. Such a redistribution will assist in counterbalancing any tendency that might exist for a renewed process of social differentiation to result from agrarian reform. It will also help to clarify to the peasantry which sector's interests the state represents. That is, the "popular" orientation of the social project being promoted by the government should become readily apparent as a consequence of this kind of reform.

A second condition for the successful incorporation of the peasantry into the attempt to push forth the transition to a socialist model of development is the organization of its active participation in that process. An ideal means for achieving such participation is through the collective organization of the production they take on with the resources they receive through the agrarian reform. This type of organization will help to prevent the emergence of an individual capitalist farmer outlook. At the same time, it will actually facilitate a greater class and social consciousness. Moreover, it will make feasible a raising of the forces of production, thereby contributing to the overall process of development in a way that would otherwise be largely impossible. Finally, given the *relatively* permanent character of collective production relations, they will aid in assuring that the involvement of this sector of the population in the transformation and development effort will be ongoing in nature.

The contrasting political impacts of the Los Patios and Plan Masaya projects eloquently illustrate how crucial participation is in this endeavor. They also suggest the pitfalls and the potential inherent in agrarian reform as a vehicle for bringing about fundamental change in the countryside. Perhaps the most important lesson they offer for those concerned with promoting development—wherein development means not only a modernization of the productive forces and expansions in production, but also includes an improved standard of living for the poor (i.e., a greater degree of social justice)—is that agrarian reform must take into account the perspective of those whose lives it affects if they are to support it. Only in this way will it be possible to achieve the illusive "popular hegemony" that must of necessity underlie the pursuit of a democratic transition to socialism.

A Brief Discussion of Methodology

A number of complementary research methods were employed in conducting the study for this book. My team of research assistants and I initiated the fieldwork with extensive interviews with representatives from the key institutions and organizations involved in planning and implementing the agrarian reform projects that were the focus of the study, and we returned to explore unanswered questions with these officials throughout the period during which the research was being conducted. We interviewed various representatives from the national, regional, and local offices of MIDINRA, BND, UNAG, and FSLN. Our purpose in carrying out these interviews was to understand the objectives that lay behind each project's implementation; projects' relationship with the larger, regional development strategy; the policy instruments that were employed in their development; and the perceived successes and failures of the projects. These officials also provided the information necessary for the preparation of a sample of each project's beneficiary population, which we employed in a survey of those populations.

The survey of Los Patios beneficiaries was carried out between February and June 1988. The Plan Masaya beneficiary population was surveyed between November 1988 and February 1989. The total number of people included in the two surveys was 121 (divided almost evenly between the project populations).

I considered approximately 120 interviews an adequate total number so as to be able to identify socioeconomic patterns within each project's respective population. This figure was also what I considered to represent the limit of feasibility given the resources available. The following discussion suggests some of the factors that set this limit.

The projects' beneficiary populations lived in hamlets (and on individual farms) that were scattered throughout the area of influence of each project. Even more important, the projects were characterized by their wide geographic dispersion—the municipalities where Los Patios was implemented covered an area of 696 square kilometers, and for Plan Masaya, 492 square kilometers. Because most of the communities in the projects' areas of influence were connected by dirt roads, the distances within these areas represented a more serious challenge than would have been the case if they had been paved. Moreover, a fair number of the beneficiaries' homes were situated on or near roads that could only be driven on during the dry season, necessitating arriving on foot to talk with them if their part of the sample coincided with the rainy season.

In addition, because the resource base of the informants was extremely limited, and because of the lack of infrastructural development and services in the areas in which they lived, none of our informants had telephones. This meant that the only way of communicating with them was to catch them at home (and neither catching them at home nor finding their homes was always easy) and to arrange a suitable time to go back and interview them.

Throughout the initial phase of this project, during which the surveys were implemented, I had an average of three to four research assistants working with me. Given our overall number, it proved impractical to contemplate living in the area under study. This was especially the case because the sector of rural society we had chosen to study, the minifundistas, simply didn't have the resources to "take us in" and have us live with them. The other option—staying with officials or representatives of the various organizations working in these areas—seemed far from ideal, as we did not want to be perceived as working for or with them. Thus, we traveled to and from our "work sites" on virtually a daily basis in the one vehicle that we had at our disposal. Needless to say, all of these factors contributed to the decision that 120 interviews (in addition to an introductory interview in each cooperative) was a reasonable and manageable number to undertake.

The sample for the Los Patios survey was divided between the two jurisdictional areas where the project was implemented (see note 2 of the introduction): Diriomo (10 informants) and San Marcos-Masatepe (51 informants). The number of cases assigned to each reflected their relative weight in the project in terms of the number of producers it benefited. Once this basic division was made, the cases were selected as follows:

Diriomo. Because all of the project's beneficiaries in this area were individual producers, this part of the sample was composed entirely of individual farmers. Eight of the informants were project participants, with the remaining two being control cases who had no relationship with it. Within the former group, three size divisions were denoted, according to the number of manzanas each farmer had planted with the project's promotional crops. The sample for Diriomo included:

   I. Beneficiaries
     1 case: less than 3 manzanas
     2 cases: between 3 and 5 manzanas
     5 cases: more than 5 manzanas

II. Control
    2 cases

The number of cases allotted to each category reflected their weight within the beneficiary population. The cases included in each category were randomly selected from MIDINRA's official beneficiary list.

San Marcos-Masatepe. Given that the project's participants in this area were drawn from the cooperative and individual producer sectors, the sample was composed of informants from both, with their numbers reflecting the weight of each sector in the beneficiary population. The sample for this area included:

I. Cooperative sector
    Cooperatives that remained in the project once having entered it
        1 case: less than 3 manzanas
        4 cases: between 3 and 15 manzanas
        23 cases: more than 15 manzanas
    Cooperatives that left the project once having entered it
        4 cases

Both the cooperatives that were included, and the specific informants within each cooperative, were selected at random from the official lists for the respective populations. The same procedure was applied with the individual producers and the control cases.

II. Individual producers
    6 cases: less than 1 manzana
    1 case: 1 manzana
    1 case: more than 1 manzana

III. Control cases
    3 cases: individual producers
    3 cases: cooperative members
    5 cases: traditional citrus farmers

This last group was included at the request of the local MIDINRA office. Those selected were chosen at random from MIDINRA's list of traditional growers.

The survey of Plan Masaya beneficiaries included 60 informants. The sample for this survey was divided between the two jurisdictional areas where the project was implemented (see note 2 in the introduction): Diriomo (with 9 informants) and Masaya (with 51 informants). The number of cases assigned to each area reflected their relative weight in the project (i.e. the area ceded to beneficiaries). Of those cases in Masaya, 27 were selected from the official lists of participants in both the Plan Masaya and PATD projects; 14 were only beneficiaries of Plan Masaya; three were only beneficiaries of PATD; and seven were control cases who had no relationship with either project. Of those cases in Diriomo, eight were beneficiaries of Plan Masaya and one was a control case. (No distinction was made between Plan Masaya and PATD beneficiaries in Diriomo because all of the cooperatives formed there through Plan Masaya were included in MIDINRA's zonal management of PATD.) The number of cases in each one of these categories was determined according to their relative weight within the total beneficiary population. The selection was further divided by the form of social organization defining their agricultural production. The final breakdown was as follows:

Diriomo
    4 cases: CCS cooperatives
    4 cases: CAS cooperatives
    1 control case: CAS cooperative
Masaya
  I. Plan Masaya/PATD
     8 cases: CCS cooperatives
    19 cases: CAS cooperatives
  II. Plan Masaya
    5 cases: CCS cooperatives
    7 cases: CAS cooperatives
    2 cases: individuals
  III. PATD
    3 cases: CAS cooperatives
    1 case: individual
  IV. Control
    3 cases: CAS cooperatives
    2 cases: CCS cooperatives
    1 case: individual

Random sampling was used to select the cooperatives that were included, and to the individual informants within each cooperative, once the categories were established.

In order to gain access to the cooperatives included in both surveys and to establish the verifiability of the information obtained, an initial interview was also conducted with one or more members of the executive junta of each cooperative prior to pursuing formal interviews with their members. The information sought in this preliminary interview included the history of the cooperative, how it was organized, what it produced, its acreage, its commercialization patterns, and so forth.

In addition, I conducted in-depth, follow-up interviews with 20 percent of the original sample population from each project between May and August 1990, several months after the 1990 elections. These were succeeded by further in-depth interviews with half of this subsample in 1991, 1992, and 1993. The number of follow-up interviews reflected what I considered to be a sufficiently large sample to provide representation with regard to the original survey populations, as well as to be a manageable size given the constraints mentioned above and the fact that during this phase of the project I was working alone.

Those included in the initial follow-up interviews were selected on the basis of several criteria. The first of these criteria arose from the kind of information that I sought to gather from them—that is, their opinion of the Sandinista government, how they voted in the 1990 elections, what their impression was thus far of the Chamorro government, and what they thought could be expected of the Chamorro government in terms of policymaking. The fact that the earlier survey had not addressed political attitudes and that the issues I hoped to discuss with them were somewhat delicate in nature meant that my selection of informants had to take into consideration which of them would feel comfortable talking about these topics with me. I began composing my list of potential interviewees by including those of our initial informants who I knew would remember me, either because I had been the one to interview them at the time of the survey or because I had spoken with them at length and developed a rapport with them when I had set up the interviews with them for my research assistants. I was convinced that if they had had no significant prior interaction with me they would be reluctant to talk about politics with me. Other criteria I took into account in composing my list of potential interviewees were the goals of covering as wide a geographical area as possible (in the projects' areas of influence) and including cases that represented the gamut of organizational forms that each project had incorporated.

The questions I asked them were designed to indirectly address each of the above-mentioned issues. Given the fiasco of the pre-election polls leading up to the 1990 elections, and my own extensive experience in interviewing the Nicaraguan peasantry, I was certain that direct questions would not illicit reliable responses. Consequently, I prepared a set of questions (which I elongated if the informant proved to be forthcoming), the responses to which would indicate his/her political inclinations.

A number of the questions addressed issues that were being hotly debated at that moment, whereas others were more broad-ranging in nature. Some of the topics addressed were: How did they view the current economic situation? How were prices—both for what they bought and what they sold—at the present time? How did prices compare with what they had been in the past? Had they taken out agricultural credit in 1990? Why or why not? How did they view the new government's credit policies? What did they think of the much talked about, but yet to be released, new currency—the "Córdoba Oro"? (The Chamorro government made the new currency the centerpiece of its early economic model, and it was held out as the symbol of what would save the Nicaraguan economy.) What kinds of services had they received from the previous government for their agricultural production? And now? How did s/he think the new (local) mayor was doing or would do? What projects had the mayor promised the community while still a candidate for office? How was his/her cooperative functioning? Had there been any changes in its functioning in the previous few months? (At this point, many informants spoke of tensions within their cooperatives stemming from political differences among members, and they often mentioned how the membership had voted.) How did s/he see the current situation of small producers? What did s/he think were the reasons that the FSLN lost the elections? How was the ambiance in their community at that moment? (There were invasions of cooperatives taking place in some of these communities—typically by UNO activists, some of whom were promised land during the campaign.) Did they think the economic and political situation was likely to improve? Had all of the parties campaigned in their communities? What were their campaigns like?

I also used the interviews to clarify any questions that might have arisen in analyzing their responses to the initial survey. In the subsequent interviews I returned to talk with those informants who had been forthcoming during the first follow-up interview (because they were clearly more comfortable talking with me about these kinds of issues). The second criterion used in their selection (which was as important as the first) was to ensure that they represented a variety of political perspectives and that the weight of their political inclinations was roughly the same as what it had been in the larger subsample for each project informant whom I had interviewed in 1990. The questions in these later interviews were designed to provide a sense of how the informants' own production was being affected by the Chamorro government's economic policies and if this had influenced their views of the new government; I also wanted to know how their cooperatives were functioning in the new economic and political environment and what impact this had on their political thinking and to hear how they felt about the overall political and economic situation and what prospects existed for small farmers, and the country as a whole, in the near future.

Finally, I undertook an analysis of the 1990 electoral data for the projects' areas of influence which evaluated precinct-level vote counts. This analysis complemented the information obtained in the follow-up interviews.

The initial stages of this study (1986–89) were carried out under the auspices of the two institutions with which I was affiliated at the time: the

Nicaraguan Food Program, which formed part of MIDINRA, and the UCA in Managua. The Food Program affiliation greatly facilitated the team's access to the network of institutions related to the Los Patios and Plan Masaya projects, while the UCA affiliation was crucial in gaining the trust of the peasants who were interviewed. The second part of the study (1990–93) was conducted while I was a President's Post-Doctoral Fellow and a member of the faculty at the University of California.

Notes

Introduction

1. It should be noted here that some analysts would disagree with the inclusion of Nicaragua, for the period of time that the Sandinistas were in power, in the category of countries that were "in transition to socialism." Vilas (1986b, 214e, emphasis in original) and Harris (1992, 19) especially fit into this camp, instead characterizing it respectively as having been "entangled in a difficult *transition to development*" or a "popular revolutionary struggle for national liberation." Luciak (1995, 3–6), who is somewhat less rigid in his definition of the term, describes Sandinista Nicaragua as having been a social formation in transition with an articulated mode of production.

Yet a number of others, including myself, choose to portray the process of social transformation that was set into motion upon the overthrow of the Somoza regime as having been the initiation of the transition to socialism (see, for example, Fagen et al. 1986, Stahler-Sholk 1990, and Ruckwarger 1988). Fagen et al. (1986, 10) argue that efforts to transform the model of accumulation to one of a socialist nature imply that "the logic of capital (the profit motive) must be subordinated to and eventually replaced by a socially determined rationality of production and distribution." They add that "the basic goals of this transformation are: (1) production and distribution oriented toward meeting the basic needs of the majority of the population; (2) an ending of class, gender, racial, ethnic, and other forms of privilege in access to 'valued goods' such as income, culture, justice, and recreation; and (3) the reconstitution of state-society relations such that the 'popular classes' have a high degree of participation in determining public policy at all levels."

In another study of socialist transformation in the Third World, G. White (1983, 1, my emphasis), posits that socialist societies "have broken . . . the autonomous power of private capital over politics, production and distribution, abrogated the dominance of the law of value in its capitalist form, and embarked upon a development path which does not rely on the dynamic of private ownership and entrepreneurship . . . [and] they have brought about (*or are bringing about*) certain fundamental transformations—in the economic, political and social realms—which reflect the long-standing aspirations of revolutionary socialist movements everywhere." Based on these two definitions, I believe that it is possible to conclude that Nicaragua, under the Sandinista regime, had initiated the transition to socialism. Although it was far from having become a socialist society, the process of societal change that began in 1979 *was* oriented toward eventually achieving this state.

2. The Los Patios project incorporated agricultural producers from the following municipalities: San Marcos, Diriamba, Masatepe, Nandasmo, Niquinohomo, La Concepción, Diriomo, San Juan del Oriente, and Diriá (see map 4). All of these municipalities are located in the same plateau region. However, they fall into three governmental jurisdictions using the traditional department boundaries referred to in some of the data cited in the text. They are also part of the same Region IV, according to a jurisdictional system set up by the Sandinista government in 1982 for the purpose of development planning. (Region IV includes the departments of Carazo, Masaya, Granada, and Rivas.) In the interest of simplicity, these municipalities will be treated as a group and referred to as the Carazo plateau region.

In the Masaya plain area the municipalities affected by Plan Masaya were Masaya, Nindirí, and Tisma (see map 4). In Diriomo, the municipalities of Diriomo, Diriá, Catarina, Niquinohomo, and San Juan del Oriente were included in this project (see map 4).

3. In recent years it has been argued that the class categories that have traditionally been used to define the rural class structure have not taken into account all of the factors that determine one's class location in the countryside (see Enríquez 1991, especially the appendix, for a summary of these arguments vis-à-vis the Nicaraguan case). The key indicator that had been used to define producer size (or one's class location) through the early 1980s was the size of one's land holdings (or farm size). Since that time, the incorporation of other factors into this definition has been suggested, such as regional differences (i.e., where the land is located) that take into consideration land quality, abundance of land, infrastructural development in the area, and so forth (e.g. Gariazzo 1984). Others have suggested that the social relations of production should also be analyzed in this equation. These are reflected in employment of paid workers on the farm and reliance on paid labor to supplement farm-earned income by the landowner (e.g., Zalkin 1988).

A number of these indicators will be utilized herein so as to specify, as much as possible, the type of producer being studied. With regard to the general description of the region on which attention will be focused, the size of landholdings and the region in which they are located will be taken into account. This will permit us to gain an understanding of the region's historical development, through an analysis of existing census data from 1952, 1963, and 1973. In the chapters describing my case studies (chapters 3–6), the employment patterns of the farm owner, which the study survey provides, will also be considered so as to be able to further distinguish producer size even within the general category of minifundista.

For the first level of analysis, the size categories employed in the 1952 census will be relied upon. These categories specify farm sizes for the central and southern Pacific regions as follows: minifundios, 1–5 *manzanas* (1 manzana = 0.7 hectares = 1.75 acres); small farms, 6–10 manzanas; medium farms, 11–50 manzanas; large farms, 51–500 manzanas; latifundios, 501 or more manzanas.

It should be noted that each of these size categories designates significantly smaller holdings than was the norm for the same categories in other regions of the country, thereby pointing to the relatively high value of land in the region under study. This high land value was due to the region's level of infrastructural development, proximity to the country's principal port and major urban markets, high land fertility, and comparative land scarcity.

4. This refers to the follow-up interviews that are described at greater length in the Brief Discussion of Methodology.

5. For lengthier discussions of the reasons for the FSLN's loss of the elections among the country's population as a whole see Conroy (1990); Spence (1990); Vickers (1990); Vilas (1990); Oquist (1990); and Zalkin (1990).

Chapter 1: The Theoretical Debates Concerning the Impact of Development on Politics

1. Burawoy (1991) argues convincingly that case studies have significant heuristic value in the effort to "reconstruct social theories," especially in circumstances in which they yield results that represent anomalies in what a specific theory leads one to expect in a given situation. Herring (n.d.) makes a similar assertion. Thus, both of the puzzles that are the focus of this study, but particularly the latter, point to the need to refine the relevant bodies of theory so that they are capable of illuminating the dynamics that underlie these puzzles.

2. Rather than present an overview of the entire field of development theory or that tradition addressing peasant politics, I have opted instead to review only those works which bring light to bear on the issues raised by this study of Nicaragua.

3. See further Booth (1985) and Serra (1985 and 1989).

4. See also Luciak (1988).

5. From the beginning, most of these scholarly works were concerned with particular cases of socialist development, e.g. Fagen (1969), Huberman and Sweezy (1969), Cliff and Saul (1972), and Bitar (1979), a phenomenon that continues to characterize the bulk of work on the topic.

6. For additional, insightful analyses of the dilemmas of the transition to socialism see White et al. (1983), *Journal of Development Studies* (1985), and *World Development* (1981).

7. See also Migdal (1974). It should be noted here that Wolf (1969) also argues that poor peasants are potential converts to the revolutionary cause if they can rely on an external force that challenges the powers that be *or* if they are located outside the physical domain of the powerful.

8. The goals to which Wolf's and Alavi's middle peasantry aspire find an echo in the writings of James Scott (see especially 1976 and 1977), who also emphasizes the desperate need of the peasantry to regain the ground it has lost to agricultural capitalism.

9. This point was also highlighted by Lenin (1966) in looking at the Russian revolution, and more recently by Herring n.d. in analyzing agrarian policies in Kerala, India.

10. See also Herring n.d.

11. This thesis is corroborated by Wickham-Crowley (1989 and 1992) in a recent study of Latin American guerrilla movements. Wickham-Crowley, however, argues that the category of receptive sectors should be further extended to also include squatters.

12. Herring n.d. found this same dynamic to have occurred among the former tenants who became small landholders in Kerala's agrarian reform.

13. Although coming from a very different theoretical tradition, one quite opposed

to that of Huntington in many respects, Herring (n.d., see especially chapter 5) reached this same conclusion based on the experience of the agrarian reform process in Kerala under the Communist Party of India.

14. In addition to those whose work is discussed in chapter 7, over the past ten years a number of studies have been published that apply the "everyday forms of resistance" framework—which had been developed to explain peasant resistance to the spread of capitalism (see especially Scott 1985)—to countries where a socialist revolution is under way (cf. Colburn 1986a and 1989, and Pelzer White 1986). The argument made by the originator of this framework, James Scott, is that the new state that is brought to power by a revolutionary movement will, in all likelihood, be more coercive and hegemonic than its predecessor. Consequently, peasant resistance to socialist regimes is virtually inevitable.

15. It was almost inevitable that conflicts would arise during the process of social transformation that was initiated in 1979, given the breadth of the forces that signed on to the platform of the provisional government less than a month before Somoza was overthrown. Two political priorities, that of national unity and that of popular hegemony, were supposed to orient the Sandinista government's policymaking agenda. What ensued over the following ten years was a shifting back and forth between these two emphases, thereby implying responding to the needs of first one sector and then the other. For more in-depth discussions of this issue see Vilas (1986b), Luciak (1987), and Coraggio (1986).

16. The productive base of these two sectors was initially constituted by the properties confiscated from Somoza and his close associates. Shortly after the confiscation of these properties, the banking system, foreign marketing companies, and foreign-owned mines were nationalized. They were then brought into the fold of the state sector, as Areas of People's Property (APP). Somewhat later, several other laws brought about an increase in the size of the APP; a law stipulating that those who had been out of the country for a specified length of time, or who were engaged in decapitalization, could have their properties confiscated. Finally, this area was later augmented by the agrarian reform laws of 1981 and 1986.

17. Two distinct analyses of the nature, purpose, and functioning of state enterprises in the agricultural sector can be found in Colburn (1990) and Biondi-Morra (1990).

18. Although the Sandinistas' stated policy was that of giving preferred treatment to the rural poor, which was composed of both workers and peasants, their simultaneous commitment to development of the state sector and national unity (read: cooperation with the bourgeoisie) resulted in dramatic swings in policy being made, with alternating sectors being benefited. See further Deere et al. (1985), Baumeister (1986), Marchetti (1989), and Zalkin (1990).

19. See Enríquez (1991) and Neira (1988) for descriptions of the characteristics of each stage and the logic behind their implementation.

20. One of the better-known English-language analyses of Sandinista agrarian policy during these first two stages is the controversial study by Forrest Colburn (1986). His analysis has drawn strong criticism on a number of counts (cf. Stahler-Sholk [1990b], Gould [1988], and Enríquez [1987]). For other assessments of the initial two stages of the reform see Baumeister (1985), Collins (1985), and Zalkin (1986), among others.

21. Interviews: No. 16, FSLN, Region IV, San Marcos Zonal Office, August 19, 1986; and No.17, MIDINRA, Region IV, Regional Office, September 16, 1986.

22. This approach to agrarian reform fits squarely within the framework of what de Janvry (1981, 224–31) has described as "rural development projects." For de Janvry, rural development projects represent one of the three types of state intervention that have composed agrarian reformism in Latin America. The other two types are agricultural development programs and land reform.

23. Thomas (1974) spoke of the drive to bring production more in line with domestic demand as an "iron law" in the construction of socialism.

24. In contrast to Los Patios, Plan Masaya clearly falls within de Janvry's category of "land reform" (1981, 224–31) as the type of intervention employed by the Nicaraguan state to promote agrarian reform in this area.

25. See also Herring n.d.

26. Herring n.d., in speaking of agrarian transformation more specifically, argues that the mobilization of the popular classes in the countryside was crucial for the relative success of the reforms of the rural social structure that were brought about by the Communist Party of India (CPI-M) in the state of Kerala during the 1960s and early 1970s.

27. The exclusion of almost all of the mass organizations from the National Assembly significantly cut back the role that they might previously have had in the policymaking process. In 1985 the recently elected National Assembly set to work preparing a new constitution for the country. Its ratification in 1987 also highlighted the now-formal nature of the process of institutionalization that had been under way for several years.

28. For more information about the changes experienced by the mass organizations during the 1980s see Vilas (1986a), Stahler-Sholk (1990b), Serra (1988), and Ruckwarger (1987).

29. For example, the implementation of the military draft greatly cut back the role of the local militias, which had been organized under the auspices of the CDS. In addition, the channeling of rationed food supplies through the workplace, which the Ministry of Internal Commerce (MICOIN) facilitated at this time, reduced the involvement of the CDS in providing this basic service.

30. Yet UNAG also cooperated with the government's draft recruitment and with its campaign to organize Defense Brigades, which were composed of cooperative members from around the country who were sent to "the north" (i.e., the central mountain region) to participate in defense-related activities. Even more importantly, however, when the economic reform was implemented in 1988, the organization was largely unable to influence government policymakers to modify it in ways that would reduce its onerousness for UNAG members. Consequently, cooperative members and their families, like the rest of the country's population, had to focus more of their attention on basic survival and less on organizational endeavors that produced questionable results.

31. It also took the initiative in the establishment of a rural provisioning network, the Campesinos Cooperative Enterprise of Agricultural Producers (ECODEPA), which was externally funded and did not have to follow all of MICOIN's dictates.

Chapter 2: How the FSLN Lost the Hearts and Minds of the Peasantry

1. In fact, even the initial measures of the agrarian reform, such as the massive redistribution of credit, the setting of ceilings on land rental prices, etc., contributed significantly to the dramatic labor shortages in the cotton and coffee harvests that characterized the early 1980s (cf. Enríquez [1991]).

2. Peter Marchetti (1989) likens this vision to that of Eugene Preobrazhenski in the early stages of the Russian revolution—a position that Stalin ultimately pursued to an extreme.

3. Marchetti (1989) drew parallels between this second vision of agricultural development and that of Nikolai Bukharin in the 1920s.

4. That is, the real shift in holdings in the 1983–88 period was between the state and peasant sectors—in favor of the latter, with little notable change taking place in the holdings of the medium and large producers during this period (see ibid.).

5. The strength with which the technocrats held onto their vision—even into the late 1980s—can be seen in Cmdt. Wheelock's position regarding the demands of the participants in the First National Assembly of the Cooperative Movement (cf. Hernández Pico [1989]). See also Wheelock Román (1990).

6. The concept of "mixed economy" did refer to other elements of the revolutionary government's model of development, in addition to its class composition. These elements included establishing the state as the center of accumulation (e.g., through its control over the banking system and foreign commerce) and the reorientation of the economy's logic away from one of meeting the needs of a small capitalist class to one of meeting, first and foremost, the needs of the majority of Nicaragua's population. For descriptions of the mixed economy model see, for example, Weeks (1987) and Gorostiaga (1986). Analyses of the manner in which the adoption of a mixed economy conditioned the course of the agrarian reform program can be found in Deere et al. (1985), Luciak (1987), and Paige (1989).

7. See especially Baumeister (1986) and Luciak (1987).

8. Ibid.

9. Moreover, even though the U.S. government made the expected pronouncement that the elections had been a Soviet-style sham (Weisman [1984]) and mounted the so-called MIGs crisis to distract international attention from the results (see Taubman [1984] and Booth [1985]), international observer groups uniformly concluded that the elections had been free and fair. For a few of the many international observer reports that reached this conclusion see LASA (1984), International Human Rights Law Group and the Washington Office on Latin America (1984), Irish Inter-Parliamentary Delegation (1984), and Canadian Church and Human Rights Delegation (1984).

10. See further IHCA (1985a).

11. Numerous opinion polls were carried out prior to the elections, the results of which were split almost evenly between a FSLN victory and an UNO victory. The split poll results largely lined up with the (perceived) political affiliation or inclination of

those conducting them. For various analyses of the polls, see Miller (1991) and Barnes (1992).

Yet, most importantly for present purposes, in the months leading up to the elections the polls were of interest to a relatively select population in Nicaragua: the pollsters, national and international election observers and analysts, and those directing the respective campaigns. For the average Nicaraguan citizen, who did not even have regular access to the principal fora in which the poll results were announced—the country's various newspapers—the polls were far removed from their daily lives. Thus, the results were, indeed, a surprise for most of the country's population.

12. For a more detailed analysis of the rural sector throughout the nation as a whole, see IPADE (1990).

13. See the Brief Discussion on Methodology. It should be noted that several of those interviewed refused to reveal their voting preference, or general political position, to the author. However, most of my informants spoke relatively freely about their political inclinations.

14. For lengthier discussions of Nicaragua's economic crisis and its impact on voting patterns see Conroy (1990), Stahler-Sholk (1990b), and Utting (1991).

15. See CEPAL (1987, 47) and CEPAL (1990, 41) for information about the rate of inflation that characterized Nicaragua throughout the 1980s.

16. Hurricane Joan struck Nicaragua in October 1988. Inflation, which had been brought down to 20 percent (monthly) by August 1988, shot up to over 100 percent (monthly) in the last two months of that year (CEPAL 1990, 42). However, beginning in February and March 1989 the monthly inflation rate was consistently lower than it had been for several years. Yet the economic reform that was begun in February 1988 had not been as successful in stimulating a rapid turnaround of the country's economic decline as had been hoped for, even prior to Hurricane Joan. Moreover, the policies that composed the reform had also resulted in the bulk of the reform's burden being borne by the popular classes. For further discussion of the economic reform see IHCA (1988a and 1988b), Conroy (1990), and Stahler-Sholk (1990b).

17. Several months after the reform was initiated the government slightly modified its position on foodstuff subsidies and began to provide a new, much more restricted food package (known for its contents, arroz, frijoles, and azucar [or rice, beans, and sugar], as the AFA) to some 160,000 public employees (Stahler-Sholk 1990b, 210). This package was intended to serve as a counterbalance for the low salary policy that remained predominant in the public sector.

18. For discussion of the impact of the economic reform on agricultural production see Stahler-Sholk (1990b), Grigsby (1989), Gutiérrez (1989), Spoor (1989b), and Utting (1991).

19. See Spoor (1989a and 1989b) for discussions of the bank's levels of recuperation for its loans before and after the economic reform, taking the inflation rate into account.

20. See further Stahler-Sholk (1990b) and Grigsby (1989).

21. See Stahler-Sholk (1990b) and Utting (1991) in this regard.

22. By early 1987 the sale of basic grains to private intermediaries was legalized after nearly three years of government control over grain purchasing. Yet, once the sale of grains to private buyers was allowed, these intermediaries no longer had to offer prices above those offered by the state because there was no longer any explicit risk in selling to them.

23. See further Hemisphere Initiatives (1989).

24. Widespread rumors that the FSLN would make a surprise announcement of the draft's permanent suspension at their final campaign rally in Managua led many to be disappointed when this did not in fact take place.

25. See LASA (1990), Spence (1990), and Vickers (1990).

26. A system of "mano vuelta" has traditionally functioned in the Nicaraguan countryside. It operates such that one neighbor will work for another for a specified period of time and then the favor will be returned. Typically no payment is involved in this relationship. Thus, it is an ideal solution for those whose cash income is limited, when they are in need of assistance on the farm. Families whose sons were drafted could resort to this system. Yet it implied providing labor services in return, thereby taking time away from work on the farm. The hiring of day laborers was also common, however.

27. Interview no. 1, Plan Masaya beneficiary and CCS member, March 12, 1987.

28. It is important to note here that in the interest of guaranteeing the possibility of making basic grains purchases for even the poorest urban consumers, the producer prices ENABAS set, as well as its sales prices, were below production costs. Thus, for many producers it proved more economically sound to purchase basic grains from the state than to grow them. It was not until the mid-1980s that producer prices began to represent an incentive to producers. Then, with the economic reform in 1988, ENABAS-set prices were once again out of balance with production costs. See Utting (1987, 1988, and 1991), Stahler-Sholk (1990b), and Enríquez (1991) for discussions of the dilemmas that emerged from government efforts to control the marketing of grains.

29. Spoor et al. (1988, 42) cite price differentials of 300 to 600 percent between ENABAS's producer prices and the market price in Managua in early 1986. See also Utting (1991, 37).

30. My research revealed that the CAS sold their produce to ENABAS more than other producer sectors. Their links with the government and the FSLN were closer than the other sectors, so their response to "encouragement" was more consistent.

31. Interview no. 118, June 29, 1990. This name—as well as all of those given for other informants and the locations of their farms—has been changed to protect his identity.

32. For example, interview no. 34, Plan Masaya beneficiary and CAS member, January 13, 1989, and interview no. 55, Plan Masaya beneficiary and CAS member, January 14, 1989.

33. Interview no. 18, June 4, 1990. It is important to note that this cooperative had been transformed from a CCS into a CAS in 1990—i.e., after our initial interview.

34. ENAPER formed part of MICOIN, and PROCOMER was part of MIDINRA.

35. Interview no. 16, FSLN, Region IV, San Marcos zonal office, August 19, 1986, and interview no. 19, MIDINRA, Region IV, San Marcos zonal office, August 23, 1986.

36. For example, interview no. 9, Los Patios beneficiary and CCS Junta member, August 28, 1987, and interview no. 6, Los Patios beneficiary and CCS Junta member, September 25, 1986.

37. Interview no. 28, Los Patios beneficiary and CCS member, June 22, 1990, and interview no. 70, Los Patios beneficiary, June 18, 1990.

38. In my experience in Region IV government production plans did not appear to contradict the interests of the producer population. These producers might have preferred to grow a greater variety of campesino crops in order to meet all of their familial consumption needs. Taking a more distanced perspective, however, it was essential that this prime agricultural land also produce food crops for the general population. Yet in Region II (i.e., León and Chinandega) producers seemed to have reason to complain about the government's frequent shifts in production priorities. Even though these policy shifts may have made economic sense, growers complained about the difficulty of shifting back and forth between crops (interview no. 8, large cotton producer, July 20, 1987.)

39. Serra (1991, 221) argues that a top-down form of treatment of agrarian reform beneficiaries generally characterized the behavior of state officials and technicians and UNAG and FSLN activists. According to Serra: "These actors were transmitters and executors of decisions that were made by higher authorities and the former had to demonstrate their compliance with those decisions or risk loosing their jobs." My own experience suggests that this is true to a certain extent. Yet I also found that at times those "higher authorities" had a much more nuanced and democratic sense of the most appropriate ways of relating to the peasantry (as will be described below), and it was the lower-level activists and officials who resorted to top-down relations.

40. This feeling appears to have been held by the campesinado more generally (cf. Hernández Pico [1989, 69]).

41. Interview no. 45, former CCS member, June 15, 1990.

42. Ibid. (it was quite evident that this issue had contributed to the decision of this beneficiary to leave her CCS), and interview no. 22, Los Patios beneficiary and former CCS member, June 16, 1990.

43. For a discussion of this issue at the national level see, Merlet and Maldidier (1987) and Porras (1987).

44. See for example, interview no. 53, UNAG Regional office, Region IV, April 26, 1989.

45. For example, interview no. 2, CCS member, Diriomo, March 16, 1987; interview no. 82, Plan Masaya beneficiary and CCS member, December 17, 1988; and interview no. 75, MIDINRA, Region IV, April 18, 1989.

46. This translates as "They Have Lent Us This Land."

47. It should be noted that this had to be done immediately upon their receipt in order to avoid the effects of inflation. See also Serra (1991, 211–13) in this regard.

48. See for example, interview no. 76, FSLN, Region IV, April 1989, and interview no. 7, MIDINRA, Region IV, May 15, 1987, in which some of the elements that would later be defined as "entrepreneurial expertise" were pointed out as missing in the cooperatives.

49. Of equal importance, even before the 1990 elections the peasantry had—in the

First National Assembly of the Cooperative Movement, which was held in September 1989—requested a formalization of the land titles they had received through the agrarian reform. They proposed the creation of an Agricultural Land Registry in order to facilitate this process. (The creation of a land registry was subsequently taken up as a project of the Chamorro government midway through its term.) However, MIDINRA—and especially its director, Cmdt. Jaime Wheelock—did not see this as a priority, as he sought to reassure those attending the Assembly that "not one inch of land redistributed through the agrarian reform would be returned to its former owners" (Hernández Pico [1989, 70]).

50. In fact, one UNAG official commented to me that the majority of those who still needed land in Region IV had previously been cooperative members. That is, upon their exit from the cooperative, they rejoined the pool of landless and land-poor campesinos. He argued that the imposition of a CAS form of production organization was the cause of high desertion levels in the cooperatives and the continuing problem of landlessness. Interview no. 53, UNAG official, Region IV, April 26, 1989.

51. See article 11 of chapter 2 of the Agrarian Reform Law (*La Gaceta*, [1981]). Until April 2, 1990, land received through the agrarian reform could only be passed on to offspring in the same (collective) form in which it was received by the original beneficiary. At that time, during the two-month transition period between the Sandinista and Chamorro governments, the law was revised to permit the sale, passing on through inheritance, etc., of this land (see República de Nicaragua [1989–90, 321–23]). Titles did, however, remain collective.

52. See further UNO (1989).

53. Interview no. 36, CAS president, Plan Masaya, July 24, 1990.

54. Interview no. 72, June 8, 1990.

55. Interview no. 60, former CAS member, June 21, 1990.

56. The Chamorro government's decrees 10-90 and 11-90 established the legal mechanisms by which former landowners could apply to have their property reinstated to them. Nonetheless, in the months following the change in government, it became increasingly common for previous landowners simply to communicate their interest in having their farms returned directly with those who had been granted the land. In some cases this communication took the form of a letter, and in others it followed the occupation of that land by UNO extremists.

57. I am including here several additional informants who were beneficiaries of these two projects, but who were not part of the original sample for the surveys conducted in 1988 and 1989. They participated in my discussions with the informants who were included in the sample. Their opinions were quite poignant, and they undoubtedly represented a position held by an important minority of the beneficiary populations. Thus, I have added their voices to those taken from our original sample.

58. Interview no. 36, Plan Masaya beneficiary and CAS member, July 1990.

59. Interview no. 36, Plan Masaya beneficiary and CAS member, July 1990, and interview no. 90, Plan Masaya beneficiary and CCS member, July 2, 1990, respectively.

60. Interview no. 109, Los Patios beneficiary and individual farmer, May 31, 1990.
61. Interview no. 89, CCS member, June 1, 1990.
62. See further UNO (1989) and *La Prensa* (1990).

Chapter 3: Los Patios: Its Roots

1. The first phase of the implementation of Los Patios roughly covered the 1983–88 period. Given the fact that the survey stage of my research was completed by early 1989, the following discussion of the project focuses primarily on its first phase.

2. See Enríquez (1991) for a lengthier discussion of the development of agroexport production in the nation as a whole. See also Squier (1972), Levy (1976), Radell (1969), and MacLeod (1973) for descriptions of the specific stages of this process.

3. See Enríquez (1991) and Lanuza Matamoros (1976) regarding the legislation that created some of these mechanisms.

4. It should be noted that this figure describes the coffee acreage located in the municipalities included in the Los Patios area of influence, which is an area slightly less inclusive than that characterized by MIDINRA (1983) and cited above.

5. Approximately 86.6 percent of the region's agroexport acreage (including cotton, coffee, and sugarcane acreage, and pastures) was located on farms larger than 50 manzanas in size by 1963 (calculated from Ministerio de Economía [1966], tables 28, 31, and 32).

6. The expansion of agroexport production stimulated an immigration towards the country's agricultural frontier, which experienced a notable increase in basic grain cultivation in the 1960s and 1970s (cf. Williams [1986], and Enríquez [1991]).

7. For discussion of Somoza's agrarian reform programs see Núñez Soto (1981), Enríquez (1991), and Enríquez and Spalding (1987).

8. The one food crop that had historically been an exception to this pattern was rice. Its production was another area of capitalist expansion in the post-WWII period (see Biderman [1982]).

9. Of the municipalities included in our study, San Marcos experienced the greatest employment benefits, with 43 percent of its available labor force being affected.

10. Coffee was the only major export crop cultivated by the cooperative sector in 1982 (Spoor [1987], table 29). It was not until 1983 that this sector also became involved in cotton production and, in 1984, sugarcane production.

11. By October of 1982, a total of 371 existed in Region IV, which incorporated 5,723 campesinos (CIERA [1989a], table 27). Of that total, 54.9 percent of those in cooperatives were members of CCSs, 43.5 percent were members of CAS, and the remainder formed various kinds of pre-cooperatives. Yet of these cooperatives, it was principally the CAS that had been formed on redistributed land, while the others had formed on land owned by their members. In fact, 82.9 percent of the land redistributed in Region IV during the 1981–82 period was turned over to campesinos who had formed CAS (CIERA [1989a], 57). This phenomenon resulted from the strong preference of the agrarian reform ministry to promote the formation of CAS through land redistri-

bution. CAS were seen as being the most advanced form of collective farming and a major step in the transition from precapitalist peasant farming to socialist agricultural production.

12. Between 1950 and 1980 Nicaragua's urban population grew from 15 to 54 percent of the total population. Managua also expanded at an extraordinary rate during this period, accounting for 10 percent of the total population in 1950 and 28 percent in 1980. See further CEPAL (1981b), 60–61.

13. See further UNRISD (1986).

14. It should also be noted that almost all of those interviewed were natives of this region.

15. This calculation, as well as those which follow, reflect patterns *within* the population of Los Patios beneficiaries, as opposed to within the sample as a whole.

16. A number of these were peasant capitalists. But a few of them had moved beyond the peasant category to be simply capitalist farmers.

17. See Murdoch (1980) and de Janvry (1981) for comprehensive discussions of the relationship between "population and poverty."

18. A third of our sample had been wage laborers (primarily in the agricultural sector) *just prior* to their inclusion in this agrarian reform project.

19. Nonetheless, only one informant had been employed in Managua in the period just before becoming a project beneficiary.

Chapter 4: Los Patios: Its Social and Political Impact

1. In fact, the expansion of Los Patios in 1986 to a new sector of producers, medium- and large-scale campesinos, was prompted almost entirely by political motivations. This sector of the campesinado had previously been largely neglected by the agrarian reform. Los Patios was adopted in Diriomo to initiate a reversal of this pattern. Agrarian reform officials had a genuine interest in expanding agricultural resources to a widening pool of campesinos. But they were also worried about the political consequences of the agrarian reform's limited reach within this sector. While the results of the 1984 elections were never mentioned as a contributing factor in the decision to extend Los Patios to the Diriomo development pole, the similarity in timing between this project's expansion and the implementation and expansion of Plan Masaya (1985 and 1986) suggests that they were one of the concerns motivating this effort.

2. The crops included in this list were chosen, in addition to the reasons described in the text, because of their resistance to the smoke from the nearby Santiago volcano that affects this region. Many other crops cannot be grown there because of the smoke.

3. See further MIDINRA (1987).

4. In quantitative terms, whereas 81 percent of those informants who had been producers previously had sold some portion of their crop, 98 percent participated in market relations after entering the project. These figures show a general increase, that while not small, is not striking. However, the quantitative data that was generated in this survey describing quantities of crops produced and sold was not entirely reliable, because this information had become highly politicized with the government's implementation of marketing regulations.

Nonetheless, on a qualitative level, our interviews pointed to the fact that this shift had been more notable than the figures suggest. That is, previously, *most* of the beneficiaries' production was destined for household consumption, although they also sold small amounts of produce to increase their cash income. After entering the project, this pattern was reversed.

5. In all likelihood, the continued use of credit was encouraged by real negative interest rates.

6. That is, as opposed to informal sources of credit, such as private moneylenders.

7. The 25 percent who had not utilized agricultural inputs previously had been blocked from doing so primarily by their lack of economic resources.

8. Data on both cooperatives were taken from MIDINRA (1986); and interviews no. 120, no. 121, no. 91, and no. 92 with the cooperatives' Juntas Directivas in September 1986 and June 1989.

9. In mid-1989 the Julio Buitrago Cooperative was divided into two cooperatives, one composed of those producing coffee and one composed of those producing pitahaya. In those cases in which a family cultivated both crops, a different family member was associated with each cooperative.

10. Scott (1985, 111) uses similar kinds of indicators to identify socioeconomic improvement among the peasantry in a small Malaysian village.

11. One could legitimately increase the number describing the beneficiary population to include—at a minimum—the spouses of the participants. Yet that would still only bring the total number to 1,300 for the whole area incorporated into the project.

12. Interviews: BND, Region IV, La Concepción branch office, August 2, 1990, and various residents of La Concepción, August 2, 1990.

13. Don Roberto also typically farmed approximately two manzanas of basic grains for the family's consumption, when he could find land to rent.

14. Former official of the CCS Harold Rosales and current BND official and La Concepción resident, interview with the author April 3, 1992.

15. Ibid.

16. It also fits with Anderson's 1994 description of the Pikin Guerrero–San Caralampio population, which is discussed below.

17. Many communities were renamed in the wake of Somoza's overthrow. In some cases, including that of San Caralampio, by 1990 at least a part of their residents had begun to refer to them by their pre-1979 names. This often reflected their political perspectives and was a statement of their rejection of the replacement of traditional names by "revolutionary" names. I am opting to use the traditional name here as that was how it was referred to in the precinct-level data from the 1990 elections.

18. Anderson's own position is that a whole variety of factors—to which she refers as the "political ecology" of a community—determine the kind of political behavior in which a given population will engage. In addition to socioeconomic factors, she argues that the degree of village cohesion, its level of internal social differentiation, its residents' access to social services, and their perception of degrees of injustice all influenced the adoption of one or another form of peasant political behavior. Such an approach offers the potential of extending our theoretical understanding of peasant politics beyond a reliance on only one independent variable for explanation. However, it would seem to be most testable at the level of individual community studies, and less useful

for analyzing the impact of major policies and strategies in policymaking that extend beyond community boundaries to cover a region—which was the objective of the present study.

19. The political orientation San Caralampio's residents appeared to have adopted prior to 1979 (one of remaining largely removed from the political turmoil that had enveloped the country until it was left with no option but to do so in self-defense) would seem to have expressed itself once again in a stronger-than-average opposition to the FSLN in 1990. There, the vote in 1990 was 31 percent in favor of the FSLN and 57.1 percent in favor of the UNO (unpublished data, CSE 1990). Anderson noted that prior to 1979 this community's residents had "not sympathized strongly with the revolution," a phenomenon that she relates, at least in part, with the *relatively* "better-off" status of the peasants who lived there. It would appear that this political inclination had not been radically undermined by ten years of Sandinista policymaking.

20. It should be noted that there did not appear to be any observable difference in voting patterns according to the form in which production was organized among Los Patios beneficiaries (see table 4.3).

21. Differentiation internal to the CCS was also an issue in the 1980s. Serra (1991, 211) found that there was a strong positive correlation between socioeconomic homogeneity among cooperative members and their degree of participation in the life of the cooperative. In contrast to the CAS, though, the CCS were found to have consistently higher levels of internal differentiation: "with a few rich campesinos—[who were] generally members of the Juntas Directivas and social leaders."

22. Serra (1991, 204–6) found a very strong relationship between the economic situation and the degree of participation of cooperative members, with participation increasing notably in positive economic circumstances and dropping off precipitously in negative ones. He also observed that the CCS were especially hard hit by the economic reform of 1988.

Chapter 5: Plan Masaya: Its Roots

1. COSEP's relationship with the Sandinista government was tense from as early as 1981; its president for much of the 1980s, Enrique Bolaños, was a vociferous opponent of the regime. For discussion of COSEP see chapter 6 of this volume; Spalding (1994); Gilbert (1985); and Sholk (1984).

2. In fact, according to three major agricultural studies, the percentage of the nation's cotton acreage there ranged from a high of 23 percent in 1952 to a low of 4.1 percent in 1963. By 1974–75, however, it had risen again, to 9 percent. These figures were calculated from the 1952 census, as cited in Blandón (1962), table 5; the 1963 census, Ministerio de Economía (1966), table 8; and a study cited in CIERA (1980d, 136).

3. In the mid-1970s, cotton covered 10,000 manzanas in Masaya, or 25 percent of the arable land (CIERA [1980c, 138 and 153]). Although pastures occupied more land than cotton cultivation—using 47 percent of the area's arable land—beef production was less central to Masaya's economy than cotton.

4. For an example of how this process took place in one rural community in this area, see Houtart and Lemercinier (1992).

5. MIDINRA (1984, 3).

6. Another phenomenon that contributed to the desertion rate that first year was the fact that some of the project's beneficiaries were not campesinos. They had been laborers and/or people involved in commerce, and they looked at their earnings from the harvest as a means of financing future informal sector activities. See MIDINRA (1984, 3), for further discussion of this issue.

7. This represented a significant shift for the most prominent of the technocrats, Wheelock, who stated in early November of 1984 (i.e., just prior to the elections) and again in early 1985, that for all intents and purposes, the agrarian reform was over (cf. LASA [1984], and MIDINRA [1985]).

8. See further chapter 6 of the Agrarian Reform Law, in CIERA (1989b, 68).

9. See MIDINRA (1988), n.d.(a), and n.d.(b).

10. These calculations, as well as those which follow, reflect the situation of the subgroup composed of Plan Masaya beneficiaries, as opposed to the sample as a whole.

11. Among the overall beneficiary population, this figure was notably lower, 29 percent.

Chapter 6: Plan Masaya: The Social and Political Impact of the Project

1. These data only describe the production practices of the informants from Masaya, as comparable data from Diriomo are unavailable.

2. See further Stahler-Sholk (1990a and 1990b).

3. The text here will be particularly focused on Masaya as opposed to Diriomo because of the former's greater weight in terms of the area affected by the project (84 percent of the acreage was located in Masaya). See further MIDINRA n.d.(a). In contrast to Masaya, the situation in this regard was somewhat more varied in Diriomo.

4. It should be noted that the price of cotton in the international market had begun to recover by 1987 (Empresa Nicaragüense de Algodón—Nicaraguan Cotton Enterprise, unpublished data, 1988). Thus by 1988 and 1989, the Nicaraguan government was once again promoting the expansion of cotton production, but only in the departments of León and Chinandega. See, for example, *Barricada* (1989).

5. See further *Barricada* (1987) and *Nuevo Diario* (1987).

6. These figures were: (1) For the pre-1979 period, calculated from CIERA (1980c, 138), and (2) for 1986–87, estimated in interview no. 80, MIDINRA, Region IV, Masaya zonal office, September 11, 1988. In contrast, the national average during this latter period was 17 hundredweight per manzana (PAN 1986).

7. See further IHCA (1985b).

8. In fact, the collapsing of "private sector" with large growers had prevailed in local parlance and domestic political circles until this time. It was not until the mid-1980s that the Sandinistas consciously expanded usage of the term to also refer to small- and medium-scale producers.

9. For a discussion of the limited possibilities of permanent employment in cotton production—which had prevailed there previously—see Núñez Soto (1981) and Enríquez (1991).

10. Cofradia and Pilas Occidentales together contained approximately 27 percent of the total beneficiary population of Plan Masaya, with a sum of approximately 273 ben-

eficiaries (calculated from interview no. 115, a local UNAG official, April 11, 1992; and MIDINRA, n.d.[a]).

11. Calculated from unpublished data from the CSE (1990). It must be noted here that Cofradia and Pilas Occidentales were benefited by the provision of additional services, including electricity, running water, and schools (or new classrooms).

12. Interview no. 116, former FSLN leader, Diriomo, February 15, 1992. It should be noted that these communities only received land and were not showered with other resources.

13. The first figure is from interview no. 115, UNAG, Masaya zonal office, April 11, 1992; the second was calculated from unpublished CSE data, 1990.

14. As indicated in chapter 4, it seems quite reasonable to assume that the spouses of the beneficiaries might well have voted in a similar fashion to their mates—as they were also benefited by the project—thereby possibly bringing this figure up to 24 percent. Given the potential still inherent in this situation for the problem of ecological fallacy, it makes sense to approach the electoral data cautiously and use it only to provide a general picture of pro-FSLN sentiment in these rural communities.

15. Thiesenhusen (1989) suggests that this is true for Nicaragua's agrarian reform as a whole, especially because it formed part of a broader process of societal transformation.

16. Interview no. 12, SAIMSA representative, January 31, 1991.

17. This was a region that had proved itself to be quite resistant to the goals of the Sandinistas' social project more generally. A discussion of the multiple reasons for this situation is beyond the scope of the present study. For such a discussion of Region V see Serra (1991) and Marvillet (1994).

18. He defines medium producers as holding between fifty and five hundred manzanas, large producers as holding more than five hundred manzanas, and small producers as owning less than fifty manzanas (Luciak [1995, 210, endnote 31]).

19. Interestingly, Quebrada Honda's early sympathy with the Sandinista revolution would seem to be reflected in its *relative* lack of support for the UNO ticket in 1990. Despite the fact that the FSLN lost the elections there (with 40.1 percent of the vote), the UNO won by only a very slim margin (42.2 percent of the vote)—a margin that was notably lower than the national average (calculated from CSE unpublished data, 1990).

CHAPTER 7: THE LESSONS TO BE DRAWN FROM LOS PATIOS AND PLAN MASAYA

1. Once again, given that the vast majority of Plan Masaya beneficiaries were drawn from Masaya as opposed to Diriomo, our attention will be concentrated on Masaya.

2. The Diriomo-based parents' group stands out in this regard, with a full 75 percent stating that this was their sole economic activity. What is crucial to remember here is that land rentals were a real option for those who did not own land there.

3. The equivalent figure for Plan Masaya's Diriomo-based participants was 13 percent.

4. Anderson's study (1994, 123 and 147), of Quebrada Honda (in the Plan Masaya

area of influence) and San Caralampio (in the Los Patios area of influence) also indicates the difference between these two areas: in the former the average landholding was of 0.9 manzanas, while in the latter it was of 3.9 manzanas.

5. Plan Masaya's Diriomo-based participants fell in the middle of the other two groups, with 63 percent having joined the rural wage labor force at some point prior to 1985.

6. Harris (1992, 141–42) makes a similar assertion when he posits that "without this form of organization [democratic self-management], socialist relations of production cannot be developed and institutionalized."

7. There also appears to have been an interactive effect between these two factors. That is, the data set forth in tables 4.3 and 6.5 suggest that the social origins of the beneficiaries influenced the degree of impact that the organizational form of their production had upon their political perspectives. Specifically, in the more proletarianized of these two populations—Plan Masaya beneficiaries—the organizational form of production had a notable effect on their level of support for the FSLN. In contrast, there is no apparent relationship between organizational form and political perspective in the case of the less proletarianized population of Los Patios beneficiaries. However, the small number of individuals included in these samples precludes a more definitive statement about this phenomenon.

8. In San Marcos the FSLN won with 55.7 percent of the vote, and in Masatepe it won with 46.5 percent of the vote (CSE unpublished data, 1990).

9. See also Luciak (1995) and Brown (1990).

10. Stahler-Sholk (1990b) analyzes the impact that Sandinista economic policies had on each sector of the popular classes.

11. The latter was evident as the government attempted to restrain popular demands for more far-reaching change, so as to sustain the confidence and participation of the capitalist sectors in the mixed economy.

12. Many of the ideas for this discussion were drawn from Deere (1986); Munslow (1984); Barker (1985); Roesch (1984); MacEwan (1981); Rodríguez (1983); and Forster (1982).

13. For discussion of the issues raised by the heavy reliance on state farms that has characterized many Third World countries engaged in a transition to socialism, see Patemen (1989).

14. On the development of Cuba's cooperative movement see Kay (1988), Valdez Paz (1981), and Deere et. al. (1992).

15. See especially Hyden (1980), Barker (1985), and Boesen et al. (1977) on the Tanzanian agrarian reform.

16. The lower estimate is from Barker (1985, 67), while the higher estimate is from Deere (1986, 119).

17. The formation of a socialist-oriented government in Mozambique triggered the closing off of labor markets in South Africa for rural dwellers and a counterrevolutionary war, which was promoted by South Africa. Both of these factors had a strong impact on the peasant economy.

18. Wiegersma (1988). On Vietnam, also see Werner (1984) and White (1985).

19. Herring (n.d. and 1989) provides an excellent analysis of the contradictory results of the CPI-M's agrarian reform.

20. Luciak (1995) describes at some length the rationale behind this combination of representative and participatory democracy as stemming from the goal of achieving popular hegemony within the context of national unity.

21. Fagen (1986, 250) poignantly states this thesis with respect to Cuba: "The Cuban revolution has survived and even prospered in adversity because the integrative and mobilizational politics of the regime have given second, third, and even tenth chances to a revolutionary state which has, in general, managed the economy poorly."

22. Herring (n.d. and 1989) speaks of this dynamic emerging even in the context of communist-ruled Kerala. Likewise, Kay (1978) found a similar situation to have developed under Allende's socialist regime.

Bibliography

Alavi, Hamza. 1965. "Peasants and Revolutions." In *The Socialist Register*, edited by Ralph Miliband and John Saville, 241–77. London: Merlin.

Alemán, M., et al. 1986. "La estrategia de sobreviviencia de los sectores populares de Managua y el impacto del mensaje económico gubernamental." *Encuentro*, no. 29 (September–December): 47–83.

Anderson, Leslie. 1994. *The Political Ecology of the Modern Peasant: Calculation and Community.* Baltimore: Johns Hopkins University Press.

Barker, Jonathan. 1985. "Gaps in the Debates about Agriculture in Senegal, Tanzania, and Mozambique." *World Development* 13, no. 1: 59–76.

Barnes, William A. 1992. "Rereading the Nicaraguan Pre-Election Polls." In *The 1990 Elections in Nicaragua and Their Aftermath,* edited by Vanessa Castro and Gary Prevost, 41–128. Lanham, Md.: Rowman and Littlefield.

Barndt, Deborah. 1995. "Popular Education." In *Nicaragua: The First Five Years,* edited by Thomas Walker, 317–45. New York: Praeger.

Barricada. 1980. "Aplastar la contrarevolución: Tarea de todo el pueblo." Speech by Comandante Humberto Ortega Saavedra, August 24.

———. 1984. "Lunes socio-económico: Plan Contingente de Granos Básicos." July 9.

———. 1987. "Solo en Occidente se cultivara algodón." June 13.

———. 1989. "Foro socio-económico: ¿Conviene sembrar algodón?" June 5.

Baumeister, Eduardo. 1985. "The Structure of Nicaraguan Agriculture and the Sandinista Agrarian Reform." In *Nicaragua: A Revolution Under Siege,* edited by Richard L. Harris and Carlos M. Vilas, 10–35. London: Zed.

———. 1986. "Estado-mundo agrícola: Una relación cambiante." *Pensamiento Propio* 4, no. 34 (July): 18–22.

BCN (Banco Central de Nicaragua). 1979. *Indicadores económicos,* 5 (December). Managua.

Belli, Pedro. 1975. "Prolegómeno para una historia económica de Nicaragua de 1905–1966." *Revista del Pensamiento Centroamericano* 147 (January–March): 2–30.

Biderman, Jaime. 1982. "Class Structure, the State, and Capitalist Development in Nicaraguan Agriculture." Ph.D. diss., University of California, Berkeley.

Biondi-Morra, Brizio. 1990. *Revolución y política alimentaria: Un Análisis crítico de Nicaragua.* Mexico City: Siglo XXI.

Bitar, Sergio. 1979. *Transición, socialismo y democracia.* Mexico City: Siglo XXI.

Blandón, Alfonso. 1962. "Land Tenure in Nicaragua." Master's thesis, University of Florida, Gainesville.

Boesen, Jannik, Birgit Storgaard Madsen, and Tony Moody. 1977. *Ujamaa: Socialism from Above.* Uppsala, Sweden: Scandinavian Institute of African Studies.

Booth, John. 1985. *The End and the Beginning: The Nicaraguan Revolution.* Boulder, Colo.: Westview.

Bossert, Thomas John. 1985. "Health Policy: The Dilemma of Success." In *Nicaragua: The First Five Years,* edited by Thomas Walker, 347–63. New York: Praeger.

Brown, Doug. 1990. "Sandinismo and the Problem of Democratic Hegemony." *Latin American Perspectives* 17, no. 2 (Spring): 39–61.

Burawoy, Michael. 1985. *The Politics of Production.* London: Verso.

———. 1991. "Reconstructing Social Theories." In *Ethnography Unbound: Power and Resistance in the Modern Metropolis,* by Michael Burawoy et al., 8–27. Berkeley: University of California Press.

Burbach, Roger. 1986. "The Conflict at Home and Abroad: U.S. Imperialism vs. the New Revolutionary Societies." In *Transition and Development: Problems of Third World Socialism,* edited by Richard R. Fagen et al., 79–96. New York: Monthly Review Press.

Canadian Church and Human Rights Delegation. 1984. *Nicaragua 1984: Democracy, Elections, and War.* Toronto.

CEE (Comité Estatal de Estadísticas). 1989. *Anuario estadístico de Cuba.* Havana: Editorial Estadística.

CEPAL (Comisión Económica para América Latina, United Nations). 1966. *El desarrollo económico en Nicaragua.* Santiago, Chile.

———. 1979. *Nicaragua: Repercusiones económicos de los acontecimientos políticos recientes.* Mexico City.

———. 1981a. "Programa de la Junta de Gobierno de Reconstrucción Nacional de Nicaragua." In *Nicaragua: El impacto de la mutación política,* edited by CEPAL, 105–20. Santiago, Chile.

———. 1981b. *Statistical Yearbook for Latin America, 1980.* Santiago, Chile.

———. 1987. *Notas para el estudio económico de América Latina y el Caribe, 1986: Nicaragua.* Mexico City.

———. 1990. *Notas para el estudio económico de América Latina y el Caribe, 1989: Nicaragua.* Mexico City.

CIERA (Centro de Investigaciones y Estudios sobre la Reforma Agraria). 1980a. *Diagnóstico socio-económico del sector agropecuario: Carazo,* vol. 5. Managua: MIDINRA.

———. 1980b. *Diagnóstico socio-económico del sector agropecuario: Granada,* vol. 6. Managua: MIDINRA.

———. 1980c. *Diagnóstico socio-económico del sector agropecuario: Masaya,* vol. 4. Managua: MIDINRA.

———. 1980d. *Diagnóstico socio-económico del sector agropecuario: Rivas,* vol. 7. Managua: MIDINRA.

———. 1985. "Investigación sobre Masaya y la Zona de los Pueblos." Unpublished report.

———. 1989a. *La reforma agraria en Nicaragua: 1979–1989: Cifras y referencias documentales,* vol. 9. Managua.

———. 1989b. *La reforma agraria en Nicaragua: 1979–1989: Estrategia y Políticas,* vol. 1. Managua.

———. 1989c. *La reforma agraria en Nicaragua: 1979–1989: Marco jurídico de la reforma agraria,* vol. 8. Managua.

Cliff, L., and J. Saul, eds. 1972. *Socialism in Tanzania.* Nairobi: East Africa Publishing House.

Colburn, Forrest D. 1986a. "Foot Dragging and Other Peasant Responses to the Nicaraguan Revolution." *Peasant Studies* 13, no. 2 (Winter): 77–96.

———. 1986b. *Post-Revolutionary Nicaragua: State, Class, and the Dilemmas of Agrarian Policy.* Berkeley: University of California Press.

———, ed. 1989. *Everyday Forms of Peasant Resistance.* New York: M. E. Sharpe.

———. 1990. *Managing the Commanding Heights: Nicaragua's State Enterprises.* Berkeley: University of California Press.

Collins, Joseph, with Frances Moore Lappé, Nick Allen, and Paul Rice. 1985. *Nicaragua: What Difference Could a Revolution Make?* San Francisco: Institute for Food and Development Policy.

CONAL (Comisión Nacional del Algodón). 1973. *Estadísticas del Algodón en Nicaragua: 1950–72.* Managua.

Conroy, Michael E. 1990. "The Political Economy of the 1990 Nicaraguan Elections." *International Journal of Political Economy* 20, no. 3 (Fall): 5–33.

Coraggio, José Luis. 1986. "Economics and Politics in the Transition to Socialism: Reflections on the Nicaraguan Experience." In *Transition and Development,* edited by Richard R. Fagen et al., 143–70. New York: Monthly Review Press.

CSE (Consejo Supremo Electoral). 1990. "Resultados de las votaciones." Consolidated, unpublished data.

Deere, Carmen Diana. 1986. "Agrarian Reform, Peasant Participation, and the Organization of Production in the Transition to Socialism." In *Transition and Development,* edited by Richard R. Fagen et al., 97–142. New York: Monthly Review Press.

Deere, Carmen Diana, Peter Marchetti S.J., and Nola Reinhardt. 1985. "The Peasantry and the Development of Sandinista Agrarian Policy." *Latin American Research Review* 20, no. 3: 75–109.

Deere, Carmen Diana, Mieke Meurs, and Niurka Pérez. 1992. "Towards a Periodization of the Cuban Collectivization Process: Changing Incentives and Peasant Response." *Cuban Studies* 22: 115–49.

de Janvry, Alain. 1981. *The Agrarian Question and Reformism in Latin America.* Baltimore: Johns Hopkins University Press.

Donahue, John M. 1983. "The Politics of Health Care in Nicaragua Before and After the Revolution of 1979." *Human Organization* 42, no. 3 (Fall): 264–72.

Enríquez, Laura J. 1987. "Half a Decade of Sandinista Policy-Making: Recent Publications on Revolutionary Policies in Contemporary Nicaragua." *Latin American Research Review* 22, no. 3: 209–22.

———. 1991. *Harvesting Change: Labor and Agrarian Reform in Nicaragua, 1979–1990.* Chapel Hill: University of North Carolina Press.

———. 1994. "The Transformation of Food Crop Production in Contemporary Cuba." Paper presented at the annual conference of the Pacific Sociological Association, San Francisco, April 6–9.

Enríquez, Laura J., and Rose J. Spalding. 1987. "Banking Systems and Revolutionary Change: The Politics of Agricultural Credit in Nicaragua." In *The Political Economy of Revolutionary Nicaragua,* edited by Rose J. Spalding, 105–25. Winchester, Mass.: Allen and Unwin.

Fagen, Richard R. 1969. *The Transformation of Political Culture in Cuba.* Stanford: Stanford University Press.

———. 1986. "The Politics of Transition." In *Transition and Development,* edited by Richard R. Fagen et al., 249–63. New York: Monthly Review Press.

Feder, Ernest. 1970. "Counterreform." In *Agrarian Problems and Peasant Movements in Latin America,* edited by Rodolfo Stavenhagen, 173–223. New York: Anchor.

FIDA (Fondo Internacional de Desarrollo Agrícola). 1980. *Informe de la Misión Especial de Programación a Nicaragua.* Rome.

FitzGerald, E. V. K. 1986. "Notes on the Analysis of the Small Underdeveloped Economy in Transition." In *Transition and Development,* edited by Richard R. Fagen et al., 28–53. New York: Monthly Review Press.

Forster, Nancy. 1982. "The Revolutionary Transformation of the Cuban Countryside." *UFSI Reports* 26.

Foster, George M. 1960–61. "Interpersonal Relations in Peasant Society." *Human Organization* 19, no. 4 (Winter): 174–78.

Friedland, William. 1982. *Revolutionary Theory.* Totowa, N.J.: Allenhead Osmun.

Gariazzo, Alicia. 1984. "El café en Nicaragua: Los pequeños productores de Matagalpa y Carazo." *Cuadernos de Pensamiento Propio* 2.

Ghai, Dharam, Cristóbal Kay, and Peter Peek. 1988. *Labour and Development in Rural Cuba.* New York: St. Martin's Press.

Gilbert, Dennis. 1985. "The Bourgeoisie." In *Nicaragua: The First Five Years,* edited by Thomas W. Walker, 163–82. New York: Praeger.

Gorostiaga, Xabier. 1986. "Economía mixta y revolución Sandinista." In *La economía mixta en Nicaragua,* edited by CINASE (Centro de Investigación y Asesoría Socio-económica), 47–71. Managua: CINASE.

Gould, Jeffrey L. 1988. "Resistance and Participation in the Post-Revolutionary Nicaraguan Countryside." *Peasant Studies* 15, no. 4 (Summer): 275–85.

Granma. 1993a. "Acuerdo del Buró Político: Para llevar a cabo importantes innovaciones en la agricultura estatal." September 15.

———. 1993b. "Avanza el proceso de creación de Unidades Básicas de Producción Cooperativa." October 2.

———. 1993c. "Mayor autonomía en la producción cañera: Nuevos conceptos en la agricultura." September 18.

Grigsby, Arturo. 1989. "El impacto de las medidas en el sector agropecuario." In *Política económica y transformación social*, edited by CIERA, 75–89. Managua: CIERA.

Grindle, Merilee S. 1986. *State and Countryside: Development Policy and Agrarian Politics in Latin America*. Baltimore: Johns Hopkins University Press.

Gutiérrez, Iván. 1989. "Situación del campesinado frente a las medidas económicas de 1988." In *Política económica y transformación social*, edited by CIERA, 90–108. Managua: CIERA.

Harris, Richard L. 1992. *Marxism, Socialism, and Democracy in Latin America*. Boulder, Colo.: Westview.

Hemisphere Initiatives. 1989. *Establishing the Ground Rules: A Report on the Nicaraguan Electoral Process*. Boston: Hemisphere Initiatives.

Hernández Pico, Juan. 1989. "De clase incomoda a pilar de la revolución: El campesinado en la Primera Asamblea Nacional del Movimiento Campesino." *Encuentro* 37–38 (July–December): 61–72.

Herring, Ronald J. 1989. "Dilemmas of Agrarian Communism: Peasant Differentiation, Sectoral and Village Politics." *Third World Quarterly* 11, no. 1 (January): 89–115.

———. n.d. "Contesting the 'Great Transformation': Land and Labor in South India." Unpublished manuscript.

Hirshon, Sheryl, with July Butler. 1983. *And Also Teach Them to Read*. Westport, Conn.: Lawrence Hill.

Houtart, Francois, and Genevieve Lemercinier. 1992. *El campesino como actor: Sociología de una comarca de Nicaragua, El Comejen*. Managua: Ediciones Nicarao.

Huberman, Leo, and Paul Sweezy. 1969. *Socialism in Cuba*. New York: Monthly Review Press.

Huntington, Samuel P. 1965. "Political Development and Political Decay." *World Politics* 17, no. 3 (April): 386–430.

———. 1968. *Political Order in Changing Societies*. New Haven: Yale University Press.

Hyden, Goran. 1980. *Beyond Ujamaa in Tanzania: Underdevelopment and an Uncaptured Peasantry*. Berkeley: University of California Press.

IHCA (Instituto Histórico Centroamericano). 1985a. "The Elections Reagan Would Like to Forget: An Analysis of the November 4 Electoral Results." *Envío* 4 (April): 1b–29b.

———. 1985b. "The Nicaraguan Peasantry Gives New Direction to Agrarian Reform." *Envío* 4 (September): 1c–18c.

―――. 1988a. "El pueblo de Nicaragua por la paz y por un modelo económico más popular." *Envío* 7 (July–August).

―――. 1988b. "More on the Economy—And More Needs to be Done." *Envío* 7 (November): 13–21.

International Human Rights Law Group and Washington Office on Latin America. 1984. *A Political Opening in Nicaragua (Report on the Nicaraguan Elections of November 4, 1984).* Washington, D.C.

IPADE (Instituto para el Desarrollo de la Democracia). 1990. "Resultados electorales en el sector rural." Unpublished manuscript.

Irish Inter-Parliamentary Delegation. 1984. *The Elections in Nicaragua, November 1984.* (November 21). Dublin.

Johnson, John J. 1958. *Political Change in Latin America: The Emergence of the Middle Sectors.* Stanford, Calif.: Stanford University Press.

Journal of Development Studies. 1985. "The Agrarian Question in Socialist Transitions." Special issue edited by Saith Ashwani, 22, no. 1 (October).

Kay, Cristóbal. 1978. "Agrarian Reform and the Class Struggle in Chile." *Latin American Perspectives* 5, no. 3 (Summer): 117–40.

―――. 1988. "Recent Developments in Rural Cuba: Collectivisation, Economic Reforms and Rectification." *Bulletin* no. 1. European Association of Development Research and Training Institutes.

La Gaceta-Diario Oficial. 1981. "Ley de Reforma Agraria," *La Gaceta* no. 188 (August 21): 1737–42.

―――. 1986. "Reforma a la Ley de Reforma Agraria," *La Gaceta* no. 8 (January 13): 57–61.

Lanuza Matamoros, Alberto. 1976. "Estructuras socioeconómicas, poder y estado en Nicaragua, de 1821 a 1875." Senior thesis, Programa Centroamericano de Ciencias Sociales, San José, Costa Rica.

La Prensa. 1990, "Agenda de Violeta Chamorro para el rescate de la economía nacional." Special supplement, February 21.

LASA (Latin American Studies Association). 1984. *The Electoral Process in Nicaragua: Domestic and International Influences.* Austin.

―――. 1990. *Electoral Democracy Under International Pressure: The Report of the Latin American Studies Association Commission to Observe the 1990 Nicaraguan Elections.* Pittsburgh.

Lenin, V. I. 1966. "Preliminary Draft Thesis on the Agrarian Question." In *Collected Works,* vol. 13. Moscow: Progress Publishers.

―――. 1980. "El socialismo y el campesinado." In *El socialismo y el campesinado.* Moscow: Progress Publishers.

Levy, Pablo. 1976. *Notas geográficas y económicas sobre la República de Nicaragua.* Managua: Colección Cultural, Banco de América.

Lipset, Seymour Martin. 1963. *Political Man: The Social Bases of Politics.* Garden City, N.Y.: Anchor.

Lowy, Michael. 1986. "Mass Organizations, Party, and State: Democracy in the

Transition to Socialism." In *Transition and Development,* edited by Richard R. Fagen et al., 264–79. New York: Monthly Review Press.

Luciak, Ilja. 1987. "National Unity and Popular Hegemony: The Dialectics of Sandinista Agrarian Reform Policies." *Journal of Latin American Studies* 19, no. 1 (May): 113–40.

———. 1988. "Participatory Development in Sandinista Nicaragua: Grass-Roots Movements and Basic Needs." *Scandinavian Journal of Development Alternatives* 7, no. 4 (December): 29–53.

———. 1995. *The Sandinista Legacy: Lessons from a Political Economy in Transition.* Gainesville: University Press of Florida.

MacEwan, Arthur. 1981. *Revolution and Economic Development in Cuba.* New York: St. Martin's Press.

MacLeod, Murdo. 1973. *Spanish Central America: A Socioeconomic History, 1520–1720.* Berkeley: University of California Press.

Mao Tse-tung. 1967. *Analysis of the Classes in Chinese Society.* Peking: Foreign Language Press.

Marchetti, Peter, S.J. 1986. "War, Popular Participation, and Transition to Socialism: The Case of Nicaragua." In *Transition and Development,* edited by Richard R. Fagen et al., 303–30. New York: Monthly Review Press.

———. 1989. "Semejanzas y diferencias en dos debates sobre el campesinado—la economía mixta y la vía al socialismo: Preobrazhenski y MIDINRA vs. Bujarin y la UNAG." *Encuentro* 37–38 (July–December): 35–45.

Marvillet, Christiane. 1994. "Peasant Counter-revolutionaries: The Case of Nueva Guinea, Nicaragua, 1965–1984." Ph.D. diss., University of New South Wales.

Marx, Karl. 1977. *The Eighteenth Brumaire of Louis Bonaparte.* New York: International Publishers.

Merlet, Michel, and Christophe Maldidier. 1987. "El movimiento cooperativo, eje de la sobrevivencia de la revolución." *Encuentro* 30 (January–April): 47–92.

MIDINRA (Ministerio de Desarrollo Agropecuario y Reforma Agraria). n.d. [a]. "Distribución zonal de las cooperativas y individuales: Plan Masaya." Unpublished report, Region IV.

———. n.d. [b]. "Informe sobre las cooperativas nuevas beneficiarias de la reforma agraria." Unpublished report, Region IV.

———. 1983. *Estrategia regional de desarrollo agropecuario y reforma agraria.* Region IV. Managua.

———. 1984. *PECOS: Año 1.* N.p.

———. 1986. "Informe Preliminar de las C.C.S." Unpublished report, Region IV.

———. 1987. MIDINRA, Region IV, Zonal III (1987); and MIDINRA, Region IV, Zonal XI (1987). Unpublished data.

———. 1988. "Informe de área, rendimiento y producción estimado del PATD." Unpublished report, Region IV, Zonal de Masaya.

Migdal, Joel S. 1974. *Peasants, Politics, and Revolution: Pressures Toward Political and Social Change in the Third World.* Princeton: Princeton University Press.

Miller, Peter V. 1991. "The Polls: A Review, Which Side are You On? The 1990 Nicaraguan Poll Debacle." *Public Opinion Quarterly* (Summer): 281–302.

Ministerio de Economía. 1966. *Censos nacionales: Agropecuarios.* Dirección General de Estadísticas y Censos. Managua.

MIPLAN (Ministerio de Planificación). 1980. *Programa de Reactivación Económica en Beneficio del Pueblo.* Managua.

Munslow, Barry. 1984. "State Intervention in Agriculture: The Mozambican Experience." *Journal of Modern African Studies* 22, no. 2: 199–221.

Murdoch, William W. 1980. *The Poverty of Nations: The Political Economy of Hunger and Population.* Baltimore: Johns Hopkins University Press.

Neira, Oscar. 1988. "La reforma agraria Nicaragüense: Balance de ocho años." In *Nicaragua: Cambios estructurales y políticas económicas,* edited by INIES, 67–110. Managua: INIES.

Nuevo Diario. 1987. "La estrategia en el algodón." June 13.

Núñez Soto, Orlando. 1980. "La tercera fuerza social en los movimientos de liberación nacional." *Estudios Sociales Centroamericanos* 27 (September–December): 141–57.

———. 1981. *El somocismo y el modelo capitalista agroexportador.* Managua: Departamento de Ciencias Sociales, UNAN.

Oquist, Paul. 1990. "Investigación 'Dinámica socio-política de las elecciones Nicaragüenses 1990': Análisis de los resultados globales." Unpublished manuscript.

Ordóñez Centeno, Rigo. 1976. "La política crediticia algodonera: El caso de Nicaragua." Senior monograph, Facultad de Ciencias Económicas, UNAN, Managua.

Ortega, Marvin. 1985. "Workers' Participation in the Management of the Agro-Enterprises of the APP." *Latin American Perspectives* 12, no. 2 (Spring): 69–81.

Paige, Jeffery M. 1975. *Agrarian Revolution: Social Movements and Export Agriculture in the Underdeveloped World.* New York: Free Press.

———. 1989. "Revolution and the Agrarian Bourgeoisie in Nicaragua." In *Revolution in the World System,* edited by Terry Boswell, 99–128. New York: Greenwood Press.

PAN (Programa Alimentario Nicaragüense). 1986. "Estadísticas básicas del sector agropecuario." Unpublished report (August).

Pateman, Roy. 1989. "Peasants and State Farms: Problems in the Transition to Socialism in Africa and Latin America." *Peasant Studies* 16, no. 2 (Winter): 69–86.

Pelzer White, Christine. 1986. "Everyday Resistance, Socialist Revolution and Rural Development: The Vietnamese Case." *The Journal of Peasant Studies* 13, no. 2 (January): 49–63.

Pollitt, Brian. 1979. "Agrarian Reform and the 'Agricultural Proletariat' in Cuba, 1958–66: Some Notes." Institute of Latin American Studies Occasional Papers no. 29, University of Glasgow.

Porras, Alonso. 1987. "El movimiento cooperativo en Nicaragua." *Economía y Revolución* 1 (October): 14–19.

Radell, David R. 1969. "A Historical Geography of Western Nicaragua: The Spheres of Influence of León, Granada, and Managua, 1519–1965. Ph.D. diss., University of California, Berkeley.

República de Nicaragua. 1989–90. "Ley de Protección a la Propiedad Agraria" (Law No. 88). In *Decretos-Leyes y Leyes de la República de Nicaragua*, vol. 16. Managua.

Rodríguez, Carlos Rafael. 1983. "Cuatro años de reforma agraria." In *Letra con filo*, vol. 2, edited by C. R. Rodríguez, 209–38. Havana: Editorial de Ciencias Sociales.

Roesch, Otto. 1984. "Peasants and Collective Agriculture in Mozambique." In *The Politics of Agriculture in Tropical Africa*, edited by Jonathan Barker, 291–316. Beverly Hills, Calif.: Sage.

Roxborough, Ian. 1979. *Theories of Underdevelopment*. London: Macmillan.

Ruckwarger, Gary. 1987. *People in Power: Forging a Grass-Roots Democracy in Nicaragua*. South Hadley, Mass.: Bergin and Garvey.

———. 1988. "The Campesino Road to Socialism? The Sandinistas and Rural Cooperatives." In *The Socialist Register*, edited by Ralph Miliband and John Saville, 220–43. London: Merlin.

Saul, John S. 1974. "African Peasants and Revolution." *Review of African Political Economy* 1 (August–November): 41–68.

Scott, James C. 1976. *The Moral Economy of the Peasant: Subsistence and Rebellion in Southeast Asia*. New Haven: Yale University Press.

———. 1977. "Peasant Revolution: A Dismal Science." *Comparative Politics* 9, no. 2 (January): 231–48.

———. 1985. *Weapons of the Weak: Everyday Forms of Peasant Resistance*. New Haven: Yale University Press.

Serra, Luis Héctor. 1985. "The Grass-Roots Organizations." In *Nicaragua: The First Five Years*, edited by Thomas Walker, 65–89. New York: Praeger Publishers.

———. 1988. "Organizaciones populares: Entre las bases y el poder." *Pensamiento Propio* 6, no. 56 (December): 42–45.

———. 1989. "Limitada por la guerra; pendiente a futuro: Participación y organización popular en Nicaragua." *Nueva Sociedad* 104 (November–December): 134–43.

———. 1991. *El movimiento campesino: Su participación política durante la revolución Sandinista, 1979–1989*. Managua: UCA.

Sholk, Richard. 1984. "The National Bourgeoisie in Post-Revolutionary Nicaragua." *Comparative Politics* 16, no. 3 (April): 253–76.

Spalding, Rose J. 1994. *Capitalists and Revolution in Nicaragua: Opposition and Accommodation, 1979–1992*. Chapel Hill: University of North Carolina Press.

Spence, Jack. 1990. "Will Everything be Better?" *Socialist Review* 20, no. 3 (July–September): 115–32.

Spoor, Max. 1987. *Datos macro-económicos de Nicaragua (1960–1986)*. Departamento de Economía Agrícola, Universidad Nacional Autónoma de Nicaragua. Managua.

———. 1989a. "Reforma económica y crédito rural en Nicaragua (1988–89)." Paper prepared for the 15th annual conference of LASA, San Juan, Puerto Rico, September 21–23.

———. 1989b. *Un inventario de políticas agrarias para los granos básicos en Nicaragua*. Managua.

———, et al. 1988. *El maíz, nuestra raíz: Estudio económico del mercado de maíz (1979–88)*. Managua: DEA, UNAN.

Squier, Ephraim George. 1972. *Nicaragua, sus gentes y paisajes*. San José, Costa Rica: Editorial Universitaria Centroamericana (EDUCA).

Stahler-Sholk, Richard. 1990a. "Stabilization, Destabilization, and the Popular Classes in Nicaragua." *Latin American Research Review* 25, no. 3 (Fall): 55–88.

———. 1990b. "Stabilization Policies Under Revolutionary Transition: Nicaragua, 1979–1990." Ph.D. diss., University of California, Berkeley.

Taubman, Philip. 1984. "U.S. Is Reported to Oppose Electoral Challenge to Sandinistas." *New York Times*, October 21.

Thiesenhusen, William C. 1995. *Broken Promises: Agrarian Reform and the Latin American Campesino*. Boulder, Colo.: Westview Press.

Thomas, Clive Y. 1974. *Dependence and Transformation: The Economics of the Transition to Socialism*. New York: Monthly Review Press.

UNO (Unión Nacional Opositora). 1989. "Programa de gobierno de la Unión Nacional Opositora." Supplement included with daily newspapers, August 24.

UNRISD (United Nations Research Institute for Social Development). 1986. "Urbanization and Food Systems Development in Nicaragua." In *Food Systems and Society: Problems of Food Security in Selected Developing Countries*, edited by UNRISD, 190–209. Geneva.

Utting, Peter. 1987. "Domestic Supply and Food Shortages." In *The Political Economy of Revolutionary Nicaragua*, edited by Rose J. Spalding, 127–48. Winchester, Mass.: Allen and Unwin.

———. 1988. "The Peasant Question and Development Policy in Nicaragua." *IDS Bulletin* 19 (July): 40–46.

———. 1991. *Economic Adjustment under the Sandinistas: Policy Reform, Food Security and Livelihood in Nicaragua*. Geneva: UNRISD.

Valdez Paz, Juan. 1981. "El proceso de colectivización rural en Cuba." *Estudios del Tercer Mundo* 3, no. 1: 121–37.

Vickers, George R. 1990. "A Spider's Web." *NACLA Report on the Americas* 14 (June): 19–27.

Vilas, Carlos M. 1985. "Unidad nacional y contradicciones sociales en una economía mixta; Nicaragua 1979–1984." In *La revolución en Nicaragua*, edited by Richard Harris and Carlos M. Vilas, 17–50. Mexico City: Ediciones Era.

———. 1986a. "The Mass Organizations in Nicaragua: The Current Problematic and Perspectives for the Future." *Monthly Review* 38, no. 6 (November): 20–31.

———. 1986b. *The Sandinista Revolution: National Liberation and Social Transformations in Central America*. New York: Monthly Review Press.

———. 1988. "Popular Insurgency and Social Revolution in Central America." *Latin American Perspectives* 15, no. 1 (Winter): 55–77.
———. 1990. "What Went Wrong?" *NACLA Report on the Americas* 24 (June): 10–18.
———. 1991. "Nicaragua: A Revolution that Fell from the Grace of the People." *Socialist Register.* London.
Weeks, John. 1987. "The Mixed Economy in Nicaragua: The Economic Battlefield." In *The Political Economy of Revolutionary Nicaragua,* edited by Rose J. Spalding, 43–60. Winchester, Mass.: Allen and Unwin.
Weisman, Steven R. 1984. "Reagan Predicts Nicaraguan Vote Will Be 'Sham.'" *New York Times,* July 20.
Werner, Jayne. 1984. "Socialist Development: The Political Economy of Agrarian Reform in Vietnam." *Bulletin of Concerned Asian Scholars* 2 (April–June): 48–55.
Wheelock Román, Jaime. 1980. *Nicaragua: Imperialismo y dictadura.* Havana: Editorial de Ciencias Sociales.
———. 1984a. *Entre la crisis y la agresión: La reforma agraria Sandinista,* División de Comunicaciones, MIDINRA, Managua.
———. 1984b. "Revolución y desarrollo: El sector agropecuario en la transformación revolucionaria." *Revolución y desarrollo* 1, no. 1: 5–14.
———. 1990. *La reforma agraria Sandinista: 10 años de revolución en el campo.* Managua: Editorial Vanguardia.
White, Christine. 1985. "Agricultural Planning, Pricing Policy and Co-operatives in Vietnam." *World Development* 13, no. 1 (January): 97–114.
White, Gordon. 1983. "Revolutionary Socialist Development in the Third World: An Overview." In *Revolutionary Socialist Development in the Third World,* edited by Gordon White et al., 1–34. Lexington: University Press of Kentucky.
White, Gordon, Robin Murray, and Christine White, eds. 1983. *Revolutionary Socialist Development in the Third World.* Lexington: University Press of Kentucky.
Wickham-Crowley, Timothy. 1989. "Winners, Losers, and Also-Rans: Toward a Comprehensive Sociology of Latin American Guerrilla Movements." In *Power and Popular Protest,* edited by Susan Eckstein, 132–81. Berkeley: University of California Press.
———. 1992. *Guerrillas and Revolution in Latin America: A Comparative Study of Insurgents and Regimes since 1956.* Princeton: Princeton University Press.
Wiegersma, Nancy. 1988. *Vietnam: Peasant Land, Peasant Revolution.* London: Macmillan.
Williams, Robert G. 1986. *Export Agriculture and the Crisis in Central America.* Chapel Hill: University of North Carolina Press.
Wolf, Eric R. 1969. *Peasant Wars of the Twentieth Century.* New York: Harper and Row.
World Development. 1981. "Socialism and Development," special issue edited by Kenneth P. Jameson and Charles K. Wilber, 9–10.

Zalkin, Michael. 1986. "Peasant Response to State Grain Policy in Post-Revolutionary Nicaragua." Ph.D. diss., University of Massachusetts, Amherst.
———. 1988. "Los olvidados: Campesinado medio." *Pensamiento Propio* 6 (November): 8–14.
———. 1990. "The Sandinista Agrarian Reform: 1979–1990?" *International Journal of Political Economy* 20, no. 2 (Fall): 46–68.

Index

Tables and illustrations are denoted by page numbers in italics.

AFA (Arroz, Frijoles, Azucar). *See* subsidies
agrarian reform, 14; definition of, 4; efforts of Somoza regime, 63–64; goals of, 2–3, 64, 97; history of, 31–37; in Latin America, 123–24; laws for, 17, 180n.51; policy shifts in, 32–35, 117; projects of, 2; role in Contra war, 145; and Sandinista development model, 1, 16–19, 31–32; and socialist regimes, 22; theories of, 59; Third World parallels of, 147–54; visions of, 32–33, 58, 103–5, 104–5, 176n.5. *See also* Huntington, Samuel P.; Los Patios project; Plan Masaya project
Agricultural Land Registry, 180n.49
agroexports. *See* export crop production
Agro-Industrial Systems of Masaya, Inc. (SAIMSA), 95, 104, 120
Alavi, Hamza, 12
Allende, Salvador, 153
AMNLAE. *See* Luisa Amanda Espinosa Association of Nicaraguan Women
Anderson, Leslie, 87, 132, 183–84n.18, 184n.19
Areas of People's Property (APP), 174n.16
Arusha Declaration (1967), 150
ATC. *See* Rural Workers Association

Banco Nacional de Nicaragua (BNN), 60
Banco Nicaragüense de Industria y Comercio (BANIC), 60
BANIC. *See* Banco Nicaragüense de Industria y Comercio
Barrios de Chamorro, Violeta. *See* Chamorro, Violeta Barrios de

beef industry. *See* cattle ranching
black-market, 45–49
BNN. *See* Banco Nacional de Nicaragua
Boaco, 131
Bolaños, Enrique, 95, 120, 184n.1
Bukharin, Nikolai, 176n.3
Burawoy, Michael, 24, 173n.1

Campesinos Cooperative System of Storage and Sales (ECODEPA), 130–32, 175n.31
capitalism, 1, 15, 21, 29, 61, 65
Carazo plateau, 17, 60
CAS. *See* Sandinista Agricultural Cooperatives
Catholic Church, 66
cattle ranching, 100–1, 108, 109. *See also* export crop production
CCS. *See* Credit and Service Cooperatives
CDS. *See* Sandinista Defense Committee
Chamorro, Violeta Barrios de, 43, 44, 53
chapiollo, 33
children, 69, 107–8
Chile, 152–53
Chontales, 131
class, social. *See* social class differences
coffee, 10, 60, 65, 181nn.4
Cofradia, 122, 185–86n.10
collective agriculture, 66. *See* cooperatives
collective production arrangements. *See* cooperatives
COMECON. *See* Council of Mutual Economic Assistance
CONARCA. *See* National Commission of Coffee Plantation Renovation

conservatism, as result of agrarian reform, 153, 158–60
Contra war, 31, 102, 131, 145
cooperatives, 18–19, 24, 49–51, 65–66, 151; attrition from, 54, 102, 180n.50, 185n.6; and collective production arrangements, 22, 24, 28, 49–51, 113, 125–28, 142–43, 158–60; formation of, 79–80, 87–88, 105, 119, 135, 150, 181–82n.11; impacts of. (*See also* Los Patios project; Plan Masaya project); resistance to, 34, 49–51, 66; types of, 125–28; weaknesses of, 52–55
Corinto, 61
COSEP: *See* Superior Council of Private Enterprise
cotton: acreage of, 3, 184nn.2; expansion of production of, 61–62; and imported inputs, 117; and land tenancy, 107–9; price of, 185n.4; production history of, 98–100; and SAIMSA, 95. *See also* export crop production
Council of Mutual Economic Assistance (COMECON), 149–50
CPI-M. *See* Kerala
credit, agricultural, 39, 40, 52, 54; in Los Patios project, 77–78, 78, 183n.5; in Plan Masaya project, 114, 119–20; and Somoza regime, 64, 99–100
Credit and Service Cooperatives (CCS), 17, 89; and benefits, 51, 105; and commercialization process, 47; internal differentiation in, 184n.21; in Los Patios project, 75, 87–88; in Plan Masaya project, 125–26, 130
CSMs. *See* Dead Furrow Cooperatives
CT. *See* Worker Collectives
Cuba, 148–50
cultivation patterns. *See* production systems
currency conversion, 39

Dead Furrows Cooperatives (CSMs), 113
debt. *See* Nicaragua
Deere, Carmen Diana, 142
Defense Brigades, 175n.30
de Janvry, Alain, 24, 175nn.22

demobilization, of population, 26, 110, 146, 151, 153
democracy, 11, 142, 155
democratization, 31, 137
devaluation, 40
development models, 154–60; capitalist, 1; Cuba, 149–50; Los Patios project, 65, 74–75, 92–93; mixed economy, 176n.6; Plan Masaya project, 101–2; Sandinista, 1, 16–19, 31–32; socialist, 1, 10–12
development theory, 4–5, 8–12, 24. *See also* Huntington, Samuel P.
Diriomo, 2, 18, 100, 122, 164–65, 182n.1, 186nn.1
dissent, in revolutionary process, 11
draft, 34, 44, 55, 83, 175n.29

EAP. *See* Economically Active Population
ECODEPA. *See* Campesinos System of Storage and Sales
Economically Active Population (EAP), 63
economic crisis, 37–43, 91, 129, 151
economic reform, 37–43, 80–81, 129
elections, 1984, 35, 176n.9; effect on Plan Masaya project, 103; results of, 34–35; as turning point, 26
elections, 1990, 35, 176–77n.11; background factors in loss of, 37–57; and impact of Plan Masaya project, 97, 122–23; post-election analysis of, 7, 36; reasons for loss of, 20–28; results of, 1, 35–36. *See also* voting patterns
employment. *See* off-farm employment
ENABAS. *See* Nicaraguan Enterprise of Basic Foods
exchange rate unification, 41, 120
export crop production, 118; changes in Region IV, 63, 69; effects on peasantry, 98, 136; increases in, 39; and labor shortages, 32; land concentration in, 62; and need for foreign exchange, 134; in Plan Masaya project, 18, 102, 132; in Region IV, 6, 60–62, 64–65, 71, 181nn.5; in Third World, 22. *See also* cattle ranching; cotton; sugarcane

Fagen, Richard, 10–11, 26, 188n.21

feminist issues, 27
food crop production, 18, 62, *118;* and basic grains, 42–43, 114, 135, 178n.22; effect of export crops on, 68–69; in Plan Masaya project, 101–2, 117–19, 120, 135; in Region IV, 64–65, 76–77
foreign debt. *See* Nicaragua
Frei, Eduardo, 153
FSLN (Sandinista Liberation Front), 1, 20; and cooperatives, 51; and 1990 elections, 35, 81, 97, 103, 122–23, 135. *See also* Sandinista government
fuel pricing policy, 41–42

government, authoritative, 8, 10
Government of National Reconstruction. *See* Sandinista government
Gross Domestic Product (GDP), 38
Gutiérrez, Iván, 42–43

Harris, Richard L., 187n.6
Héroes y Mártires cooperative, 79
Herring, Ronald J., 12, 173n.1, 173nn.1, 174n.13, 175n.26, 188n.22
Huntington, Samuel: development theories of, 8–9, 91, 129, 136, 157; flaws in development theories of, 154–55; on peasantry, 14–15

identification-building: failure of, 147; with land, 52, 55; with landowners, 21, 23, 88–89, 124, 141; in peasant sector, 91; with Sandinista government, 97, 136
illiteracy. *See* Nicaragua
income levels: changes in, 79–80, 116, 141
individualism. *See* identification-building
inflation, 37–39, 42, 47, 116, 177n.16
infrastructure issues, 67, 100
inputs, agricultural, 40–41, 48–49, 79, 117, 119
institutionalization, of revolutionary process, 26
interest rates, 40, 183n.5
interviews, 19–20, 36, 82–83, 167–68. *See also* methodology
INVIERNO, 64

Julio Buitrago cooperative, 79, 183n.9

Kay, Cristóbal, 188n.22
Kerala, 152–54, 174n.13, 175n.26

labor patterns, 75, 178n.26. *See also* wage labor
labor shortages, 32, 176n.1
La Concepción, 81–86
land: inherited, 140; and *latifundios,* 14, 60; rental of, 101, 186n.2; takeovers of, 83–85, 124–25, 180n.56; tenure, 107–9; titles of, 53–54, 102, 125, 179–80n.49
landless campesinos. *See* peasantry, landless
landowners: peasantry identification with, 21, 88–89; power of, 55; reclamation of distributed land, 83–85, 124–25, 180n.56
land redistribution, 17, *111–12;* drawbacks to, 32; and land ownership, 55; and land titles, 53–54, 102, 125, 179–80n.49; in Los Patios project, 20–21, 79, 83–86, 143–44; in Plan Masaya project, 102, 105, 110, 113, 114, 124–25; shifts in policy for, 50–51. *See also* land
Lenin, Vladimir Ilyich, 12
Los Patios project, 17–18, 25, 58–72, 182–83n.4; background of, 59–64; benefits of, 59, 77–81, 93, 141; contrasts with Plan Masaya project, 138–44, 158, 159; cooperative formation in, 79–80, 87–88; economic activities of beneficiaries, 68, 69; effect of economic reform on, 41–43; flaws in, 72, 88–91; identification-building in, 94, 147; map of, *18, 82;* model of, *21,* 74–75; objectives in, 17, 58–59; policy instruments in, 77–80; political impact of, 72, 81–94, 138–44; project participant profiles, 67–70, *139,* 172n.2; socioeconomic impact of, 75–81, 92; transportation costs in, 74–75; voting patterns of beneficiaries, 20, 36–37, 184n.20
Lowy, Michael, 11, 155
Luciak, Ilja, 130–31, 188n.20
Luisa Amanda Espinosa Association of Nicaraguan Women (AMNLAE), 27

mano vuelta labor system, 178n.26
Mao Tse-tung, 12
Marchetti, Peter, 3, 176nn.2
Masatepe, 165, 187n.8
Masaya, 18
mass organizations, 26–28, 110, 146, 156, 175n.27
methodology, 53–54, 180N.57; data sources for study, 81–83, 122–23, 172n.3, 186n.14; outline of, 163–69; in phases of research, 5; surveys, 19–20, 75–76, 105–7. *See also* interviews
MICOIN. *See* Ministry of Internal Commerce
MIDINRA. *See* Ministry of Agricultural Development and Agrarian Reform
minifundistas, 2, 18, 20, 51; increase in numbers of, 62; in Los Patios project, 73, 74, 86; in Plan Masaya project, 102, 121–22
Ministry of Agricultural Development and Agrarian Reform (MIDINRA), 32, 43, 65; and cotton production, 99; and land tenure, 104; and technical assistance, 48–49, 52
Ministry of Internal Commerce (MICOIN), 31, 45, 175nn.29
mixed economy, 33, 93, 144, 176n.6
mobilization, of population, 25, 91; effect of agrarian reform on, 15; importance of in land reform, 14–15; importance of in societal change, 94; importance of in transition to socialism, 9–10, 156–57; in Kerala, 153–54
models. *See* agrarian reform, visions of; development models
modernization, 8–9, 15
Mozambique, 149, 151, 187n.17

National Assembly, 26, 28, 175n.27
National Commission of Coffee Plantation Renovation (CONARCA), 65, 66, 71, 78, 96
National Opposition Union (UNO), 35, 43, 55–57, 92, 130, 143
National Perishables Enterprise (ENAPER), 47

National Union of Farmers and Ranchers (UNAG), 27–28, 52; on collectivization, 51; membership of, 120; mobilization efforts of, 146–47, 175n.30; and *Tiendas Campesinas,* 130, 131
Nicaragua: Contra war, 31, 43–45, 102, 131, 145; debt, 38, 77; economic crisis in, 37–43; *el puño de hierro,* 45–49; foreign debt, 38; illiteracy, 63; population growth in, 67, 182n.12; standard of living, 10, 67, 75, 116–17, 135; trade deficit, 38; unemployment, 38
Nicaraguan Enterprise of Basic Foods (ENABAS), 29, 30, 42–43, 45, 46, 178nn.28
nutritional requirements, 39, 63

off-farm employment, 69, 116. See also wage labor
Ortega, Daniel, 7

Paige, Jeffery M., 13, 23, 133–34
participation. *See* mobilization, of population; political participation
party politics, 10, 26
PATD. *See* Program of Directed Technical Assistance
Patriotic Military Service (SMP). *See* draft
peasantry, 66, 182n.16; attitude toward draft, 44–45; attitude toward Sandinista government, 3, 88–90; development potential of, 12–14, 136, 138, 160–61; Huntington on, 14; landless, 23, 66–67, 100–1, 132; marginalization of, 42, 71, 100, 107, 109; middle, 12–13, 87, 152, 173n.8, 186n.18; politics of, 12–16, 29, 87–88, 157–58; poor, 12, 157–58; resistance to socialist regimes, 153, 158–60, 174n.14; and social class differences, 48–49, 87, 127, 131–32, 152; subgroups of, 3–4, 12; voting patterns of, 3, 36. *See also* repeasantization
PECOS. *See* Special Project Camilo Ortega Saavedra
Perishables Marketing Promoter (PROCOMER), 47

Pilas Occidentales, 185–86n.10, 186n.11
Plan Masaya project, 2, 17–19, *114;* as "Agricultural development and Agrarian reform Zone," 104; background of, 98–101; benefits of, 96, 123, 125, 128–29, 134–35, 141, 146; and confiscation of company property, 95, 120–21; contrasts with Los Patios project, 95–98, 138–44, 158, 159; cooperative formation in, 105, 119, 135; economic activities of beneficiaries, *106;* effect of economic reform on, 41–43; map of, *19;* political impact of, 97, 120–34, 138–44; project participant profiles, 105–9, *139;* proletarianized peasantry in, 23; and shift in land distribution, 50–51; socioeconomic impact of, 113–20, 135; technical assistance in, 18, 41, 115, *115;* voting patterns of beneficiaries, 20, 36–37, 122–23, 130, *130,* 135
political participation, 10, 11; and change process, 146–47; in cooperativization, 141–42; importance of, 161; Serra on, 184n.22; and transition to socialism, 23–25; and wage labor, 13. *See also* cooperatives, collective productive arrangements; mobilization of population
popular opinion, 11
population growth. *See* Nicaragua, population growth
Preobrazhenski, Eugene, 176n.2
price increases. *See* inflation
private sector, 95, 120–21, 174n.16, 185n.8
PROCOMER. *See* Perishables Marketing Promoter
production plans, 15, 48, 179n.38
Program of Directed Technical Assistance (PATD), 78–79; impact of, 118, 119; mission of, 105; and production plans, 48; relation to Plan Masaya project, 18, 41, 115
proletarianization, of peasantry, 15, 23, 31, 133–34, 136, 148
propeasant vision, of agrarian reform, 32–33, 58, 104–5
property, private, confiscation of, 95, 120–21, 174n.16
puño de hierro, el, 45–49

Quebrada Honda, 132, 186n.4, 186n.19

recampesinización. *See* repeasantization
Region II, 99, 179n.38
Region IV, *63,* 64–67, 69, 110, 117–18, 179n.38. *See also* export crop production; food crop production
Region V, 119, 131
Region VI, 131
repeasantization, 34, 73, 93; in Cuba, 148; in Los Patios project, 75–76, 90–91; in Plan Masaya project, 96, 113
rice, 181n.8. *See also* export crop production
road block inspections *(tranques),* 46. *See also puño de hierro, el;* Nicaraguan Enterprise of Basic Foods (ENABAS)
Roxborough, Ian, 8
Rural Credit Program, 64
rural-urban migration, 67, 103
Rural Workers Association (ATC), 104

SAIMSA. *See* Agro-Industrial Systems of Masaya, Inc.
San Caralampio, 86–87, 183n.17, 184n.19, 187n.4
Sandinista Agricultural Cooperatives (CAS), 19, 24, 65, 105, 130
Sandinista Defense Committee (CDS), 26–27, 175n.29
Sandinista government: black-market grain sales clamp-down, 45–49; composition of, 16; economic record of, 56; goals of, 64; as illustration of Huntington's theories, 8–9, 22; legitimacy of, 34; peasants' attitude toward, 3, 82–86, 88–89, 183n.17, 186n.17; political priorities of, 174n.15, 174n.18; prioritization of peasantry, 110; project of popular hegemony, 144–47; support for, 8, 36–37, 56–57, 122–23, 130, 143, 187nn.7. *See also* FSLN
Sandinista Liberation Front. *See* FSLN
San Marcos, 165, 187n.8

Scott, James C., 174n.14
Serra, Luis Héctor, 23–24, 128, 179n.39, 184n.22
SMP. *See* draft
social class differences, 139–41; in data analysis, 172n.3; in ECODEPA project, 131–32; in Los Patios project, 87, 89–91; and MIDINRA technicians, 48–49; in Plan Masaya, 127; and social transformation, 152
social equity, 15, 86
socialism, transition to, 9–11, 155–57, 171n.1
social services, 22, 38, 43, 67
social wage. *See* social services
Somoza Debayle, Anastasio, 16
Special Project Camilo Ortega Saavedra (PECOS), 102
stabilization program. *See* economic reform
Stahler-Sholk, Richard, 146
standard of living, 10, 67, 75, 116–17, 135
state farm sector, 31, 33, 65, 149
subsidies, 41, 177n.17
subsistence production. *See* food crop production
sugarcane, 61. *See also* export crop production
Superior Council of Private Enterprise (COSEP), 95, 120–21, 184n.1
surveys. *See* methodology

Tanzania, 150–51
technical assistance, to project beneficiaries. *See* PATD
technocratic vision, of agrarian reform, 32–33, 103–5, 176n.5
technology, in agricultural production, 41, 105, 115, 119. *See also* Program of Directed Technical Assistance (PATD)
Thiesenhusen, William C., 186n.15
Third World, 10, 11; export production subsidization in, 22; Huntington on, 154–55; parallels of agrarian reform in, 147–54
Thomas, Clive, 10
Tiendas Campesinas. *See* Campesinos System of Storage and Sales
Tisma-Masaya, 135
trade deficit. *See* Nicaragua
tranques (road block inspections), 46
transition, to socialism. *See* socialism
transportation costs, 41–42, 47, 74–75

UNAG. *See* National Union of Farmers and Ranchers
unemployment. *See* Nicaragua
United States, 43–44, 56. *See also* Contra war
UNO. *See* National Opposition Union
UPANIC, 120

Vietnam, 152
voting patterns, 3, 20, 35, 35–36, 184n.20. *See also* elections; Los Patios project; Plan Masaya project

wage labor, 132–34, 140–41, 187n.5; decrease in, 80, 116; increase in, 38, 70, 107, 108; relationship to political participation, 13; rural dependency on, 13, 63
Wheelock, Jaime, 32, 185n.7
White, G., 171n.1
Wickham-Crowley, Timothy, 13, 173n.11
Wolf, Eric, 12, 173n.7
women's rights, 27
Worker Collectives (CT), 19